Booktalk!

Booktalk!

BOOKTALKING AND SCHOOL VISITING
FOR YOUNG ADULT AUDIENCES

by Joni Bodart

THE H. W. WILSON COMPANY
NEW YORK
1980

Library of Congress Cataloging in Publication Data

Bodart, Joni.
    Booktalk! Booktalking and school visiting for
young adult audiences.

    Bibliography: p.
    Includes index.
    1. Book talks. I. Title.
Z716.3.B6   028'.5'5   80-16461
ISBN 0-8242-0650-9

Printed in the United States of America

To Mama, with a big hug,
because your late-blooming prickly porcupine
has finally smoothed her prickles and bloomed—
just as you've always said she would . . .
And to Christy, Ceci, and Mike,
who also love late-blooming porcupines,
because you all believed in me
until I finally believe in myself . . .
This one is for you.

CONTENTS

Acknowledgements   xi

Introduction   ix

Chapter 1.   Why Booktalking? What's All the Fuss About?   1

Chapter 2.   Writing a Booktalk: "Gettin' Down to the
               Nitty-Gritty"   5

Chapter 3.   Doing Booktalks in Schools: "Takin' It
               To the Streets"   22

Chapter 4.   Preparing a Class Presentation: Behind
               the Scenes   37

Chapter 5.   Giving a Booktalk: How to Hold a Roomful of
               Uncaged, Untamed Adolescents in the Palm
               of Your Hand   47

Chapter 6.   Hassles, and How to Handle Them: Murphy
               Was Right!   58

Chapter 7.   How to Tell When You're a Success and What
               to Do About It, Without Getting a
               Swelled Head   69

Chapter 8.   Teaching Booktalking: Spreading the Word   74

Chapter 9.   Other Ways of Doing It: "Diff'rent Strokes"   82

Booktalks   85

Bibliographies   217

List of Publishers   237

Index   241

Figure 1.   Class Visit Information Card   40

Figure 2.   Teacher's Class Visit Evaluation Form   49

Figure 3.   Class Visit Summary Sheet   72

ACKNOWLEDGEMENTS

No BOOK is ever written in a vacuum, and this one certainly never would have become a reality without the help of a lot of friends:

Jerry Stevens, whose idea it was, and who, with his talent for arm-twisting, eventually persuaded me to "Do something!" about it;

Elizabeth Talbot and Sue Tait, who read the various drafts and offered gentle and constructive criticism, generous amounts of encouragement when I needed it, and who in general kept me going over all the roughest spots;

Carol Starr, who also offered help and criticism, and who in addition showed me through her own example what a good young adult librarian should be, and then helped me toward that goal;

Harry Madden, who said, "Of *course* you can do it!" every time I needed to hear it, even when I called collect, in the depths of depression, after I'd cancelled our weekend plans because I'd had to write and then spent the whole time staring at a blank page;

Mary Moore, who put up with a frequently rather preoccupied partner who had a new crisis every other chapter;

Dorothy Taylor, who deciphered the pages and pages of scribbled handwriting and scrambled typescript that made up my rough draft to produce the final manuscript on time;

All the YA people in the Alameda County Library, BAYA (Bay Area Young Adult Librarians), and elsewhere who contributed ideas, booktalks, and lots of encouragement;

Linda Lapides, who came up with the title at a moment's notice, and in the nick of time;

And last, but certainly not least, from H.W. Wilson, Jean Mester, who was the first to hear about my then half-baked idea for a book and who didn't once laugh at me; Bruce Carrick, who encouraged me with both tact and patience to keep working until I actually had a book and not a half-baked idea; and my editor, Norris Smith, also a person of great tact and patience, who not only kept me up to date with what was going on but who also knew what I wanted to say—sometimes better than I did!

My thanks to all of you—I couldn't have done it without you!

JONI BODART
March 17, 1980

INTRODUCTION

THIS BOOK contains my ideas about booktalks: what they are, and how to write them, deliver them, and make them work. It's not meant to cover all the ways you can do a booktalk or every style you can use, although I have given examples of different approaches in some cases. But mainly this book describes how I and other YA librarians that I've known and worked with do booktalks. There are as many ways to do booktalks as there are people who do them. These are the ways I know about—what works and what doesn't. You may or may not be able to use all the details on preparation and presentation, but the basic outline may be helpful. Adapt it to suit your own personality, and if one way doesn't work, try another. This book isn't meant to be the final word, but rather the first few words you need to start you off on your own career as a booktalker.

Therefore I've included a lot about how to do booktalks but not so many of the talks themselves. It *is* possible (and practical) to exchange talks with other people, but very seldom do you find someone with a style and delivery so close to yours that you can lift an entire talk verbatim. So to those of you who wanted hundreds of ready-made booktalks, all I can say is, I'm sorry, and take a look at Elinor Walker's *Book Bait* (third edition, 1979) and the ALA's *Doors to More Mature Reading* (1964). I hope all of the how-to information will help you build up your own collection so quickly and easily (though probably not effortlessly) that soon you'll have hundreds of booktalks on file. And those will probably be several times as useful to you as mine would have been.

The talks I have included (both my own and those contributed by other YA people) are meant to serve as examples, to give you a place to start. They are not supposed to represent the only way to write booktalks. Some of my talks were successful, others weren't. Some have been through many changes since I first wrote them. For several titles I've included a couple of talks, since different people saw these books from different points of view, and this seemed interesting and possibly helpful to beginners.

In order to know what a good booktalk is, you need to know what a bad one is. Telling too much about the book is probably the most common fault, followed by telling too little. A talk that doesn't make the book interesting or isn't true to the book's contents isn't a good one, nor is one that makes the book sound more interesting than it really is. However, the majority of my bad talks are simply the ones the kids don't like. Sometimes it can be traced to something specific, sometimes not.

Don't feel that the talks in this book are carved in stone, never to be changed. That's just not so—adapt them, use them. The end result will be your talk, not someone else's. There are two major ingredients to a successful booktalk that you must provide yourself: enthusiasm and experience. If you enjoy what you are doing and are genuinely excited about the books you're discussing, your presentation will most likely be a success, even if your technique is not perfect. Conversely, you can have booktalking technique down pat and still not be able to sell the books, if you don't care about them. You need to like the books you're talking about (or at least, like *something* about them) and care about the people you're talking to. Both these concerns are essential, and there are no substitutes. *You* are the person who makes books fun.

Experience will make anyone a better booktalker, providing he or she is willing to learn from it. Every booktalker has a first time out—and we all have horror stories to tell about the mistakes we made. I did my first booktalks in my alma mater, Del Rio High School. I still have those talks, and they are *not* memorable. My mother arranged for me to talk to twelve classes in two days when I was home on vacation during my senior year in college. (She was the librarian and ex-head of the English department, which gave her a lot of leverage in arm-twisting.) On the first day I talked to a class of sophomores with my sister in it. She and I did not get along well anyway. She'd heard me practicing, and she was bored with everything I had to say. She spent the entire time I was in the class inciting minor riots. I ended up stopping in the middle of a talk to tell her to shut up! I don't remember much about what I said except that I was *awful*! I went to the teachers' lounge afterwards and cried for half an hour. It was mortifying. It took me several years (and many more minor riots) to forgive her. Then several years ago she visited me and heard me do booktalks again. Her comment: "Of course you were good. I knew you would be—I heard you do them before, remember?" So much for minor riots.

The main thing is just getting out there and doing it, even if you bomb six times in a row. Find out why you bombed and try again. Eventually, you'll make it. And you may still be selling books along the way. The best measure of success is the number of kids who want to read the books you talk about. If you can convince kids to read, you're a success, no matter how frightened you may feel.

In giving how-to information, I have aimed at the novice who has no idea where to start or what to do. I have tried to cover all the details in order to give that person as much help as possible. For more experienced booktalkers, though, some of the information may be extraneous. I have focused on the school library or school classroom presentation, but much of the material in this book could be adapted for other situations as well. Booktalking is very flexible and totally portable. The techniques can always be used in one-to-one reader's advisory work, for example. And just as everyone enjoys storytelling, everyone can enjoy booktalking. (Yes, there are *always* exceptions!)

1

WHY BOOKTALKING?

What's All the Fuss About?

FOR ME, reading is a way to explore new worlds, new ideas, new people, new experiences. If people, especially teenage people, don't read, it's because they don't think it's fun, or interesting, or "in," or "cool," or "bad," or *necessary*. I do booktalks because I have found this to be the quickest, most effective way to change their minds, as effective with the avid readers as it is with the reluctant ones. Booktalking can turn students on to things they may never have thought of before, and introduce them to books that will broaden their horizons. Reading can be vitally important to troubled kids, as well. Although solutions to problems are not always found in books, teenagers can at least find there the reassurance that they are not the only people who have ever had to face those problems. And even with the increasing influence of movies and television, the ability to read is still essential to an individual's functioning adequately in our society.

Reading is also recreation—it is fun, funny, entertaining, and emotionally satisfying. It can be an individual or a group experience. It is something to enjoy by yourself or to share with friends. It is portable and adaptable, something you can do almost anywhere with almost no preparation. I see it that way, but then I've been reading easily since I was five years old. Many people see reading only as a chore; they are not able to read easily enough to truly enjoy it. To me, that's where booktalking comes in. In booktalking, you try to emphasize the fun and excitement of reading. Even if the kids don't listen, or don't check out the books, at least you will have shown them that somebody (an adult who is not a teacher) thinks that books are important, and is willing to visit their class to say so. That's the least you can accomplish. But perhaps you'll convince a kid to try reading. Let me tell you about a boy at the Stanislaus County Juvenile Hall whose experience demonstrates what a difference booktalking can make.

I hadn't noticed Billy until he picked up *The Haven*. I'd been curious about whether anyone would pick it up—the cover was certainly a "grabber," showing a huge dog's head with slavering jaws, teeth bared in a snarl. Unfortunately, the cover had little to do with the story, a clumsy imitation of Tolkien. I asked Billy to tell me what he thought of the book when I came back next week, since I hadn't given it to any kids before and I wanted his opinion. The next week he was one of the first to come running up to me—he not only loved the book, he'd been reading it out loud to the other boys in his room, and they loved it too! He was nearly through, did I have anything else just like it? My favorite book at the time was Gordon Dickson's *The Dragon and the George*, which I did a booktalk on and which he was equally enthusiastic about. *The Hobbit* was next, then *Star Wars, Splinter of the Mind's Eye*, and several books on body building. I was rejoicing at having found not only a real reader but also one who could inspire his peers. *The Haven* was so popular it didn't surface again for months, and *The Dragon and the George* soon disappeared as well. Imagine my shock when Billy came up to me the week before he was transferred to CYA (California Youth Authority) Camp and said how much he appreciated all my help and suggestions—before he came to Juvenile Hall, he said, he didn't read much and almost never finished a book! Now he really liked to read, and was reading faster than he ever could before—and he planned to keep on even after he got out!

That's what booktalking can do, and that's why I do it!

What Is a Booktalk?

In the broadest terms, it's what you say to convince someone to read a book. It's what I was doing as far back as grade school and as recently as yesterday when someone said, "Joni, you've read a lot, tell me a good book to read." It's sharing your enjoyment of a book with other people and convincing them that they would enjoy it too.

A booktalk is not a book review or a book report or a book analysis. It does not judge the book's merits; it assumes the book is good and goes on from there. As a dramatic art, booktalking has something in common with storytelling, although in content it more nearly resembles an unfinished murder mystery—it doesn't say "who dunnit," but it makes you want to find out. A good booktalk reaches out to the listeners and involves them so they become not merely listeners but participants. It makes them care enough about the people in the book to want to read it and see what happens after the end of the talk.

A good booktalk is enticing. It is a come-on. It is entertaining. And it is fun, for both the listener and the booktalker. However, a booktalk should not be better than the book it's about. Overselling a book merely means that your credibility will be reduced for future talks. If the first three chapters are slow and the rest of it is great, say so. Don't let your audience think it's great from page one—they may not make it to Chapter Four!

Booktalks fall into two general categories, long and short. A long booktalk is five to seven minutes long, is presented in a somewhat formal manner, and requires preparation ahead of time. A short booktalk is thirty seconds to two minutes long, informal, and is usually either an adaptation of a longer talk or extemporaneous. The former is used in classroom presentations, the latter in reader's advisory work or between the longer talks in a classroom presentation. Both kinds of booktalk give a glimpse of the book, ensnaring the listener's attention, and then drop the story at a climactic moment, never giving away the ending.

Another type of booktalk, which I will not be concerned with here, involves memorizing a section of a book and reciting it word-for-word. People who use this technique swear by it, although I cannot personally recommend it. Its major weakness lies in the fact that the excerpt has to be memorized. If at some point you forget the next word, you may blank out and lose the entire rest of the talk. Memorized talks also tend to sound memorized, and quoting characters can lead to problems for the person who finds dialects difficult. My first experience hearing someone do booktalks was with Judy Kuykendall at the Dallas Public Library in 1969. She and her staff did talks of this kind and did them very well. Mary Kay Chelton, a former YA librarian and now a faculty member at Rutgers University, uses this method also, and recommended it in an article on booktalking in *School Library Journal*, April 1976. There are advantages—the author's style is easily conveyed, as is the flavor of the book. No writing skill is necessary, since the speaker doesn't have to use his or her own words. However, the passage must be learned so well that it is instinctive. (Techniques used by storytellers in memorizing stories can be very helpful here.) This type of booktalk can be extremely effective when well done, but can be just as ineffective when done poorly. I feel that the people who can succeed with this type of booktalk would be even more successful using the method I shall describe in the next chapter. It's also possible to include an excerpt from a book *within* a long booktalk, but there are special problems involved in this approach too, that will be discussed later.

2

WRITING A BOOKTALK

"Gettin' Down to the Nitty-Gritty"

How to Prepare a Long Booktalk

THERE ARE two unbreakable rules in booktalking:
1. Don't tell the ending of a book.
2. Don't talk about a book you haven't read.

There are good reasons for these rules. In a booktalk, you are trying to persuade people to read a book by telling them just a little bit about it, and if you tell the whole story, including the climax, there will be no reason for them to read it. The idea is to make them want to read the book by withholding information, so that their curiosity is piqued. The reasons for the second rule are just as obvious. How can you talk about a book you haven't read? If you're using someone else's booktalk, and you learn it and do a marvelous job giving it, all your work will be wasted if, afterwards, someone comes up and asks a question you can't answer. Then, on top of that, if you are really lucky, there'll be a bright kid around to listen to you fumble that first question and say (loudly): "You didn't *really* read that book, didja?" I know it happens because it has happened to me—and I can categorically state that there are no holes in classroom floors to sink through in such a situation. In addition, your credibility goes down the drain in that class, and occasionally, if word gets out, in the entire school.

It's simply not worth it, so read the book you're talking about, even if you are using someone else's booktalk.

The first step in building a collection of booktalks is to read as much as you can. There is no danger of reading too much. You will not be able to write talks on everything you read, and probably not all of the talks you write will be successful, at least the first time you give them. As you read, jot down notes about the book. These can be written on three by five cards for a file box or just on a piece of paper, to be stuffed in a drawer with all the other miscellaneous pieces of paper on booktalking. However you take the notes, try to keep them all together, so that when you have a chance to start writing booktalks or need some new ones you'll only have to look in one place. Your notes should include the author's name, the title, a brief one- or two-sentence plot outline, the names of important characters, incidents you thought were funny, interesting, or intriguing—and don't forget the page numbers, so you can find the scenes again.

All this note-taking may seem somewhat forced at first, and time-consuming as well. However, it saves time in the end, when you don't have to search the new-book shelves for that elusive title you can't remember, but would be perfect for the class you're talking to next week—or for the eager kid who's standing at your elbow! If extensive notetaking is something you will simply not do, try just keeping a list of the titles and authors of books that look like possibilities. Anything that will jog your memory will help. If I can, I set aside a copy of the book so I'll have it when I want to start writing—that way I don't have to take notes either! (I do need to be careful I don't re-read each book completely as I skim it for ideas—it's easy to forget why I'm reading it, slow down, and enjoy it all again. But booktalks don't get written that way.)

How can you tell what books will be easy to booktalk? Basically, the ones you liked yourself. (How can you convince someone else that reading a book will be a pleasurable experience when it wasn't for you?) The book you choose doesn't have to be a literary gem, or one that can stand the ravages of time and reviewers. However, the qualities that make any book a "good" book are important—a strong, fast-moving, believable plot, life-like characters that fit into the setting, emotional impact of one kind or another, a chance for the reader to become involved in the story, a way to identify with what's going on in the book. Phyllis Anderson Wood's *A Five-Color Buick and a Blue-Eyed Cat* is one example of a book that booktalks well. Others are Richard Peck's *Are You in the House Alone?* and *Ghosts I Have Been; No Language But a Cry* by Richard D'Ambrosio; *The Boys From Brazil* by Ira Levin; *Raise the Titanic!* by Clive Cussler; *I Know What You Did Last Summer* and *Killing Mr. Griffin* by Lois Duncan; all of Stephen King's novels, including *Carrie, 'Salem's Lot* and *The Shining*; and *The Intruders* by Pat Montandon. I've included a list in the bibliography section called "Books Someone Thought Were Easy to Booktalk." It may give you some more ideas.

Episodic books are usually easiest to talk about. James Herriot's books are an excellent example of this. You can start with a sentence or two about Herriot and how he ended up in the Yorkshire Dales. Then go right into one of the anecdotes about the animals he treated. In *All Creatures Great and Small*, Nugent's troubles with his "little jobs" is a funny scene, or perhaps you could tell about the mistreated dog whose love was able to give an old woman a new lease on life, in *All Things Bright and Beautiful*.

Basically, however, it is the book *you* like that you will be able to sell. This rule holds true almost without exception in regard to long booktalks. In a one-to-one situation, though, especially when you're acquainted with the person you're talking to, you can say, "I didn't like this book, but I know you like books on this subject, so I think you will. It's about...." Do be honest with kids—they are startlingly perceptive most of the time, scorn lies, and respect honesty.

Now that you have an idea of the kind of book to choose, have selected one and read it, and maybe taken notes to jog your memory, you're ready to plan your talk. How do you pick out a scene or series of scenes to build your booktalk around? Since booktalking is essentially just sharing your enthusiasm about and enjoyment of a book with someone else, imagine what you'd say to friends about the book to convince them to read it. Why was it funny, exciting, suspenseful, intriguing, frightening? Why did you keep on reading it? Was there a point at which you realized you couldn't put it down? Maybe that would be a good place to stop your booktalk, if it's not too far along in the story, since kids will want to pick the book up to see what happened next.

The scene you choose may or may not be a major one, but it should be one you can enjoy and identify with. It may not be the same one someone else would choose, but if it works, it's the right one for you.

Generally, look for a short scene with lots of action, perhaps something funny or suspenseful, that takes place early in the book so you don't give away too much of the plot. The scene should be complete in itself and should convey the feeling of the book. For example, in Harold Krents's *To Race the Wind* a good scene would be the description of how he learned to drive when he was a senior in high school. Another funny anecdote is his being classified 1-A for the draft (you could read the poem he wrote about fighting for Uncle Sam, if someone will just tell him which way to shoot).

Other examples of good scenes to use are: learning how to play Chicken in *Red Sky at Morning*; Anne Webb's arrival in Chicken, Alaska, in *Tisha*; Blossom Culp's ghost imitation or how she suddenly got second sight in *Ghosts I Have Been*; the first seance in *Psychic Summer*. Lead up to the scene by sketching the plot so far, if that's necessary. Then concentrate on the episode itself. Try to capture the excitement, humor, or human interest of the scene, and don't forget to mention any interesting or odd details. Then stop at a crucial point or after the punch line, and you have a booktalk.

You don't have to build a booktalk around one particular scene. Another method is to summarize the plot up to a climactic moment, and then stop. If you do this well, it can be extremely effective (as well as frustrating for the listener who wants to know what happens next). It can sell the book immediately. This kind of booktalk is definitely a teaser, a come-on, and so shouldn't reveal too much. Action, suspense, or adventure novels lend themselves to this treatment. Some examples of books you can use this way and the points at which you can stop your talk are: *Are You in the House Alone?* (Gail wakes up in the hospital, realizes that she's been raped and that no one will believe her story); *Ammie, Come Home* (Ruth is thrown down the stairs by the spirit in possession of her niece Sara's body); *Deathwatch* (Ben starts to walk across the desert without food, water, or clothes); *Bid Time Return* (Richard lies down on his bed in 1975 and begins to convince himself he will wake up in 1896); *Ordinary People* (Con realizes that his brother's death was *not* the cause of his own suicide attempt—but what was?); *The Chocolate War* (Jerry decides to defy both the school administration and the Vigils); *The Boys From Brazil* (Liebermann feels Mengele's hate emanating from the phone, and knows that unless he can stop it, ninety-four men will die); *The Dragon and the George* (Jim /Gorbash discovers Angie has been imprisoned in the Loathly Tower and he must lead a quest to rescue her). Booktalks on some of these novels appear in a special section (page 85).

How much of the story to tell is up to you—a few pages may be enough to involve the audience in some books. Others may take longer, up to half the book, as in *Are You in the House Alone?* The point is to involve and to entice, not to reveal all. You need to tell enough about the book to interest and involve the audience, and then make sure they know something else exciting is going to happen. But do not tell them what. It's better to tell too little than too much. You never want to give your listeners the feeling that they don't need to read the book because you've already told them all about it. When you say, "To find out what happens next, read . . .," the response should be, "Oh, no! Go on! Go on!" If the book has a complicated plot, it's not necessary to give all the details. You should sketch in the main highlights, leaving out more than you include. Include action; leave out most descriptive details. Remember also that you have a time limit to consider. Let your listeners discover some things about the book themselves. Don't go on and on and on. You'll suddenly discover your audience hasn't come along with you.

You may occasionally find that all you really need to do is "set the stage" rather than actually get into the story. *Interview With the Vampire* by Anne Rice can be handled this way. I describe how the young man meets the vampire in a dimly-lit bar, then actually sees him in his hotel room, and I read the vampire's first statement: "I was a twenty-five-year-old man when I became a vampire, and the year was 1791. . . ." David Wagoner's *Road to Many a Wonder* can be introduced by describing how Pa curses the farm and Ike resolves that night to leave home and seek his fortune in the Pike's Peak gold rush.

Lists of things are also interesting: For example, the items that the Robertsons took with them when their boat sank (*Survive the Savage Sea*), or the bits of food found in the plane after it crashed in the Andes with a soccer team on board (*Alive!*). Or, in *The Poseidon Adventure*, a list of the people who tried to get out, or a list of mixed-up classes from *The Alfred G. Graebner Memorial High School Handbook of Rules and Regulations* or of Isabel's religions and diseases from the same book.

Just a note here about reading an excerpt, and the dangers involved. Reading is not a substitute for learning a booktalk. It can easily become boring to kids and shouldn't be done at all unless you're extremely good. Even then the amount of reading should be strictly limited, within both the individual booktalk and the entire presentation. If you aren't sure how good you are, read to someone who you know will be critical rather than tactful, or try reading one excerpt before a class and gauge their reaction. If they listened and wanted to read the book, okay—but don't get too enthused. If they were bored and didn't want to read the book, forget it. You also need to be aware that the author's style of writing may not fit in with your style of booktalking. In that case, what you have written and the excerpt you have chosen could clash. If the transition is awkward, the talk would probably be smoother and more flowing if you told the scene entirely in your own words.

Poetry, on the other hand, must be read. But limit yourself to one or two, possibly three, short poems—no more.

I used to read quite a bit, until I realized I was enjoying it much more than my audience was. Now I do it less and less, and try to keep it to only a few sentences, such as the actual description of the vampire in *Interview With the Vampire*, rather than the whole scene, several pages long. What you're trying to do in booktalking is sell the book: if reading doesn't sell it, and for most people it doesn't, don't do it.

You can add "inside information" to your booktalk if you know something about the author, or how the book came to be written. Richard Peck's inspiration for one scene in *Representing Super-doll* was what happened in the Green Room backstage just before he appeared on *To Tell the Truth*. Elizabeth Talbot, of Alameda County Library, describes her own raccoon, Sassafras, when she booktalks *Frosty*, by Harriet E. Weaver. Watch the media for information—according to *People*, June 6, 1977, Hal Krents and his wife divide up the household chores (he takes out the garbage) and he reads Braille picture books to his son, Jamie. These sidelights on the author now a part of my *To Race the Wind* booktalk. An article on James Herriot in the March 1979 issue of *Good Housekeeping* gives not only his real name but a new view of him as a veterinarian, as distinct from an author.

You can also say something personal to introduce the book: "After I stayed up all night to read *Carrie*, I slept with a light on for weeks." "I was so interested in finishing this book I snapped at my supervisor when she interrupted my break, and nearly got fired!" This kind of recommendation is an attention-getter, and makes both you and the book seem more "real."

Some booktalkers think being impersonal is best, but I disagree, up to a point. Since booktalking is an individual art, you should always work towards what is right for you and what works for you. If you can handle including personal touches, and the audience responds to them, fine. But if this makes you uncomfortable, don't do it. Both approaches are valid and defensible. If you do decide to include something personal, remember to be matter-of-fact rather than cutesy or coy about it. Your straightforward attitude will make it okay for the kids to accept and enjoy a reference to your private life. Be aware that they will immmediately pick up whatever emotion you project. If you aren't completely at ease with yourself, your audience, and what you're saying, forget it. This is one of the things that's either a huge success or a total flop. Be prepared, and be careful.

Now you have a book and an idea of how to organize your talk on it. It's time to start writing. At this point, there are several things to remember.

As I've said, a booktalk is not an evaluation or a book review. It is not a discussion of the book's literary merit. One of my friends is a former English teacher and constantly has to be reminded that all the reasons he thinks a book is interesting are not necessarily what a teenager wants to hear about. Teenagers appreciate realistic characters, believable settings, good writing, symbolism, and a plot they can identify with too, but they just don't use these terms. All these things don't need to go into a booktalk. The center of a booktalk is *action*—what is happening in the book, who does what, and what happens then. Analyze the symbolism with your colleagues, but don't discuss it in a booktalk.

The title and author of the book should be the first and last things mentioned. Give this information before you start your talk and after you finish—and don't read from the cover of the book. Know the correct title and the author's name.

The two most important sentences in a booktalk are the first and the last. The first sentence should be a "grabber"—something that will catch and hold the interest of your audience. The first sentence determines whether everybody or nobody will keep listening to you. If the word "grabber" is intimidating, let me say it another way. The first sentence should be interesting, catchy, and attention-getting. It should also provide an immediate lead-in to the book's action. If the first sentence isn't too long, it can set the scene, with the second sentence getting into the action. But don't wait longer than the second sentence to get into the meat of the talk, or you'll lose your audience. You can lose them in the first thirty seconds of a talk and never get them back, which makes first sentences very important! Some examples of a good first sentence are: "Rob was running away from school just as fast as he could go!" (*A Day No Pigs Would Die*). "When Karen was twelve years old she walked into the girls' restroom at school and saw this rhyme written on the mirror . . ." (*Through a Brief Darkness*). "Elizabeth *hated* Lincoln, Nebraska!" (*Bird on the Wing*). "George and Kathy Lutz moved into their dream house on December 18, 1975, and on January 14, 1976, only twenty-seven days later, fled in fear for their lives" (*The Amityville Horror*).

I also think the first sentence is the hardest one to write. Once I've made a start, the rest of the talk seems to flow more smoothly. If you're stuck on the first sentence, there are several things you can do to help you get started. Try writing an annotation. Because it has to accomplish some of the same things, it can give you a place to start. If you've done a short talk or told someone about the book off the top of your head, think about what you said. Or try reading the dust jacket or back cover blurb. It's a ready-made come-on, and that's what you're looking for. Maybe you could write a short booktalk—it might be easier than a long one, since you don't have to make so many decisions about what to put in and leave out. You can always start in the middle of the action, going back to fill in the details in your next few sentences. "Elizabeth *hated* Lincoln, Nebraska!" is the first sentence of a booktalk on *Bird on the Wing*, by Winifred Madison. The reasons why she hated it, how she ended up there, and what she did about it come after, once the audience's attention has been caught. A less effective way to present this same book would be to start off by explaining why Elizabeth was in Lincoln: "Elizabeth lived with her parents in Sacramento until they got divorced. Then she lived with her mother for a year or so, until she was sent to live with her father in Lincoln, Nebraska." By the time you've said all that you may have lost some of your audience. Begin with an action, not the explanation of it. Let the details wait until you have your audience's attention.

Action can be delayed only so long, and no longer. Consider this introduction to *Red Sky at Morning*, by Richard Bradford. "After Pearl Harbor, Josh Arnold's father decides to send his family someplace safe. Safe is Sagrado, New Mexico, a little town up in the mountains, about as far from Atlanta's shipbuilding yards as you can get. It's the kind of place that has a population of six cows, four dogs, seventeen chickens and almost no people. Josh has to get used to a whole new way of life, and he gets into trouble his very first day at school."

The last sentence of a booktalk is also important—it may be all some kids remember, so make it a grabber, too. It should imply that something else will be happening but not say what. Leave them hanging in mid-air, or at least aware that they're missing some of the action if they don't read the book. Some good final sentences are: "To find out if Ben made it back to town and if Madec's plans worked or not, read *Deathwatch*, by Robb White." "Someone had found out that the four of them were responsible for killing that little boy, and now that same someone was going to kill them!" (*I Know What You Did Last Summer*). "It's not easy to become a legend in your own time, but Cattle Annie and Little Britches did just that!" (*Cattle Annie and Little Britches*). "Suddenly Peggy realized she'd just seen her first ghost!" (*The Sherwood Ring*).

The ending should come at a specific point. Unless you plan an ending, you may ramble on and on, completely losing your audience as you do. A booktalk needs to have a definite structure. First sentence(s): a lead-in to the action; middle: what happens in the book; last sentence(s): the action stops without any conclusion, letting the audience know something else will be happening. A booktalk isn't a speech—you can't afford any extra words. It must be concise—at the most, you have only six or seven minutes to make your point. If you don't plan what to say and when to stop, you can easily just go on and on and on, not realizing what you're doing until your audience starts to snore. Avoid such embarrassing moments by knowing when to stop.

When you write your talk down, it should be in a form that is convenient for you to use in a classroom. Opinions on this format vary widely. Booktalkers each have to decide what will work best for them in their own situations. I usually do my rough draft on a yellow legal-size pad but my final copy on a five by seven card, which is what I take to the class with me. I write down my rough draft, correct it, and sweat over it; then, when it's as good as it's likely to get, I put it away for several days to see what it sounds like cold. The difference is amazing sometimes, and the strengths and flaws are suddenly very clear. If the draft needs changing, I make the final revisions and then copy the result onto a five by seven card. When I write the talk down I try to limit myself to one and a half pages of legal-size lined paper for my rough draft and to both sides of the card for my final copy. That way, I know my talk will be about the right length (five to seven minutes), and thus I no longer have to time each talk. I write down everything I intend to say, word for word. Practice reading your talk aloud before you make a final draft. It should be only four to six minutes long in rehearsal, to allow for hesitation and a different pace when you actually give it. Work out how long your written talk should be to equal five to seven minutes in the classroom. Once you know that, you shouldn't have to time yourself so carefully. But don't let your talks get too long either—shorter is usually better.

Other methods include using three by five cards that can be filed in a box or drawer later; using sheets of paper rather than cards; writing down only an outline or key words and phrases to jog your memory; and writing down the first one or two sentences but using an outline from there. Some people type their notes, some don't. Marianne Pridemore, of the San Jose Public Library, uses a combination of methods. She writes out her whole talk and uses that version to practice with; then she condenses it to an outline written on one or two index cards, which she takes into the class with her. Several of her booktalks are included in this volume, both the complete talks and her briefer notes.

In the classroom, I always have my notes with me, so I can refer to them right away if I get stuck. That way my lapses of memory aren't quite so obvious. Mary Moore, a YA librarian in Stanislaus County, writes her very brief notes (sometimes only characters' names) on slips of scratch paper or three by five cards, which she leaves in the book she's talking about. Marion Hargrove, from

Prince Georges County in Maryland, doesn't take her notes with her at all, just reviews them before she goes out to visit a class. Use the method that works best for you. The purpose of notes is to keep your booktalk flowing as smoothly as possible, even if you suddenly go blank. And that does happen, even to the most experienced booktalker, although if you're good it's usually possible to cover up. Ad-libbing takes a lot of experience, however, and occasionally even experience doen't help. Several years ago I was visiting a freshman high-interest /low-reading-level class with one of the other Alameda County YA people. It was all going along as usual—neither of us was nervous, and we were both experienced with class visits and familiar with the teacher and the school. In spite of this, halfway through one of her favorite booktalks my partner forgot what her next sentence was. She stopped, looked horrified, struggled through one more sentence, then told the class that she had forgotten, and went back and started the whole talk over, using the exact words she had before. She stopped at the same place she had the first time. This time there were more than the few scattered snickers there'd been at first. She gave up and went on to another book, saying, "Well, I just can't tell you about that book, I guess." Needless to say, her impact on that class was somewhat lessened, not only for that booktalk but also for her other ones, which were shaky too.

That's the worst horror story I've ever heard about what happens when your memory evaporates and you don't have any notes. It's always been an inspiration to me to take mine along, even when I'm very familiar with the talk. There are, however, a few ways of coping with a suddenly blank memory. I'll cover those in Chapter 6.

Once your talk is down on paper, it needs to be practiced and polished before you present it the first time. (It's not necessary to be able to do it in your sleep, but practicing while in a light doze is a definite advantage!) More polishing will take place after you've done it as part of a class presentation several times, and discovered that it doesn't sound quite right, or that the kids respond better where you emphasize one thing instead of another. Just because a booktalk is written down doesn't mean it can't be or shouldn't be changed. Most of my older talks had to be re-written for this book, because what I say now bears little resemblance to what I wrote down several years ago and hadn't bothered to change.

There is no substitute for practice, something I rediscover every time I think I can do without it. An audience can be distracted from the talk itself if the speaker is fumbling for words. The audience then get nervous *for* the speaker, hoping he or she won't forget what to say. The audience can relax when they are sure the speaker is in control of what's happening. How you practice really isn't important, although you will need to rehearse aloud, just as if you were actually talking to a class. Some people use a tape recorder or videotape when practicing. Both can be helpful, and a videotape can show you not only how you sound but also how you look to the class. The only disadvantage to either of these methods is that you have to be detached enough to learn from them. Hearing and seeing how you actually look and sound can be a rather disturbing experience, which can prevent any real learning. I have found this to be true in my own case, so I use neither of these methods, although they have been very helpful to other people. If you are uncomfortable with video equipment or don't have access to it, a full-length mirror can be an adequate substitute, letting you see immediately how you look and stand.

I merely read my talks aloud over and over again, and at least one time in front of someone else, in case there's some glaring error I haven't noticed. For instance, my ability to remember numbers is nil, and if I forget one I tend to plug in another that seems appropriate—only someone else can catch me on that. It's better if it isn't a class member who's already read the book.

While practicing your talk, practice not only the words but also the way you deliver them. In a booktalk, eye contact is essential, so practice looking around the room as you talk. Making eye contact with chairs, windows, plants, and so on may make you feel a little foolish, but it will help you to remember to look around when you're in front of a class, from habit, if nothing else.

You should also practice speaking in the tone of voice you will use during the actual talk, if you possibly can. This is especially important for people who speak softly and need to remember to practice speaking more loudly and enunciating clearly, making sure to project the voice all the way to the back of the room. Breathing deeply from the diaphragm will help do this. Modulation and tone of voice should be pleasant and easy to listen to—this is also a time to practice that. If you have trouble with any of these things—enunciation, tone, projection, or modulation—practice with a tape recorder is very important, at least until these problems are corrected. Don't change your voice when you do talks, either in practice or performance. Many people tend to talk down to children or teenagers, and one way of doing this is by raising the pitch of the voice. It's obviously patronizing, and teens are aware of it.

Any time you practice, you should work to make it seem as close to the real thing as possible. Begin to form good habits in your practice sessions, and they will stay with you in front of a class. For instance, I am now practicing talks standing up in the center of the room, because my new worst fault is the way I stand and what I do with my hands. Working in front of a mirror can also help you eliminate various kinds of awkward postures and poses. If nothing else works, be creative. I make sure that if I'm going to a class where I'll be the least bit ill at ease I wear something with pockets—that way I'll know where to put my hands! I try not to juggle the books around. I hold them up briefly and then set them up on a table, so I won't distract the audience by demonstrating my lack of dexterity. I usually pick up each book and show it to the audience again at the end of the talk as I repeat the author and title. I only pick up a book during a talk if I want to show pictures, which should, of course, always be marked ahead of time to avoid fumbling.

Rayme Meyer (Alameda County Library) practices her talks on tape. She writes a talk out, records it, and then throws out the written version, keeping only brief notes on cards. She listens to the tape over and over again, at any convenient time, until she's learned it. If she decides to change something, she makes a note on the card for that book, but doesn't change the tape. These tapes are her permanent records, to help her first learn her talks, then review them later, if it's been a while since she did them. She takes nothing into the class with her, but doesn't memorize her talks and so feels relaxed about changing them.

You should practice a talk until you feel comfortable with it and don't really need to check your notes to see what comes next. You may or may not have memorized it. If you haven't, it may not always be the exact same talk every time you give it, but it will seem more spontaneous. And you will have more freedom to tailor your words for the people you're talking to. I also think knowing rather than memorizing a talk makes it harder to forget or go blank. If you've memorized a booktalk and then forget one sentence, you can't go on, since the missing sentence is the key to the next one. If you haven't memorized it, you can simply use different words to express the same idea. In learning a talk, you might try to remember a series of scenes or ideas rather than specific words, visualizing a comic strip or TV show in your mind as you speak. Pictures are harder to forget than words. If you can actually *see* what you're describing as you do it, the picture you create for your audience will be more vivid, and you will help them create their own interior "visual aids."

When you know your booktalk well, set it aside and go on to another one. Which brings me to a point I have become adamant and rather cynical about. I keep all my booktalks—I still have the very first ones I did, back in 1969. A booktalk represents several hours of hard work and creativity. Replacing or rewriting a talk that I have not given in several months can take just as long or longer than it did to write it the first time. I know because I have had to rewrite several talks I naively loaned to people who never returned them. I am all in favor of sharing booktalks, and often exchange with other people. But now I only share *copies* of my talks. The three hundred or so booktalks I have represent several times that many hours, and while I don't mind if someone else uses my talks word-for-word, I want to retain the ability to give them myself as well, and so the original stays with me.

I also keep my talks in title order—it makes it much easier to locate a specific one quickly. This sort of filing may not be necessary at first, but as you write more and more talks, you may find that locating something filed in random order can be very time-consuming. Arrange your talks in the way you find easiest to deal with—maybe even by your own system of subject headings.

The Short Booktalk

A short booktalk can be used in several ways: in on-the-floor reader's advisory work with one or more people; for a change of pace from long booktalks during a school visit; in radio or TV spots to promote YA services or the library; or as a basis for a longer booktalk.

The method for writing a short booktalk is basically the same as for a long one; the difference is simply that the short talk doesn't include as much. A short booktalk is close to a long annotation, or a dust-jacket blurb. For example:

> *To Race the Wind*, by Hal Krents, is his autobiography and tells how he refused to let blindness stop him from doing anything— including learning how to drive a car when he was a senior in high school and playing touch football with his friends when he was in college.

> In *Slake's Limbo*, by Felice Holman, Aremis Slake gets tired of being beaten up by all the gangs in New York City and so escapes by going to live in the subway for 121 days.

> When Gail wakes up in the hospital examination room with her parents and doctors hovering over her, she knows what's happened. She also knows no one will believe her when she tells them she's been raped by the son of one of the town's most influential families. *Are You in the House Alone?* by Richard Peck.

Although short talks can be written and planned, they are

more often brief, spontaneous re-tellings of what was to you the most important part of the book. This is especially true for books you've already done long talks about. Include a good first sentence and something about what happens—that's all. This isn't always as easy as it sounds, since the tendency is to go on and on, making a short talk into a long one. Pick out the crux of the plot—what scene or character does the story move around? (*Not* the scene that gives away the ending, though!) Tell about that scene in just a few sentences, as in the examples given. Your remarks ought to be short, snappy, and most of all intriguing. You have only those few sentences to hook your audience—they have to really count!

Giving short booktalks isn't difficult for some people, but others may find that they need preparation until they get the hang of it. It becomes easier with practice. A question Mary and I answered over and over again during our visits to the Juvenile Hall was, "What's this about?" Not many kids wanted to listen to more than about 30–45 seconds' worth, so we became, of necessity, adept at the short booktalk.

3

DOING BOOKTALKS IN SCHOOLS

"Takin' It to the Streets"

For a number of reasons, school visiting is one of the most effective and popular ways of reaching teenagers. It is the way to reach a maximum number of teenagers in a minimum amount of time. (In Stanislaus County, two of us visited schools between February and May, 1978, and reached over 3,000 students.) The results are measurable and often immediate—circulation figures go up, reference questions increase, requests for particular titles given wide coverage can skyrocket. So the staff can usually tell right away how effective the school visits are (especially if the books requested are already in short supply). The image presented to the students of the library and librarians is a new one—less staid and conservative; more fun, relevant, and interesting. Talking about the various AV materials the library has can bring in kids who would never ask for a book, but might check out the latest rock record or maybe an 8mm or 16mm film. The kids also know that they'll recognize at least one face when they get inside the library, and that face will be a friendly one. Teenagers are tomorrow's taxpayers—the very life of libraries may depend on convincing them the library is good for something other than school assignments. And who knows, someone sitting at one of those desks may be inspired to become a librarian because of you! (It sounds corny, but it does happen!)

A successful school visiting program takes time, energy, and dedication, but it does bring results. Occasionally, when you have a waiting list of fifteen for a popular title and no more money for duplicate copies, you may even wish the results weren't quite so good! Because of the effect the program can have, school visiting should involve not only the YA or children's librarian who makes the actual visits but also the whole library staff. Without support from staff members, the program will fail. Include them as much as you can, from making sure they know what books you'll be talking about, to inviting them to go with you, either as participants or observers.

The first essential for school visiting is a lot of booktalks. You need a collection to work from so you don't do the same ones over and over, or spend hours frantically writing new ones by the dozen for each new class. Between twenty and thirty booktalks covering an assortment of subjects and age levels is a starting point. If you will be visiting both junior and senior highs, be sure you have included talks appropriate for both. Twenty or thirty booktalks may sound like a lot, but isn't in actuality all that many. Each time you select books for a class, try to add a few new ones to supplement the ones you already have. That way you should have, at any one time, only three or so books to prepare for a class. As your booktalk file grows, this number will decrease, although you should continue to add new talks to keep up with the new books being published and also to spread out the number of requests over a larger number of books. If you have only a few talks and have to do them over and over, you'll get so tired of those books you won't be able to convince anyone to read them. The essential spontaneity and joy of sharing will be gone, and with them your effectiveness. A variety of talks averts boredom for everyone, booktalker and audience alike.

The second essential for a successful school visiting program is books. Unless you can buy multiple copies of hardback books, you should do most of your talks on titles available in paperback. If you talk about a book in short supply, tell the kids they'll have to wait for it and give them some substitutes, if possible. Assume there will be requests for the titles you talk about frequently. At

Alameda County, I bought popular titles by the case so I'd have enough to fill requests from the five schools in the area. It's not really fair to generate interest in something you can't provide, and it is bad public relations besides. But there's always the exception, and sometimes kids are willing to wait for a title. I talked to a psychology class just after I'd gotten my review copy of *Why Am I So Miserable If These Are the Best Years of My Life?* by Andrea Boroff Eagan. I couldn't resist mentioning it. Although my talk was very brief, five girls requested the book. (At the time, I was taking ten minutes at the end of each class presentation to collect requests for the books I had talked about.) I explained that I'd just ordered several copies, but that it would take them a long time to arrive and be processed. Would they be willing to wait six months or a year? They all said they would be, and I saved the requests until the books arrived, a year later. I called each of the girls, and they were all *still* interested. They all picked up the copies I reserved for them, and a couple even came back to say how much they'd enjoyed it. It had been worth waiting for!

Cases like that are unusual. More often, if a book isn't readily available, kids will lose interest.

Contacting schools to let them know you are available can be done in a variety of different ways. A letter to the principal or the school librarian—perhaps both—explaining who you are and what you'd like to do can be a good beginning, especially if you have a large number of schools to contact. Include details of what you are able to do for the school—for instance, visit classes to talk about books and the library, to encourage recreational reading; give ideas for class assignments, such as book reports; provide booklists or bibliographies to support your visits; work with the school librarian—whatever you are prepared to do. If you are willing to visit special subject classes, say so—for instance, sociology, ancient history, business, law, remedial reading, poetry, creative writing, psychology, sex education. The list is bounded by only three things: your creativity, your willingness to work, and the amount of time you have available. Finding twelve or fourteen books on psychology for hi/lo readers is *not* my idea of the easy life! You might want to also point out your willingness to work with teachers and the school librarian on finding materials for mass assignments to make them easier on all concerned. Suggest a meeting so you can discuss these things with the department heads or with the whole faculty. Such a presentation will probably take about fifteen minutes, and could include a demonstration booktalk.

If you have fewer schools to contact, I have found a phone call to be a very effective and more personal method of conveying the same information. If you aren't sure about school policies, I would suggest contacting the principal first, either by phone or in person, to explain what you'd like to do. If the response seems favorable, ask if you can speak to the teachers, at a faculty meeting if possible. Ask for no more than fifteen minutes at the beginning of the meeting. If there are no faculty meetings, then see if you can speak to a meeting of department heads, on the same basis. Find out the name of the school librarian, and before you speak at that meeting, call or visit to make sure she or he knows what you're planning to do and what you'd like to accomplish.

Include the school librarian as much as possible in your school visiting program. Some librarians will be willing to do a lot for you—contact teachers, spread the word about you, help schedule classes, etc. Cultivate these people: They are rare. Other librarians will be less helpful, and you'll have to do more work in their schools. Occasionally, you may even find a librarian who has enough time to visit classes and do booktalks with you. These librarians are also rare, and should be appreciated, even if they just introduce you or do only one or two booktalks per class.

When you speak to any faculty group, you should take no more than fifteen minutes. Be as informal or formal as seems appropriate, but remember you are trying to convince your audience that you can make a lively presentation that will "turn the kids on to the library and books." If you bore the teachers, they'll never believe you won't bore the students. It has been my experience that large faculty meetings allow more freedom to be expressive. I have a fast, lively presentation for the teachers, including an explanation of what I can do for them and what they can do for me. I give some information about what's available in general at the library, outside the YA area, and mention any current programs they might be interested in. I usually include several comments that should make them laugh, and always the challenge: "I dare you to show me a kid that I can't persuade to read one book. Maybe not the first, or even the fifth—but sooner or later, I'll find the book he'll read!" So far, I'm batting a thousand. Tailor your presentation to your own personality. Maybe you can't be as flip as I can and get away with it. If formality is what you are most comfortable with, then be formal. Just be sure you're interesting. Until you're in their classroom, all these teachers see of you is that presentation. You have to sell yourself. Try several approaches—if one doesn't work, maybe another will. And the same technique may not be equally successful every time. Be flexible. The same approach may not be right for all schools. Be sure to mention how you can be contacted and leave a minute or so for questions. I've never included a demonstration booktalk in my faculty meeting visits, since I have always had to deal with a very limited time period and frequent pauses for laughter. However, if you have time, a demonstration can be a very effective way to let teachers know what you're going to be doing in their classes, and also give some validity to your claims of being able to persuade or inspire kids to read. If you can persuade teachers to read a book, surely you can persuade their students. Tie in current events and interests whenever possible: the Superman craze, the campaign to save the whales, the controversy over nuclear energy. Avoid boredom at all costs! Elizabeth Talbot once decided to convince a faculty group that she was serious about wanting to talk to their classes and made her point by wearing a clown mask to show she *wasn't* just "clowning around"!

If the entire faculty isn't meeting at a convenient time or at all, you can give a presentation at a meeting of department heads. For some reason, these gatherings are usually more formal than teachers' meetings, so be ready to tailor your presentation accordingly. If you arrive a bit early so that you have a chance to watch people come in and listen to the conversations preceding the meeting, you should be able to read the ambiance of the group and make an appropriate presentation. It should include the same information as the one for the faculty.

Make sure you meet the heads of the English and social studies departments. These two departments will probably give you most of your booktalking business. However, you don't have to limit yourself to booktalking. If you have display space, the art department head should know about it, not only for students' pictures but for any objects that might be produced in that department or other departments: wood carvings, jewelry, models, quilts, clothes—anything that would fit your display space. Working with the journalism department could get you a book review column in the school paper, or at least a list of the books you talked about at that school. Mention these possibilities, or, at least, note the appropriate people to talk to at a later time. Also ask if you can go to an English or social studies departmental meeting and talk to the teachers directly.

After you have talked to the whole faculty, the main reason for going to a separate department's meeting will be to schedule teachers for individual classroom presentations. Be sure to take your calendar, and check before you go to make sure you've got all your commitments on it. If you haven't visited a faculty meeting, or have only gone to a department heads' meeting, a single department's meeting gives you a chance to tell teachers directly what you'll be doing, as well as schedule your visits. You should probably include more detail about exactly what you can and can't do, and why you should be allowed to speak to their classes. Give both serious and not-so-serious reasons, from encouraging kids to read to giving the teachers a chance to relax, a no-effort class, and some ideas for their own reading. These meetings tend to be informal, and you should be able to form some opinions about various teachers from what they have to say in the meeting, so you can adapt your final class presentation to what they want. Teachers vary in the amount of freedom/discipline they allow/ impose on their classes, and a booktalker has to be aware of this.

Students do what the teacher expects, and their response to outside speakers is definitely included. Be aware of teachers' personalities as much as possible, but don't forget that first impressions can be very deceiving. (Some of my most enjoyable visits in Stanislaus County were to four classes taught by a woman whom I had been dreading. I was sure she would be very much into control, so that I would have to work three times as hard as usual to get a response. In fact, she was able to blend freedom and discipline so well that her classes were eager to respond and yet ready to be polite. She was at the top of my list the next year, needless to say!)

If you've done a good job selling yourself, you may find several of the teachers in a department wanting you to go to all five or six of their classes. If you try to schedule all those classes during the departmental meeting when your time is limited and you're therefore working under pressure, you'll never make it. Just make a list of class times and pertinent information (given later in Chapter 5) and arrange to leave each person a message saying when you'll be there. Ask them to get back to you if it isn't a convenient time. Do not depend on the department head to deliver these messages for you after you've given him or her a list of all the visits. The department head should have the complete schedule, but you also need to notify each teacher individually. The school librarian should also have a schedule of all visits. In some schools the librarian or one of the teachers may volunteer to set up your school visit schedule and let you know the results. This is only practical when you have large chunks of free time, so that as few conflicts as possible develop.

If this isn't your first year at a school, you may be able to skip some or all of these meetings by merely letting the teachers whose classes you've visited previously know that you're ready to come back again. A personal note might be easier than a phone call, since teachers are occasionally rather difficult to reach. Do be sure to notify the principal and the school librarian that you'll be in the school in any case.

There is always the question of when to make these contacts

and go to these meetings. If you can get yourself included in the agenda for the first week the teachers are back in school in the fall (without the students), that might be a good time. You might type up an information sheet on YA and reference services at the library, and include information on how the library as a whole (not just the YA department) can help teachers. Another logical time to start acquainting them with what you can do is at the beginning of a semester or grading period—probably two or three weeks into the semester, to give teachers and students a chance to settle down.

When you're planning visits and contacting teachers, it's very handy to have a copy of the faculty roster. If you can't get one from the school secretary, the librarian should have one you can copy. It's better to know the name of the person you want to deal with, rather than just the title.

Scheduling school visits can be compared to doing a jigsaw puzzle—sometimes it's very frustrating when all the pieces don't go where you'd like them to! Before any school contacts have been made, you and your supervisor or administrator should establish priorities. Is school visiting your first responsibility, or does it fall somewhere further down the line, to be fitted in around more important things? Will you be able to schedule as many school visits as you like, or will you be limited to visiting only a certain number of hours, days, or classes per week or month? Are you responsible for staffing a public desk a certain number of hours per week? Does this have a higher or lower priority than school visiting?

Once you have listed your various job responsibilities in order of priority, give each of them an hour-per-week value. After you complete this analysis, you should be able to tell how much time you can spend preparing for and making school visits. I usually spend one to three hours of preparation per class, depending on how many booktalks I have to write.

The two county libraries for which I have done most of my school visiting are good examples of the different priorities school visiting can be assigned. In Alameda County, where I worked under the direction of Carol Starr, I was responsible for service to young adults in four branches and at five high schools. School visiting came third, after book selection and collection maintenance. I was also assigned to the reference desk about twenty hours per week, occasionally more, and I was not allowed to cut down on this time to increase the number of school visits I made, although my desk time was usually fitted in after my visits had been scheduled. At a maximum, then, I could do school visits only three days a week, three classes a day. I usually did do this maximum during most of the school year. I could switch the days of the week around but not increase the number of days per week or classes per day. Because the person doing the scheduling usually worked several weeks in advance, I had to require at least two weeks' notice from the teachers. I turned in a schedule of planned school visits every two weeks. School visiting was given a fairly high priority in Alameda County, but had to be worked in around other things. I talked to about 150 to 200 classes a school year, reaching approximately 3,000 to 4,000 students. Some classes I did alone, some with one of the two other YA people in the region.

Priorities were set differently in Stanislaus County. Mary Moore and I were the only YA librarians in the county, and we had the freedom to set up our own schedules and priorities. During the school year, we each worked one night (four hours) a week on the reference desk, and we spent one afternoon a week together at the County Juvenile Hall. (We did the latter twelve months a year.) Our other duties were fitted in around school visiting, which took 35–40 percent of our time during the school year, including preparation time. From February through May, 1978, we visited about 250 classes and talked to over 3,000 students. We visited junior high and high schools throughout the entire county (a total of about 30 schools), and were occasionally visiting as much as four days a week, one to four classes a day. Usually we went separately, but occasionally together.

There are advantages to each approach. In Alameda County, I was more often visible when kids came in looking for the books

I'd talked about. There was a smaller area to cover, and it could be covered more thoroughly; however, the number of classes that could be visited was set ahead of time. In Stanislaus County, there was no set number of classes to visit; consequently, Mary and I were, some weeks, out of the library more than we were in it. Kids usually didn't see us when they came in, though we tried to encourage them to come on Monday or Tuesday nights, when at least one of us would be working, and to ask for us if we weren't right there at the desk. A heavier burden was placed on the reference staff, who sometimes couldn't tell what book a kid wanted from a vague description without a title or author. We would leave a list of the books we had talked about most frequently at both the children's and reference desks, but this didn't always solve the mystery of an elusive title. With such a large area to cover, we were forced to do fewer visits per school and could not get to every school every year. With no limit on how many classes we could go to, we had to be very aware of over-scheduling and burn-out, especially near the end of each semester, when we were tired and teachers wanted to be sure and schedule us before the term was over. "No" was the word we had to learn to use, frustrating as it sometimes was, for both us and the teachers.

The number of school visits a person can do depends upon individual stamina. A beginner shouldn't try to do more than one or two a day, two or three days a week. While booktalking is fun, it is also true that a forty-minute presentation to a group of teenagers is very tiring, both mentally and physically. It is very difficult, if not impossible, to psych yourself up enough to do a good job if you're tired. Until you know your limits, try to stay well below them, and progress slowly. Some classes will be more tiring than others, depending on how much work you have to do to get and hold the class's attention. If the kids are right there *with* you, interested in what you're saying, you'll find it takes less effort to booktalk than it does if you're talking to a group that isn't interested and doesn't want to listen, so that you have to work just to get the class's attention, never mind putting the books across. It's difficult to describe the difference between a group that's with you and one that's not, but even an inexperienced speaker can recognize it.

Therefore, it may be fine to schedule three or even four classes in one day if you're talking to kids who love to read and want some new ideas. It's not such a good idea to schedule three or four classes of reluctant readers on one day, since you'll be expending more effort and energy per class and may not have enough left to do a good job with the third or fourth group. However, responsiveness doesn't always correlate with reading ability. A seventh-grade group of interested nonreaders, even though they may be full of wisecracks, is easier to talk to than a group of senior honor students who are too blasé to react or let any emotions show. A teacher who allows a class the freedom to react to your comments (while still maintaining discipline) will have classes that are more fun and easier to talk to than the teacher who demands absolute silence from the students. If possible, schedule the classes you think will be the most difficult first, so that you'll give them your best shot. If you have a good class later, you will usually be able to psych yourself up from the positive feedback during your presentation. In other words, even when your energy is running low, it's easier to put on a good show for an appreciative audience than it is for one that doesn't care.

When you begin scheduling classes, remember you'll have to allow for a lot of preparation time writing and learning new booktalks, maybe for every class. Increase your school visits slowly. It's better to say No and give everyone full measure than it is to accept every invitation and end up so tired that some classes get a less than first-rate presentation. The teachers who sit through a poor presentation won't ask you back, and will probably tell their colleagues that you don't do a very good job. You are your own best advertisement, so you need to be sure you do the best possible job with every class. You will be working more effectively and your reputation will be better if you do a modest number of very good visits instead of a lot of mediocre ones.

If your supervisor doesn't set limits, set your own and stick to them. It is difficult to do talks at more than one school a day, especially if travel time is more than five or ten minutes. I can do an absolute maximum of four classes a day, and I have to have a break sometime in between so I can relax. I cannot be onstage for four hours straight and still do as good a job with the fourth class as I did with the first. (Some people can, however. Marion Hargrove, from Prince Georges County Library, does a whole day of classes—six or seven periods, with a break for lunch—and does it with great success. She has had a lot of experience and must schedule herself heavily in order to cover the number of schools she has to visit.) You will need to consider how many days a week you will be visiting as well as how many classes you will talk to a day. You may want to limit yourself to two or three days a week. It is easier to do four classes for two or three days than for four days, especially if you need a lot of time for traveling. Consider your own convenience as well as that of the teachers when you plan your schedule. Make it as pleasant for yourself as possible. If you have several classes you think will be difficult to talk to, schedule them next to or between classes you think will be easy. Try to schedule all the classes for one day in a block, so you don't have to make several trips to the school or kill a great deal of time between appointments. For example, classes at 8:00 A.M., 9:00 A.M., and 11:00 A.M. would be fairly easy to cope with, and three in a row easier still, unless you prefer not to do three at one time. When you have extra time between classes, you might take the opportunity to talk to the librarian and let her know what you're doing, not only in class visits but in your whole YA program. You can get a cup of coffee and sit in the teachers' lounge, maybe drum up some new business or just rest your voice and not talk for awhile.

I usually stay in a class for the whole period—35–55 minutes. Teachers seem to prefer that to an interrupted class period, and it also gives me time for a more relaxed presentation. Some librarians simply don't have time to spend a whole period with each class and so only take 20 minutes, meeting two groups per class period. This method works, but is more wearing, means more hassles and more pressure, and can cause burn-out. For these reasons, I can't really recommend it. Sue Tait, of the Seattle Public Library, points out that there *are* advantages to doubling up, though. It is not very tiring if there are not many schools to visit, and beginners often find it easier to prepare a 15-minute presentation than a 40-minute one. Also, teachers may prefer not to lose a whole class period. At the end of the year, you may use short presentations to do a quick blitz of all the schools you can get to—an effective way to remind kids that there will be things going on at the library during the summer or to give them summer reading ideas.

As you get more experience you may find that you have more endurance than I do, and can go virtually all day, every day. I envy you. However, if you don't built up to that gradually, you may end up doing a poor job, not having a good time, and disliking booktalking altogether.

When you know you're going to be at a school all day, be sure to take your lunch, or scout out a convenient fast-food place so you can get away from campus if you want to. A toothbrush, deodorant, and a few basic toiletries are also important. A few minutes of "freshening up" can make you look and feel more presentable.

Burn-out does happen with school visiting. It usually starts for me about a month before school's out, when I have a very full schedule. I start counting down on the number of classes I have left. By the time the last one is over in May or early June, I'm sure I never want to do another booktalk again! That feeling lasts about a month or six weeks; then I start looking forward to school again and writing new booktalks as fast as I can. The best way to combat burn-out is not to do too much, so you don't get too tired. If you feel yourself getting tired of school visiting, slack off for awhile until you can get your enthusiasm back.

How far ahead of time should you require teachers to ask for a class visit? Again, this depends on your experience and on how much preparation time you need and have available. In Alameda County, I required two weeks' notice for "standard classes"—straight English classes, with no special subject to work around, just recreational reading. For "special classes" (ones I would have to read many new books for—history, psychology, religion, poetry, fantasy, mythology, anything not standard), I asked for four to six weeks, since I needed time to read the books (up to a dozen new ones for each class) and write the booktalks. In Stanislaus County, with a substantial file of booktalks, Mary and I still asked for a week or so advance notice, so we could be sure of having some preparation time, even for a standard class. When we were heavily booked, teachers were sometimes forced to schedule us up to three or four weeks ahead, simply because our time prior to that was already taken. Since we were both experienced and had complete freedom to do our own schedules, we did not always require much advance notice. The main thing to remember in setting up a schedule is to allow yourself enough time to plan the visit carefully, and to write and practice any new booktalks you may need.

When you schedule visits, try to have them on the days of the week when the students will be the most receptive. Friday afternoon is probably the worst time, followed by Monday, both morning and afternoon. Try to do most of your visiting on the three middle days of the week, especially to those classes you think may be most difficult. Likewise, the beginning and middle of a semester are probably the best times for heavy visiting. Toward the end of the term, everyone's worried about finals and more interested in vacation than you.

The school librarian can be very helpful in working out the best times for you to visit and may even be willing to do all or most of the scheduling for you, especially if you've been to the school before and the teachers all know you already. The librarian can also leave reminders with the teachers about your forthcoming visit several days in advance, if you have scheduled it several weeks previously. (You should do this yourself if the school librarian won't do it for you.) Work with your school librarians; include them in the program as much as possible, even to doing one or two booktalks with you, if they are interested and have time. They may be willing to let the class meet in the school library, so that the students can browse and maybe check out some of the books you talked about. Always let the school librarian know when you'll be in the school, and provide a list of the books you intend to talk about so the library can be prepared for requests. The librarian may want to purchase some of the titles for his or her own collection. You might even consult with the school librarian when you plan your presentation, so that you can include as many books as possible that are already in the school library. Then the students will have access to them there as well as in the public library.

Don't ever make the school librarian feel that you are competing. While your basic function is the same, your areas of emphasis are different. You should complement each other and work together.

If your schedule gets very full, some teachers may ask you to talk to their combined classes—eighty or ninety kids at one time. Don't do it! I have nightmares remembering the times I agreed to do this and then bitterly regretted it. A larger group is harder to control, and is likely to include more kids who enjoy making trouble. Even the kids who usually listen or at least keep quiet will find new people to talk with when two classes meet together—people who seem more interesting than their familiar classmates. You will have less chance for eye contact, and you will have to speak louder than usual just to be heard in the back row. Teachers who may be able to keep a class quiet in their own rooms aren't always able to do so when there's another class present. In short—noise, hassle, and a less than effective presentation. Perhaps someone somewhere can communicate as effectively with large groups as with small ones—try it if you think you can. But if you can't don't hesitate to refuse!

4

PREPARING A CLASS PRESENTATION

Behind the Scenes

WHEN YOUhave decided to visit a specific class, you need to find out certain things about the class so you can choose books that will be interesting to them.

1. *Subject of class.* What is the class title? What is the teacher teaching? What books have they read in class recently—you will want to avoid these. The subject of the class will affect your scheduling as well as the content of your talks, since you may need more preparation time for some subjects.

2. *Purpose of visit.* What does the teacher expect of you? Why have you been asked to come—to give recreational reading ideas or book report suggestions, provide background information for an assignment, or explain what is available on a particular subject? You should let the teacher/librarian know what you can and cannot do, and what your standard presentation includes, if this is not clear already. You may also want to more or less tailor your appearance to the teacher's expectations. If you look too much like a teenager yourself, you may have trouble getting support or cooperation.

3. *Composition of class.* What is the age level, the reading level, the ratio of boys to girls? Does the class have a long or short attention span? How large is it? What are some books class members have recently read and enjoyed? Does the class have

any special interests? How much informality is appropriate? These are things you will need to know when selecting books to talk about. If there are more boys, you will need more male-oriented books. If their attention span is short, longer booktalks won't work as well as a series of short, snappy ones. Age and reading levels are important to consider, since you want to select something that the students will be interested in *and* able to read.

4. *Length of class.* How much time will you have to talk? Do you want to talk for the whole period or only a part of it? What would the teacher prefer?

5. *Room number and location.* Be sure to get this. It's very embarrassing to be late because you got lost or had to go to the office first and find out where you were going.

6. *Exact times class starts and ends.* Teachers and school librarians run on a totally different schedule from the rest of the world. They go by periods—first, second, fifth, and so on—not by hours. And knowing you have to talk to a third period class does not tell you when to be there! Be sure to find out if third period starts at 9:15 or 10:27—there's usually no rhyme or reason to it, and every school is unique. You also need to know exactly when the class is over so you can wind up your presentation before the bell rings, and not get caught in mid-sentence as your audience rushes past you to the door.

A school visit can have a variety of purposes, which will determine the content of your presentation. Are you advertising the library or just promoting books? If part of your purpose is doing PR for the library, you will want your introduction to include information on what materials are available there (magazines, records, films), the rules and regulations for using them, the library's hours, its location, and so on. Including some actual reference questions that were particularly funny or unusual can make the point that the library is a place for adults as well as students to find information. This introduction can be very brief or as long as ten minutes. If you have mentioned various materials, you may also want to include samples of them either as part of your introduction or after your booktalks, in a wrap-up. For me, the latter way works best. After my last booktalk, I show a variety of magazines students can check out, adding the names of others I don't have with me as I go. I also talk about "adult picture books"—big books on a variety of subjects that are more pictures than text. This works well with hi/lo classes, so I usually talk about more of these for them.

If you do not want to include any general library information, your introduction can be very brief. You should include your name, your title, where you work (which branch), and where the books you're going to talk about can be found—the location of the young adult areas in your branch and in any other nearby libraries. Then just go right into your first booktalk. My introductions, whether I am pushing the library or just books, are usually only about five minutes long, since I have noticed that kids are less interested in hearing about the library than in the books I've brought.

Choose books for each class with its composition in mind. Vary long and short booktalks, so you don't talk an equal length of time about each book. Otherwise, you may create static and measured presentation, when a more interesting one is what you want. Keep in mind the amount of time you will have, and be sure to plan to include enough books to fill it up. Underestimating can create problems, such as being left with twenty minutes at the end of the class and nothing to say. Depending on the length of the class period and the other things I want to present (a long introduction about the library or samples of various things available there other than books), I can do from six to fourteen talks of varying lengths per class. I usually have one or two books left over if I do fewer talks. Some people deliberately take more books than they plan to use so that they can choose titles according to the class's response. To do this, you have to find the right balance— not carrying too many books but still giving yourself maximum flexibility as a performer.

Keep a list of the titles you plan to talk about for each class. I make a separate Information Card for each class, listing the school, teacher, class, time, room number, date, any other miscellaneous information I might want, and the books I plan to talk about (see Figure 1). I keep these cards clipped together in date order in the drawer with all my other booktalk materials, where I can find them at short notice. I try to keep three weeks or so ahead of myself when I fill out the cards, so I don't have too many last-minute decisions to make. After the visit is over, the cards provide a record of what I talked about, in case I want to do the same or different books the next time I do that class. The cards are also handy if you have a subject that is difficult to locate books on, and you have to do that particular class every year. You have something to build on, and only have to start from scratch once.

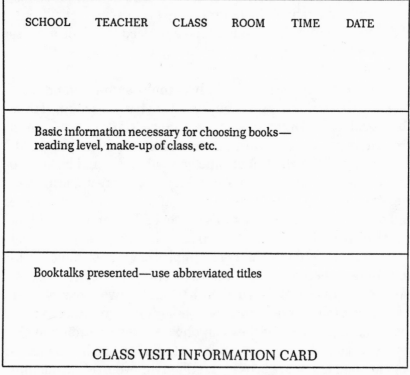

SCHOOL	TEACHER	CLASS	ROOM	TIME	DATE

Basic information necessary for choosing books— reading level, make-up of class, etc.

Booktalks presented—use abbreviated titles

CLASS VISIT INFORMATION CARD

Figure 1

When I first started booktalking I also listed the sequence in which I planned to talk about the books, although as I became more confident I did not bother to do this. But planning can be very helpful for the beginning booktalker, or for anyone who needs the security of a set program. It also helps in making a more flowing presentation, with fewer pauses or hesitations between booktalks and smoother transitional sentences connecting them.

Some people find this method too rigid, because it does not allow for last-minute changes or the idiosyncrasies of individual classes. Beginners may find it easier, however, to start with more structure and move away from it when they have more experience. Structuring is one way to minimize last-minute panic, hassles, and mistakes. Knowing exactly what is coming next can also combat stage fright, by helping you just grit your teeth and carry on without having to make any decisions of the what-do-I-do-now variety. Such structure can be useful as a crutch, to be discarded if it doesn't help or when it's no longer necessary. (I hung onto it for almost five years!)

Whether or not you decide on an exact order for all the books you use, it is a good idea to plan at least the first one or two and the last one you will talk about. These are just as important as the corresponding sentences in a booktalk. The first book you talk about should always be one that will interest both males and females. It should also be a booktalk with which you are totally familiar and comfortable. If you are a beginner, choose one you particularly enjoy doing. This first talk is the one you will be judged on. During it, your audience will decide whether you are worth listening to. The talk should be exciting, and also one you are able to do well in spite of encroaching stage fright, to which even experts are not immune. Perhaps you can find several books you can use as your standard openers, as I have. I have used *Deathwatch, The Shining, I Know What You Did Last Summer, Death in Canaan, The Boys From Brazil,* and *The Amityville Horror* as some of my openers.

I also make sure that my second book is a "grabber," just like the first one, to make absolutely certain I have everyone listening. However, if the students are mostly girls, my second book will probably be more female-oriented, though still something boys

might read. Two of Richard Peck's novels fit in well here—
Through a Brief Darkness and *Are You in the House Alone?*

The last book you talk about needs to be one that will end the
presentation on an upbeat. Whether the book is funny or suspenseful, it should definitely leave your audience wanting more.
It's the last thing you're going to say to them. It should leave a
definite impression, preferably good. *Ammie Come Home, Ice
Station Zebra, House of Stairs*, and *Jay J. Armes, Investigator*
are all good examples of this.

Within the body of your talk, try to alternate male-oriented and
female-oriented books. Usually boys are the hardest to hook and
the easiest to lose. The quickest way to make them lose interest is
to talk about several books in a row they wouldn't want to read—
love stories, for example. Put *A Distant Summer, Beginnings*,
and *My Darling, My Hamburger* together and nine times out of
ten you'll lose the male part of your audience. All this sounds
sexist, I know, but I have also found it to be true. And as we know,
many teenage boys *are* sexists. I'm not saying that we should
cater to their attitudes (in fact, we have a real responsibility to
counter them in the books we talk about), only that it doesn't
matter what you say if your audience isn't listening.

The 1979 BAYA (Bay Area Young Adult Librarians) Hip Pocket
Reading Survey (*Top of the News*, Summer 1979) showed that a
number of teenagers are interested in classic authors, such as the
Brontës, Dickens, and Steinbeck, and in "semi-classics" such
as Agatha Christie. You might try including one or two of these,
especially if you are in an English class with a conservative
teacher.

You can also use films as a part of your presentation. Many YA
librarians do so with great success. The best time to show a film is
after your booktalks, since it is very much a "dessert" and the kids
may not be interested in listening to you after they've seen the
film. Interruptions such as: "Hurry up! We wanna see the film!",
"If you don't quit talking, the class is gonna be over!", "Forget the
books! Bring on the movie!" showed me it is better to make them

wait. This may not be everyone's experience, however, so show the film at the point it works best for you.

Lists of short films for use in school classes are published by NICEM (National Information Center for Educational Media) and by *School Library Journal*, among others. The all-time favorite short is probably *Bad Bad Leroy Brown*. When we showed it to a freshman English class in an open classroom school, we attracted not only that class but kids from all the classes around it. They crowded in six deep and had a marvelous time. Their teachers were somewhat less appreciative, and requested that we please *not* bring that film again. Oh well, I guess you just can't please everyone! The best films to use are short (no more than ten minutes), fast-moving, and fun—pure entertainment. Animated cartoons work well for lower grades, and *Frank Film* has been used very successfully with juniors and seniors. Two spoofs—*Blaze Glory* and *That Rotten Teabag*—and two sports films—*Turned On* and *The Olympia Diving Sequence*—were very popular in Alameda County. But any good film will remind the kids that the library can be fun.

Before scheduling a film, be sure to get the teacher's approval. Also ask if you can use a school projector, since you already have to lug around a film, a stack of books, and other stuff. Allow enough time before your presentation to set up the equipment and rewind the film, so all you have to do later is turn on the projector. It should be all ready to go when you start your presentation.

Of course, there may be technical problems. The film may break, the projector may not work—be prepared for the worst. If anything does go wrong, try to keep your sense of humor. Don't panic—it happens to everyone. If you can't remedy the situation, forget it. Teachers show enough films these days for kids to know that occasional mishaps are inevitable. But they usually yield to the inevitable somewhat less than quietly—be ready for that, too.

Some YA librarians do a slide show as part of their presentation, showing the library, the YA area, and various programs and activities. Although I have never tried this, I'm sure a snappy, fast-moving presentation of this sort could be very effective.

Another AV aid you can use is rock music. Tape selections from the library's popular records and play them before and after your presentation, or as background for a slide show. You could either tape a few complete songs or excerpts from a variety of songs, performed by different groups. This can be a very effective way of letting the kids know something different and *fun* is happening.

You can also take a box of paperbacks into the class with you and let kids check them out right there. These can be either copies of the books you've talked about, or other titles, or both. The major disadvantages to doing this are the poor return rate and the amount of time even the most minimal processing takes. I feel however, that with a sufficient supply of paperbacks, the advantages far outweigh the disadvantages. It is fun, and the kids love it. It is the ultimate way of striking when the iron's hot, especially with hi/lo classes. If they don't get the book they want to read *now*, they may lose interest and never read it at all. This is, of course, true of any class, but especially of hi/los. At Alameda County, we didn't require a library card. We just stamped the books with a date due, and kept a record of how many went out to add to the branch circulation. We also found that it was a good idea, when talking to several classes in a row, to hold back copies of some of the most popular titles so the last class would have just as good a selection as the first one.

If you have to cancel a visit, do so as far ahead of time as you can. If something comes up at the last minute, it is especially important to let the teacher know you won't be there. So if you wake up with laryngitis on the day you have three class visits scheduled, starting at 8:00 A.M., don't just call the school and hope someone in the office will tell the teacher what's happened. Call the school librarian as well, and ask him or her to go over and tell the teacher personally or have one of the library aides do it. The librarian should always know about cancelled visits, anyway, because she or he may be able to provide valuable help in a last-minute emergency. School visits are supposed to create good will for the library. Not showing up for a visit without letting anyone know you won't be there is bad public relations (and bad manners, too). If you tend to oversleep, try using two alarm clocks or get someone to give you a wake-up call.

The library staff needs to be prepared for the results of a successful school visiting program: Kids, kids, and more kids, all wanting the same books, most of which they can't identify by either title or author, only by bits and pieces of the plot, and the fact that "somebody came to my class and talked about it." Children's and reference staff members can get very annoyed, to say the least, if they are caught unprepared for the onslaught.

A list of the books you talk about should be on hand at both the adult and children's reference desks. If you are not doing too many classes, it could be organized by teacher and school. If possible, this list should be annotated, at least briefly, since titles and authors may mean little or nothing to the kids who come in. Don't forget to make sure all branches near the schools where you talk have lists, as well as the main branch.

Have as many copies of the books you talk about ready in the library as possible. Borrow from other branches ahead of time if you can't buy enough copies, especially of hardback books. If you have space to do it, you can set aside several shelves in your office or work area for multiple copies of the books you talk about. That way the library staff has to look in only one place for extra copies.

You can also make a separate display in your young adult area for "Books Everybody's Talking About," and use it only for book-talked books. Again, it means the staff has only one place to look. At Fremont Main, I had all the hardback books I talked about stamped "Booktalk Display," and the pages automatically shelved them in that area. It saved a lot of wear and tear on everyone concerned, and, once it was set up, was easy to maintain.

Since you will be taking copies of the books with you when you visit classes, you need to pull them ahead of time and keep them by your desk or in your office. You should start doing this toward the end of the summer, if you plan to begin giving talks in September or October. The copies you pull should be nice looking, with dust jackets if they are hardbacks. But use as many paperbacks as possible. Kids usually prefer them, they're easier to carry, and you're more likely to have multiple copies in the library, so the one you pull won't be missed. You should keep these sample books during the whole time you're doing book-talks, so that you know they'll always be available when you need them. Make sure other staff members understand that these copies are not to be moved for any reason. At 8:15 in the morning, when you're running late for a 9:00 class, suddenly noticing that three of your booktalk books are unaccountably missing can wreak havoc with your carefully planned presentation and with staff relations as well, not to mention what might have been a beautiful day! If you explain to staff members precisely why you must have these books available at all times, and add a "*Please* Do Not Touch, *Ever!*" sign to your shelves, you should have no problem.

If you are handing out booklists to the classes you visit, you should probably have a copy of each book on the list in your desk collection. You will be booktalking some or most of these, and the rest are your potential talks. If you want to change the program at the last minute, these copies will be useful.

5

GIVING A BOOKTALK PRESENTATION

How to Hold a Roomful of Uncaged, Untamed Adolescents in the Palm of Your Hand

PRACTICE is the first step in giving a successful presentation. Polish your booktalks until they are perfect. Plan what you're going to do, including how you'll display the books, where you'll stand, and what you'll do with your hands. Work out what you're going to say in your introduction, writing it down if that is easiest; if not, just making notes to remind yourself what comes next. Practice until you are completely at ease with what you'll be saying.

Make doubly sure you have copies of all the books you'll be talking about, especially if they are books you haven't used before. Kids are going to be more interested in a book that they can actually see. Also, you may discover that it's easier to talk about a book if you have it with you. Sometimes I only remember what I want to say when I pick up the book itself. If I have to talk about something I don't have on hand, I flounder, forget what to say, and generally do a rotten job.

I carry all my paraphernalia for school visiting in a large, sturdy canvas bag, which provides, I feel, the easiest and least awkward means of transporting all this gear, and eliminates juggling several different packages. The book bag is used only for school visits, and usually stays at work, so I know where it is. Make sure that any sack you use is sturdy enough to carry the weight of everything you'll be putting into it, and large enough so that you *can* put everything into it. It should also be shaped so that it's easy to carry when full.

The day before a visit, I load books, booklists, a film if I'm using one, class visit information cards, teachers' evaluation forms (Figures 1 and 2), request cards, booktalks, and calendar into the book bag. If I'm going to an early class, the bag probably goes home with me, so I don't have to stop by the library and pick it up the next morning, when I could have slept fifteen minutes longer. If it's a later class, I'll take home the talks I need to practice and leave everything else at work. (Occasionally I find time to practice booktalks at work. More often I don't, and have gotten into the habit of practicing at home. It's not the best of all possible arrangements, but it involves me in the fewest hassles.)

I have reasons for carrying along everything I take, in spite of the fact that I occasionally have rather a heavy load. Books and booktalks, films and the Teacher Information Cards are obvious items to take. Booklists are nice to hand out to the class, to suggest other things the kids might like to read. These lists should be bright, eye-catching; and annotated. Almost any format will do. Some people want to include a larger number of books on these lists and skip the annotations, but the kids seem to prefer annotations because they give an idea of what the book is about. More information on booklists is included in Chapter 7.

When I was at Alameda County, some of us on the Fremont YA staff worked up a class visit evaluation form that's been used there ever since. (See Figure 2.) Mary and I also used it in Stanislaus County. It offers a chance to get feedback, encouragement, and occasionally, helpful pointers about how to improve your performance. It's relatively simple, and I always tell the teachers they can spend as much or as little time on it as they wish. Replies vary widely, from the casual to the meticulously detailed. (And do be prepared for criticism. Nine times out of ten, all you get is positive feedback—but do watch out for that tenth reply! Not all teachers or students are careful to be tactful.)

Bringing enough copies of the books you have mentioned to fill requests in class is a nice touch that many kids will appreciate. Or

TEACHER'S CLASS VISIT EVALUATION FORM

Teacher _____ Librarian(s) _____

Class and Grade _____

School _____ Date _____

Please be honest—our feelings won't be hurt—and we really need to know how to improve.

1. How would you rate the visit?

EXCELLENT   SATISFACTORY
UNSATISFACTORY   HORRIBLE

2. In what ways was it satisfactory or unsatisfactory?

	GREAT	OKAY	AWFUL	OTHER
General Presentation	——	——	——	——
Length of Booktalks	——	——	——	——
Interest Level	——	——	——	——
Number of Talks	——	——	——	——
Appropriateness of Titles	——	——	——	——
Reading Level	——	——	——	——
Other (specify)	——	——	——	——

Comments on any of the above:

3. What things did you particularly like about the visit?

4. How could the visit be improved?

5. Would you be interested in further visits?

6. Would you recommend to other teachers that we visit their classes?

7. What opinions/reactions did your class have after we left?

8. Other comments/questions.

Figure 2

you can take requests in class and fill them later. Allow about ten minutes or so for checking out books, or for passing out the request cards and getting them back. Usually all that the students really need to put down on a card is the title of the book they want and their name, address, and phone number. Fill the request cards when you get back to the library and call the kids as soon as the books are available. My record number of requests was fifty-seven from three classes, but student response can vary widely from class to class. These procedures *are* time-consuming. Finding all the books and calling each person can take hours, and many of the books may never be picked up. You may have to go through the request shelves a week later and retrieve all the orphans to fill other requests. When the kids respond, the request cards can work very well, and the kids will appreciate the special attention. But every person has to decide individually whether the response is worth the trouble involved.

Be sure you always take your calendar. Teachers frequently want to know when their next visit will be, if they can schedule another one, or if they can change to another day. Other teachers may drop by the classroom, the staff lounge, or the library to schedule new classes. The one day you forget your calendar is the day when all of the above will happen, I guarantee!

When you are deciding what to wear to the school, remember that you're going to have a whole roomful of kids staring at you. Wear something comfortable that will stay in place without adjustment and allow you to move naturally, something you can forget about once you've put on. Your individual style will determine exactly how you dress, but no matter how you look, you should give that roomful of kids something nice to look at. Be attractive. That can mean wearing your newest outfit or the old standby that always makes you feel good. I usually dress up a little and make an effort to wear something at least close to the latest thing. (I feel an obligation to do my part to change the stereotypical librarian image.) However, if the latest thing isn't right for you, wear whatever is. Some people prefer to be as unobtrusive as possible, in order not to distract from the books.

Unexceptional or "classic" clothes can save you from being labeled "unprofessional" or "hippie" by either the class or the teacher and since an "unprofessional" image can jeopardize your position in the school, you should consider your appearance from this angle as well. There are even more practical considerations: Pockets can be useful if you have trouble deciding what to do with your hands. And no matter what else you wear, be sure to choose comfortable shoes. Four-inch heels or new boots may look super-chic, but don't wear them unless you can stand up in them for four hours at a stretch without falling off or getting grumpy! It's difficult to think about anything else when your feet hurt, so make sure they don't.

In summary, try to feel comfortable and look attractive. Be aware enough of how you look that you can forget about it.

Get to the school ten or fifteen minutes early so you have a chance to find the room or go by the library and say hello to the librarian. You might also be asked to stop at the office so the school administration knows you're on campus. Don't interrupt a class if you arrive before the bell rings. Wait in the library or in the hall near the room. When the period is over, gather up your things and go in.

Introduce yourself to the teacher. Make sure part of a desk or table can be cleared off so you have a place to display your books as you talk about them. Ask the teacher not to leave the room, and explain to him or her that you can't be both a disciplinarian and an entertainer. There is usually no problem about this; most teachers assume they'll stay in the room. However, it's a good idea to mention it when you're visiting a teacher for the first time or if a class looks as though it might be particularly loud and difficult to handle. You might also ask the teacher to introduce you, so that there will be a definite beginning to your presentation. This is more effective than the teacher just taking roll and wandering off to the back of the room, leaving you to get the kids quiet and introduce yourself. Even "This is _____ from the library who's going to talk about books" is better than nothing. Carol Starr tells a funny story about a teacher who introduced her the first time she went to his class with a five-minute speech on the theme "I've given up my valuable class time for this speaker, so you better be quiet or else!" The second time she spoke to his class, he said merely, "This is Carol Starr, and she's going to tell you about some really neat books." A one hundred percent improvement!

Set your things up in the order you are going to need them. Give the teacher an evaluation form, if you intend to use one, before your presentation starts, in case he or she wants to make notes while you're talking. If you plan to talk about the books in a certain order, stack them up in that order. Stack your notes or booktalks the same way. They should be where you can unobstrusively glance down at them if you need to do so. Decide where you're going to stand—behind or beside the table where your books are is best if you have to refer to your notes at all. If you aren't using notes, you can stand in front of the table or desk and lean or even sit on it. Make sure the way you move or stand will not make you look awkward—practicing or just taking thought will help here. Women need to be aware of how they sit when they wear skirts. "Keep your knees together" may sound like something your mother used to say, but not doing so can be distracting and embarrassing for your audience and for you.

Just as the clothes you wear to a class should be those that make you feel comfortable and at ease, the best way for you to act in front of a class will also depend partly on your own personality. Move and stand in a way that feels natural and right for you. Leaning against the backboard, against the side or front of the desk where your books are, or standing away from the desk in the open are all equally good. Sitting on the desk, either on the edge or completely on it, is more difficult to carry off, but if such a position is one you like, try it. (However, you need to be aware that the informality such a position suggests may make some teachers and even an occasional student uncomfortable.) Standing away from walls and desks makes it easier to use body language as a part of your talk, but also makes your unconscious body language more obvious. Standing with your hands on your hips or arms folded can convey the idea of "parent" or "lecture" without your intending it. If you are ill at ease with your hands at your sides, link them loosely in front or in back of you; put one hand at your side, the other in back of you; or put one or both of them in your pockets. You can use gestures during your talks, but be very sparing. A speaker with windmilling arms can be easy to mock, amusing and distracting. Remember to look pleasant as you talk, and smile when you can. Your facial expression, as well as your body language, can turn kids on or off.

The last thing to do before you start talking is relax. Remind yourself that you are going to be fine, and that even mistakes can be dealt with and are not major crises. Remember you are promoting books for recreation, even if the reason you're there is to help the class find something for a required book report. You have to enjoy yourself; *you* have to have a good time too. Take a minute to be aware of that. The kids you're in front of want to enjoy the program, and no matter how monstrous they look right now, they're just people. Most of them are probably pretty nice. Wait until everyone is quiet and the attention is on you, take a deep breath, *smile*, and begin.

As you begin to talk about each book, pick it up and show it to the class, giving its author and title as you do so. Then stand it up facing the class, so they can see the cover. Sometimes the teacher will insist that the kids write down all the authors and titles you mention, but try not to delay your talks any longer than necessary. Point out that kids can get the information off the book jackets when the presentation is over or from the lists you will distribute. Or just go on holding up the book as you start your talk, so that everyone can copy from the cover (try to hold it steady!). As you set down one book after another, make an effort to display them in an attractive arrangement, with as many titles visible as possible. If some books have to be obscured, they should be the ones that you talked about first. The cover of the book you are currently talking about should always be visible.

If there is a picture you want to show the class, walk in front of the whole class, holding the book just above their eye level. Be sure to hold the book straight up and down, *not* with the top tilted back toward you. Give the class as long and clear a look as possible without losing the sense of your talk. It isn't necessary to talk the whole time you're showing pictures, but don't let silences build up for more than thirty seconds or so. If someone says, "Hey, wait, I didn't see it!" remind the kids that they'll have another chance to look at the books after you finish talking.

When you finish your last booktalk, invite the kids to come up and see the books and ask any questions they may have. If you are taking requests, explain as briefly as possible how to fill out the cards and be ready to hand them out. Talk to the kids who come up about the books, and be ready to suggest other titles to students who have already read the ones you talked about. Responses to your invitation to come up and look at the books can vary widely, to say the least. Usually a junior high class will have an enthusiastic response. Kids may even elbow you to one side in their eagerness to get to the books. Many times, in a junior high class, all the kids in the room have come up to examine the books and talk to me. (And examine is the accurate word. There was one nude photo in *The Rock Almanac*—I didn't have any idea it was there until it was found by a rather gleeful eighth-grader. Someone found it and made a big deal about it in almost every junior high class I went to. I finally gave up and quit taking that book!) It doesn't seem to matter much whether the kids are good readers or not, either, on a junior high level. They *all* want to see what's going on. High school classes are much more blasé. You hardly ever get a stampede even out of sophomores. Maybe one or two kids will, oh-so-casually, drift up to look at the books and pick up a booklist. Leaving the booklists for kids to pick up from the table where the books are displayed seems to work better than passing them out. Fewer lists will be made into airplanes or just dropped on the floor. Besides, the booklists provide an excuse for kids to get closer to the books (sometimes it even works!).

Don't judge your presentation by the number of kids who come up to talk to you afterwards. There are many factors besides the presentation itself that may influence them. If the teacher is a strict disciplinarian, they may not be inclined to move without permission. Or they may be waiting for someone else to go first—no one wants to appear too eager by being the first person to move. If that's the case, a few more comments can break the ice and put them at their ease. Hand someone a book he's been eyeing or strike up a conversation. Listen to what the kids are saying and watch what they're doing for a clue about why they're pretending to be bumps on logs. It may or may not have anything to do with you.

If two people can visit classes together, that makes booktalking easier in almost every way. The preparation is divided in half, as is the pressure. With two different personal styles, there is more variety in the program. Each person has a chance to relax and catch a breath while the other one is talking. One person can do the introduction, the other the final wrap-up, and the two can alternate booktalks in between, each person doing one or two at a time. I prefer alternating to having people do all their talks at once, but every team needs to work out its own arrangements. After the visit, you can also take the opportunity to get feedback from your partner. It's easy to just let a booktalk get longer and longer, unless someone reminds you to keep it short. Your partner can help you realize how you affect other people. It was Mary who recently told me that while putting my hands on my hips might call attention to the ten pounds I'd just lost, it was also making me look like a lecturing parent, and alienating my audience. I was able to tell her that part of one of her favorite booktalks was really too graphic for some kids, and she toned it down a bit. You can also learn new booktalks and tricks of the trade from your partner, and pick up some new ideas.

It's also interesting to take a non-YA person with you, either as a participant or an observer. If staff members are cynical about your exhaustion when you get back from a school visit, have them go with you and perhaps do just one talk. Unless they are very unusual, that one talk will exhaust them as much as all of yours do you. (This isn't always true—the person may already be an experienced public speaker.) Even if you do the whole presentation yourself and the visiting staff member just observes, the amount of energy and preparation required should be obvious.

If you are asked to do a presentation on how to write a term paper in a particular subject (such as business, law, history, biology, biography, or psychology) or on what is in a specific section of the reference collection, have a reference librarian who knows about that subject and section go with you to make the presentation. For instance, suppose an American history teacher asks you to come to class and explain how to do research for a major term paper. The students need to have an idea of where to start, how to proceed, and what reference tools they may find in the library. You should request a copy of the assignment sheet, if there is one, and poll the reference staff to see who would like to go. (This often translates as whose arm can be twisted until they yell uncle and agree to go.) Try to get someone who can speak effectively to a group, and who doesn't have strong negative feelings about teenagers. Since this is a history class, someone whose special interest is in that area would be the best person to ask. When you give booktalks, you talk about what you enjoy reading. If at all possible, make sure the reference person you take with you has an interest and some expertise in the subject under discussion. Give the reference people all the information you have about the class and let them choose which books to talk about. If they have never spoken to a class before, explain what they should do. The easiest approach is probably to take a sample question and follow it through several reference books, using as many kinds of tools as possible. The speaker should include both basic and specialized tools and spend from two to five minutes on each one, explaining the kinds of information it covers and how to use it. You should take as many of the books with you as possible, and allow about ten minutes for the class to examine them after the presentation. Passing them around during the presentation can be very distracting for both listeners and speaker—don't do it.

You may want to supplement the reference talk with general information on the library—where it is located, the reference phone number, what kinds of questions can be answered over the phone, where the reference desk is, how to ask a reference question and request a book, what interlibrary loans are and how they can be used, and the problems inherent in trying to do a major assignment that is due the next day, since specialized or even sufficient information isn't always immediately available.

If the class is also required to do a book report or can do one for extra credit, you might give one or two of your short booktalks after the reference presentation. The books you choose can be fiction or nonfiction, tied into the sample question or on an entirely different aspect of the subject.

You can take a wide variety of staff members into a class to observe for just as wide a variety of reasons. Beginning booktalkers will have a better idea of what it's all about if they've actually seen one or more class visits. An added advantage is that the beginners' mistakes won't seem so earthshaking to them after they've seen an expert fumble, recover, and go on. And even the most expert booktalker can and does make obvious mistakes that aren't always easy to cover up! The novice needs to know that everyone can recover, gracefully or not (more about that later in Chapter 6). If kids have been generating piles of requests for the books you talk about, perhaps the ILL department would be interested in seeing just what you're doing that has increased their workload so suddenly. The same holds for the circulation and reference staffs, since they're the ones actually facing the kids who come in after books. Include the rest of the staff in your booktalking program as much as you can. The impact of school visits is not limited to the YA people—it affects everyone who works in the library. If everyone knows what you're doing firsthand, and why the kids are so excited about certain books, they may be more understanding about the fifty-first request for *The Amityville Horror*, or more sympathetic to the tenth kid who walks up and asks for *Killing Mr. Griffin*, when the first two got the last copies, and nobody wants to put in a request, everybody wants the *book*!

6

HASSLES AND HOW TO HANDLE THEM

Murphy Was Right!

MURPHY'S LAWS are, for me, a statement of reality. If anything can go wrong, it will, and in the worst possible way as well. Preparation can avert some problems, but others are unavoidable. Even the most expert and experienced booktalker occasionally falls on his or her face. When it happens to you, all you can do is to get up as inconspicuously as possible, dust off your bruised nose, knees, and pride, and go on as if nothing unusual had happened. The mark of a professional entertainer, whether storyteller, actor, comedian, or booktalker, is the ability to cover up all but the most obvious mistakes and not let them affect the rest of the performance. It has also been my experience that when I am nervous, I am almost waiting to make a mistake. Once I've made it, however, the waiting is over and I can get on with what I'm doing. The feeling is "if-I-make-one-mistake-the-whole-world-will-fall-apart!" But then, once I've made that mistake and gotten it over with, I discover that neither I nor the world have been shattered, that I have been neither booed nor lynched by my audience, and that as long as I laugh at myself, they won't laugh *at* me but *with* me.

Recently, I was talking to an eighth-grade class of reluctant and non-readers and, in the course of my talk on William Sleator's *House of Stairs*, mentioned that there were three boys and two girls in the story. This sentence had occasionally elicited giggles from the front row, but I'd ignored them. After I'd finished my presentation, and the kids were milling around the table where I'd set up the books, one of them picked up *House of Stairs* and said, looking at the cover of the paperback copy, "Where's the other boy?" I looked at the cover, and sure enough, there were three girls and two boys. The reason for the giggles was obvious. I admitted my mistake, thanked the boy who'd pointed it out to me, and laughed about it. In another class of eighth graders, which I had visited the previous year, I asked if they'd already heard me talk about *Through a Brief Darkness*, by Richard Peck. Only one girl had, and she'd read the book too, so I began by saying I'd have to be really careful, since she'd catch any mistakes I made. Everyone laughed. I began, and as I progressed, the girl who had read the book kept smiling and nodding. In the middle of my talk, she suddenly stopped smiling and shook her head. Since this was a class I had a good rapport with, I felt it would be okay to stop and see what I'd said wrong. (This would *not* be okay in every class, since it breaks the continuity of the presentation and focusses the class's attention on something besides your talk.) I couldn't get her to say what I'd done, so I shrugged, passed it off, and got back into my booktalk. End of incident.*

Obviously, mistakes aren't limited to the inexperienced or the nervous. Everybody makes them. All you need to know is how to recover with a maximum amount of ease and grace. The most important thing to remember when trying to achieve this is, *Don't panic*! Panic can make you freeze and forget what to do. It makes any mistake seem worse. If you keep your wits about you and stay calm, you can recover one way or another from *any* mistake.

The worst, or at least the most obvious, mistake is forgetting what comes next, in the book or the booktalk. This is for me the most nervewracking thing that can happen when I'm in front of a

---

*Until I re-read the book, that is. Then I discovered that about half my talk had nothing to do with Richard Peck's novel. Over the years, I'd gradually invented a story of my own—no wonder she'd been shaking her head! The talk in this book is a new one.

class. It takes all my will power not to run screaming from the room. My first line of defense is my notes, which I always have unless I've been doing the talk for a year or so. I keep the notes on the table where my books are, and if I feel I'm going to need them, I move around to stand in back of the table so I can see the notes by just glancing down. This position is a little more "teacherish," but seems to be the best stance for checking notes inconspicuously. You should know your talk well enough that you don't actually need to read it, just glance down at it two or three times to make sure you're on the right track. If you realize you aren't sure what's coming up, glance down and check *before* you completely run out of words, if you can. If it's not the next sentence you have forgotten but the next word, you may not be able to keep talking as you check your notes. *Don't panic* when silence falls. Find your place and go on. A break of a few seconds in a talk isn't a tragedy. Usually the kids are so impressed at all you're remembering that they don't really react much when you have to check your notes. And sometimes kids will be too embarrassed about an adult making a mistake to laugh immediately, especially if you maintain your poise. The silence is probably much louder and longer to you than to anyone else anyway. (Warning: This is a sweeping generalization, of course. Some kids *always* notice *everything*. Don't worry about them—they seem to be in a minority, and are occasionally not even appreciated by their peers!)

If you don't have notes to fall back on, recovering from a suddenly blank mind is more difficult. Again, don't panic. Slow down and stay calm. If you know that you have a sentence or two to go before you run out of words, take as long as possible to say those sentences, to give yourself a maximum amount of time to remember what you've forgotten. *Think* about what you're saying—after all, you've read the book. You *know* what comes next. This is where knowing rather than memorizing a talk comes in handy, since all you have to remember is a scene, rather than an exact sequence of words. If you have memorized your talk and have lost the exact words of the next sentence, try paraphrasing until you can remember. Sometimes a couple of extra sentences elaborating on the last thing you remember will give you enough time to recover. Struggle on as far as you can before you give up completely.

If you can't remember anything about the book no matter how calm you stay and how carefully you think—admit it! Say something like, "I've suddenly gone blank; I have no idea what comes next! To find out, you'll just have to read (title)." Or, "This is ridiculous! I didn't intend to tell you the ending, but now I can't even remember the middle! But it's still a neat book; read it yourself and find out." Be as casual and un-nervous as you can. Laugh about it, make a joke. You want the kids to laugh with you, so *you* must laugh first. If they laugh first, they may be laughing *at* you instead. Do whatever you are most comfortable with, but don't make a big deal about having forgotten something. It *isn't* a big deal, unless you make it so. Be brief in what you say to wrap up the talk you don't remember, and immediately go on to your next one. No matter how colossally bad your mistake was, it should only involve that one booktalk and not the rest of your presentation. Work to wipe out the memory of that mistake with the rest of your performance. The show must go on, no matter what. It should go on superlatively!

If you leave something out, and don't realize it until several sentences later, you can always fix it then. There are several ways to do this—the most obvious way is to be obvious. "Oh, I forgot . . .", add whatever you left out, and pick up your booktalk again. You can also work in whatever you left out in a more subtle way if you can think quickly. This means not stopping to add what was left out as soon as it occurs to you but waiting until you reach an appropriate place in the talk to insert it. Or you can assess the importance of what you've left out and decide not to include it after all. An experienced booktalker will find it easier to add to or rearrange a booktalk while giving it than will a novice. For a novice, the least awkward tactic may be to either admit something was left out or not mention it at all. There are actually few details in a booktalk that are one hundred percent essential, and if you leave one of *those* out, you will soon realize it. Listen to what you're saying—make sure it makes sense. Then you'll include all the really necessary parts.

There are two schools of thought about what to do if you forget names or numbers. One suggests that you insert any handy name or number and go on. The other holds that you should not make up what you've forgotten but just do without. For a number, use "many," "several," or "a few." Instead of giving a name, describe the character by personality, role, or appearance, or use only "he" or "she." Each method has its pitfalls. Too many nameless characters can be confusing, but it's embarrassing to get caught when you've inserted any handy number in place of the correct one. I hadn't re-read *Deathwatch*, by Robb White, for years; I'd just talked about it. After a while, Ben wasn't walking fifty or sixty miles back to town but two hundred! Mary had to bring me back to reality.

Forgetting part of your talk is only one of the problems you will run into. The other big ones are an uninterested class, a series of unexpected interruptions, and an uncooperative teacher.

Teenagers have myriad ways to expressing their lack of interest. Ostentatiously reading a different book, doing homework, writing notes or letters, daydreaming, talking, whispering, looking at magazines, making noise, fiddling, and generally acting as if you were a minor annoyance that might go away are only a few of their tactics.* Any behavior of this sort will make it harder for you to get the books across. You will feel that you are using up mental energy without getting anything back in return.

Just hope that the teacher won't let things go too far, so the class doesn't get completely out of control. If there are more than one or two troublemakers, things *are* getting out of control, and if the teacher doesn't do anything (in spite of the fact that you explained ahead of time that you couldn't double as a disciplinarian), there

---

*Of course, some teenagers use the same techniques to disguise a genuine interest. Just as I've seen kids do homework, listen to the radio, and watch TV at the same time, I've also found that they can follow a booktalk closely while combing hair, staring into space, twiddling pencils, etc. It's just unfortunate that it's usually hard to tell whether they are actually listening or not, because you'll be tempted to assume the worst—they're bored!—when in fact they may be hoping to hear more.

is one simple technique that usually works quite well. Stop talking, preferably in the middle of a sentence to make it more obvious, and look at the ringleader. Wait till she or he quits talking, then go on as if nothing had happened. If you get any smart remarks like "Whatcha lookin' at me for? I ain't doing nuthin'!" you can say, "I was just waiting till you finished talking" (or "making noise," or whatever). Maintain your cool and self-possession, in spite of your ardent desire to wring the kid's neck—hard—or to run out of the room screaming. The troublemakers are trying to hook you into their game—don't let them.

Another way to make the noisy group quieter, if not silent, is to get the rest of the class interested, so the other kids will tell the noisy ones, "Shut up, I can't hear!" Aim your talk at the kids you can reach, especially the ones who look as though they might be class leaders. Or try to get the troublemakers themselves interested. You may be able to do this by talking directly to them or by choosing books they will like. Perhaps rearranging the order of your talks will catch them. Work harder to make your talks interesting—build suspense as high as possible, and make the funny parts even funnier. If only the best will interest them, do your very best. Try using body language; come out from behind the desk or table and use your whole body to show what's going on in your talk. Use a book with pictures, such as *Jay J. Armes, Investigator*, since everyone will want to look at them. If conversations continue afterwards, they may be about the book; many times the talk will stop altogether. If one thing doesn't work, try something else. Be aware of what you were doing when the noise stopped, if only for a minute. Try doing that again, if you can. There are some classes that are going to talk and not listen no matter what you do, and these classes always seem to have teachers who let them get away with it. (Remember Murphy's Laws?) Don't let these classes discourage you. Just grit your teeth, smile, and struggle through. Every booktalker gets a fair share of classes like this—no one gets left out. It is a good idea to remember the teachers who allow this kind of behavior, so that in the future you can remind them again that your primary function is entertainment, not discipline. If they are still not willing to do their part, schedule their classes in tandem with good ones, psyche yourself up, and valiantly ignore the uproar. Do-nothing teachers are, in my experience, few and far between. Most teachers want to make sure their classes act properly, and will take the steps necessary to quell unruly students.

But even the most conscientious teacher can have students who turn into demons as soon as you're alone with them. A junior high (eighth-grade) reading class gave me one of the worst times I've ever had. I was just getting over a cold, it was my third class that day, and my voice was giving out. I asked the teacher to get me a glass of water before the class started. I'd hoped she would send one of the students out for it, but she didn't. She trusted her class and had faith in me (I had done talks for her several times), and so she took roll, introduced me, and walked out to get my water. I had ten seconds of sheer panic as she disappeared in the middle of my introduction, but I kept talking. The trouble started with the first booktalk—the main character's name was the same as a smart-aleck's in the front row. "Oh joy!" I thought, and kept on going. Then pencil-tapping, hair-combing, face-making, and talking erupted all over the room. I struggled along for a minute or so, then stopped. After several eternities, the racket quieted down a bit, and I went on. So did all the students. I stopped again. Several comments were made by the two or three kids who were listening—"Shut up, I can't hear!" I said, "Come on, y'all, I can't talk over you." New comments about my "y'all." I went on, holding on to the shreds my dignity, but now all was lost. More racket! Then I got out the heavy artillery (not really a good idea, actually a *bad* idea, but I was desperate): "If you don't want to listen, I'm sure Ms Silva will be glad to assign you some homework when she gets back." (Where *is* she, anyway?) Rude comments, made by the kids who were listening to the noisy ones, but the noise level stayed about the same. I finally stopped one last time, "Come on, guys, mellow out, *please!*" That elicited a lot of imaginary joints and appropriate noises, but they got reasonably quiet. About the time they all settled down, of course, the teacher came back, and they transformed themselves into little angels. The rest of the period was blessedly unremarkable, but if the teacher hadn't come back when she did, I might have been up for manslaughter!

Noisy-rude classes are to be distinguished from noisy-interested ones. Loud comments about your talks or a discussion with another kid can be signs of interest. An interested class can be almost as noisy as a rude one, and yet be right there with you, giving you the support, attention, and feedback you need. The difference is especially noticeable in the timing of the noise. In an interested class, the noise may rise between talks, starting after a talk is over, as kids comment on it, and last sometimes even into the first part of the next talk. But by the end of each talk, the noise will have died down completely, as more and more kids get involved in the story. Then it will rise again in the interval between the talks. You can't expect a responsive class to remain totally quiet and motionless. Noise and movement can mean interest as well as uninterest. The class's attitude makes the difference, and is almost immediately obvious.

You can respond to interested comments and questions. If possible, don't stop your talk, but respond in between talks. If you have to answer a question in the middle of a talk, make the interruption as brief as possible and get right back into your talk. Classes in which a dialogue goes on can be the most fun for both you and the kids. Don't shut the kids off—take part in the fun! But don't go too far. Here again, you need to remember your role: You are the one in charge. Be sure you don't give up that position.

A class can show its lack of interest by a total absence of response. It's as if you were playing to a vacuum. Nothing comes back to you. Perhaps you brought inappropriate books. You're looking at a class of mostly boys, and two-thirds of your books have female leads. You didn't realize these kids all had heard you last year—and you're doing the same talks they heard then. Occasionally you'll find a teacher who doesn't really communicate to you the actual make-up of the class you're going to address. "Good readers" can mean almost anything, and result in your bringing grade-level books for non-readers. *Disaster*! Suddenly you realize all those blank looks mean that no one has any idea *what* you're talking about—no one in the class could possibly read any of the books you've mentioned. In cases like this, try to pick the few books that are appropriate, talk about them, and either omit the others or do them quickly. You may end up doing a shorter presentation. Since the class has a lower reading level than you expected, concentrate on magazines and "adult picture books," if you have brought any. You can also talk about appropriate books that you don't have with you but are available from the library. When you do this, though, remember to write the author's name and the title on the board, in case anybody wants to copy down the information. In other words, play it by ear and try to make the best of a difficult situation. But if you feel that the situation is impossible, ask the teacher if you can come back another day with more appropriate books, rather than struggle through with ones that aren't right.

The responses you'll get from junior high and senior high school students will vary from class to class and from grade to grade. Even a lackluster response during and after a presentation doesn't necessarily mean that you've been a flop or that your books were inappropriate. In a high school class, it may just mean that no one wants to be the first person to go up and look at the books, or that they're all practicing being cool and blasé and you're a perfect target. If you want a really enthusiastic response, the kind where you're trampled by kids grabbing for books, go to a junior high class—the need to be "cool" doesn't usually take over until about the tenth grade. Older high school students are probably just as interested as the younger ones in the books you're talking about, but they are much less direct about expressing it.

Another thing you're going to have to deal with is interruptions from the outside. These come in all forms, but never the one you're expecting or are prepared for. Kids straggle in late or have to leave early. Someone comes from the office with a note telling a class member to go somewhere else immediately. There's a fire drill. The public address system comes to life with interminable announcements just as you reach the most exciting part of your talk. Bells ring for unknown reasons in the middle of the class. The easiest way to deal with all of these interruptions is to ignore them, as far as possible (obviously, you can't ignore a fire drill!). The student who comes in late or with a message can be directed to the teacher, who may be in the far corner, with just "Mr. Soandso is over there," said very quietly, while pointing to the teacher. Teachers usually catch on to this quickly, and may call the student's name and/or stand up to attract attention, so that you can get back to your talk as quickly as possible. There's no way to escape bells or PA announcements. Just shrug and wait. A comment about good timing or not being able to shout over the noise can bring the class's attention back to you when the interruption is over. After a long interruption like an announcement, you should probably repeat your last sentence or idea, to make sure even the kids who quit listening a little early know where you are. This isn't always necessary after a brief interruption.

My "favorite" interruption comes from the kid who is either too dense or too preoccupied to respond to quiet instructions. This student walks in and tries to hand me a late pass, sick excuse, or whatever, and doesn't respond to "She's over there," "Ms Soandso is in the back of the room," or even "I'm not the teacher; she's right over there." Finally, I usually give up, take whatever is being handed me, and worry about it after my presentation is over. By that time the whole class is giggling, and the thread of my talk has been lost.

Teachers can be difficult or uncooperative in a variety of ways: for instance, by leaving the room, not keeping the class quiet, interrupting a talk with questions or comments that are not relevant, or whispering to a teacher's aide while you are trying to make your presentation. Explain to the teachers, if you can, what you expect of them and why. I have never been able to bring myself to tell a teacher in class not to whisper, or stop my presentation to eject a student who has been allowed to cause trouble. But I have gotten up the courage to speak to teachers between periods and remind them that I need a quiet, orderly classroom to work in. Fortunately, teachers who whisper during a talk are uncommon, for their rudeness can have a devastating effect. Once you realize that a certain teacher is likely to present problems of one kind or another, you can schedule his or her classes for times when you will be most able to deal with those problems. Try not to do more than two classes in a row for this teacher, and schedule them, if possible, when you'll be fresh and alert. Don't try to handle three classes for a difficult teacher after you've just gotten off a two-hour shift on the desk, without lunch or even a break. You'll be asking for trouble, and you'll probably get it. When it comes to problem teachers or problem classes, make it easy on yourself.

CHAPTER

7

HOW TO TELL WHEN YOU'RE A SUCCESS

And What To Do About It

Without Getting a Swelled Head

IT'S EASY to tell if your school visiting program is a success. Kids will appear at the school and public libraries asking for the books that were talked about, requests will pile up, circulation will increase. Kids will recognize you in a variety of places, from the library to the grocery store to a movie theatre lobby, and come up to ask you about a title they've forgotten or to tell you how much they enjoyed reading one of the books you mentioned.

There's also a ripple effect, as kids tell other kids about a book they've liked and the news reaches kids who never even heard you talk. Teachers have a grapevine, too, and successful visits to one or two teachers' classes can prompt the rest of the faculty to ask for visits. Encourage teachers to spread the word—a colleague's recommendation can be much more effective than your own assertion that you can interest their classes.

Some of these signs of success can be very annoying to other library staff members, who have to deal with multiple requests for the same book, incorrect title or author information, and urgent demands for another book just like the one you talked about in Mr. Soandso's class. There are a number of ways to make life easier for everyone inundated by hordes of demanding kids. A separate display area for booktalk books is one way I've already mentioned. Booklists and bibliographies of various kinds can also help.

Annotated booklists to pass out during a class visit can let the kids know that there are other good books in the library besides the ones you talked about. Be sure these lists are also available in your young adult area and at the public service desks—reference, children's, and any other desks where staff might be asked for the books you've been talking about. Very often booklists can confirm a title or author, or help a librarian locate something else when the specific book wanted isn't on the shelf. In Alameda County, I used three booklists at the same time, each including some books we talked about regularly and some we didn't talk about that were more likely to be on the shelf. Lists like these should be kept current and revised about every other year, if possible. In theory, the more lists you use, the wider the requests will be spread, because there will be more titles for the students to choose from. In fact, requests still pile up for the books discussed in class, but the lists are a good source of second choices.

Booklists should be just as attractive as possible. Bright colors and catchy covers will help ensure they'll be read and not made into paper airplanes. Ask an art class to design some lists for you as a class project. Maybe you have a graffiti board in your library—use part of it as the cover, or perhaps as a half-tone background for the entire list, with the annotations typed on top. It can really be fun when people in the class recognize their own artwork! Play up current popular movie themes—"It's a bird! It's a plane! It's Superbook!" with an S-emblazoned book emerging from a phone booth was on one of the Stanislaus County YA lists. TV shows can be used as well—pick something "everybody" is watching. Humor always attracts attention. One of my favorite booklist titles came from Carol Starr and completed a cover with a large shark and a skindiver on it—"Books you can sink your teeth into!" Collect booklists from other libraries, not only for ideas about titles to include but also for covers. If someone else has a good idea, see if you can adapt it for your list.

Annotations are easier, too, if you have someone else's to work from. Be careful not to use anything without asking permission first. Most of the time people are quite willing to share.

If you don't have the time or money needed to produce an annotated booklist to pass out to classes, you should prepare a typed bibliography for the staff at the various public service desks. The bibliography can be annotated or not, depending on the time you have to spend on it and the extent to which the people using it will have to depend on it, rather than on YA staff members. It can be arranged by author, title, or subject, depending on which seems most useful. It should include all the books you plan to talk about frequently, and also others to suggest when those are checked out. If this list is not annotated, notes on similarities between books can save valuable time. A few words are all that's necessary—"for fans of _____" or "A book like _____"—just enough to get the idea across.

Both booklists and bibliographies should be made available to the school librarian, who will get requests also. Teachers may appreciate having copies, too. Many will post them in their classrooms so that kids will be able to refer to them.

Another way to let library staff members and school librarians know what you have talked about is to xerox your class visit information cards or summary sheets—your own records of what you've talked about in each class, with the names of the schools and the teachers. If a kid can't remember the title of the book, all the school librarian or staff member has to do is find the correct sheet or card. Elizabeth Talbot uses a Class Visit Summary sheet to record not only what books she talked about but other information she may want to refer to in the future (see Figure 3). A clipboard or notebook with copies of these sheets, filed by school or by date, would be easy to maintain and handy to refer to at any or all of the information desks.

A subject file of booktalks cross-indexed by author and title is useful, though time-consuming to prepare. It can be made on three by five cards for a desk file drawer, and used not only for booktalk information but also for reader's advisory help. I spent

CLASS VISIT SUMMARY SHEET

DATE OF VISIT: _____ TIME: _____

SCHOOL: _____ ROOM: _____

TEACHER: _____ DEPARTMENT: _____

TYPE OF SERVICE REQUESTED: _____

_____

_____

NUMBER OF STUDENTS IN CLASS: _____

NUMBER OF REQUESTS TAKEN: _____ (List titles below)

BOOKTALKS (List titles below)

COMMENTS:

Figure 3

one whole summer making such a file at Fremont Main, where it was used frequently. This type of file is as time-consuming to update as it is to create, however, which may mean that the updating doesn't get done.

You may be asked by school librarians or teachers to draw up bibliographies on various subjects for classroom use. Whether or not you do this should depend not only upon the time you have available but also on your relationship with the school in question. If you are having trouble getting into a school and would like to get a department head or school librarian on your side, making future visits easier, then your time and energy will probably be well spent compiling such a list. Otherwise, you might want to consider refusing. The problem is one of time. I have yet to meet a YA librarian who had more than enough, or even sufficient. Consider your priorities when deciding whether or not to take on extra work that could conceivably be done either by the school librarian or by the teacher. In refusing, you can point out the time factor—and offer to help when or if they do come in to work on the bibliography.

Another way to deal with this question is to start collecting a file of bibliographies and booklists, arranged by subject. Then, when someone asks you for a bibliography, say, "I can't do one especially for you, but you can look at my file of materials on that subject," and the blow will be softened. You will have given them something to look at and build upon, without spending too much of your own valuable time in the process. Be sure you get all your file materials back. It's very annoying to see your files shrink little by little, as other people make use of them.

Being a successful booktalker is fun, but it means making everyone involved, both library staff and faculty members, think it's just as good a thing as you and the kids do. Ensuring that the information teachers and librarians need is readily available will help make this possible. A booktalk hasn't really *worked* until a kid has the book he or she wants to read. You won't always be there to hand the book to the kid, so you have to make sure someone else will be able to.

8

TEACHING BOOKTALKING

Spreading the Word

THE NEXT STEP in booktalking is, of course, proliferation—*not* doing it all yourself. Offer to share your skills with other staff members. Everyone who works with teenagers needs to know how to do booktalks, but the YA staff aren't the only ones who can profit by developing these skills. The reference staff will be able to deal more easily with the reader's advisory questions from all ages if they know the basics of the short booktalk. The children's staff can use booktalks along with storytelling in programs and in school or class visits, as well as in readers' advisory work on the floor. Some children's librarians use booktalks with kids as young as third graders. The techniques I've outlined work just as well with young children as with teenagers, with one proviso—both the individual talks and the presentation as a whole must be tailored to the younger group's shorter attention span. School librarians from elementary to high school can make wide use of booktalking skills, and perhaps do some booktalks with you or with a children's librarian. Teachers of reading and English will find it easier to persuade their classes to read if they say something to introduce the books that are available instead of just handing them to the students. Check with your local and state library associations to see if they can sponsor and organize a booktalk workshop of some kind for librarians or teachers, or both.

There are several ways of teaching booktalking, depending on the group you're working with. A workshop with several sessions, where all the participants have a chance to write and give book-talks and also see themselves on videotape, is perhaps the most effective way to train people who will be doing large numbers of school visits. Both Carol Starr and Virginia Carpio, Young Adult Coordinators for Alameda County Library and San Jose Public Library, use this method to train their young adult staffs.

A less elaborate program would be more appropriate for staff members who simply want to improve their readers' advisory skills. One session with a demonstration and detailed, specific instruction might suffice, as long as participants had a chance to do two or three short talks themselves. Teachers could also be included in a program like this.

However, workshops like these are only effective with relatively small groups, of ten or fifteen at the most. If a group is too large to be subdivided into smaller units, so that all the members of the audience can participate, then a lecture with a demonstration beforehand and a question period afterwards is the only practical format.

Multi-Session Workshops

A workshop with a goal of training YA librarians or other staff members to begin an extensive booktalking/school-visiting program should have at least three sessions, four if possible. Participation should be limited to fewer than ten people; six or eight is best. Then the audience won't be so large as to be intimidating. With a small group, a feeling of camaraderie is engendered, and members feel more comfortable about being evaluated. In addition, the sessions when members all give their own talks don't last too long.

The first session should consist of detailed instructions on how to write and give booktalks, with demonstrations by various people. If videotape is available, a number of people can be taped giving talks and the tape used (over and over) to show various styles of writing and delivery. It's also interesting to see the workshop leader both on tape and live, to show the members the difference between a live presentation, when the audience can interact with the speaker, and a "canned" one. Carol uses several tapes in the workshops she gives to new staff members. One is of staff members doing their favorite talks, another is an actual class visit, and a third is a training tape made by a group of Bay Area young adult coordinators, which is sold nation-wide.* Each of these tapes gives a different view of booktalking, and shows various styles of both writing and presentation.

The other sessions should be about two weeks apart, and each of the members should write and practice one to three talks to give for the group each time. If it is possible to have these sessions videotaped, that can be very helpful. It is much easier to become aware of your mistakes and remember to correct them when you've seen them on TV. However, a videotape may be threatening to some people. If they can see only their mistakes, their self-confidence will be destroyed. It is the responsibility of the workshop leader to make sure that their strengths are pointed out to them as well as their weaknesses—things that need improvement or change.

Praise should have a prominent place in any critique, especially of people who are not very confident or outgoing. Correct their mistakes gently, being sure to say something nice as well. It's a good idea to begin and end with something good, sandwiching any criticism in the middle. Criticism should always be constructive and corrective, focused on specific points that need to be changed. Members of the group should have a chance to comment on each other's talks, but be sure the discussion doesn't go on too long. The leader should be aware of the ways different people are reacting to being criticized, and should temper or end the discussion if someone seems to be uncomfortable.

Self-confidence is a big part of booktalking, and the purpose of a workshop of this type is not only to teach technique but also to instill confidence and help people feel at ease in front of a group.

*To obtain copies of this excellent videotape, called "Easy YA Booktalking," contact Virginia Carpio, Young Adult Coordinator at San Jose Public Library, 180 W. San Carlos St., San Jose, CA 95113.

Any method you use should build up ease and confidence and not contribute to fears or stage-fright. Many people say that some of their most difficult presentations were done in a workshop, talking to peers who were looking for mistakes to correct. (Teenagers, on the other hand, are eager to be entertained and aren't looking for mistakes—they are often much less intimidating than librarians.)

An extended workshop with more than one session of booktalking and videotaping gives members a chance to correct their mistakes in both composition and delivery. They can repeat booktalks they have done before or give new ones at each meeting, and finish the workshop with a core collection of usable talks. It's also possible to provide the experience of choosing books for a particular group by having each person prepare a list of books for full-length presentation to a specific imaginary class, and then actually write booktalks on several of them. Lists of the books chosen and copies of all the booktalks actually given should be available to all the workshop participants. That way each person will have access to many talks immediately, even if not all are usable without adaptation.

Single-Session Workshops

A single-session workshop can accomplish some of the same things as a multi-session one, but it also has certain disadvantages. The participants have less time to write and polish their talks and no way to improve performance in practice sessions. However, if time is limited, and more is necessary than just a demonstration and lecture, a one-day workshop is the answer. It can work well as a conference program, a preconference seminar, or an inservice training program for teachers or library staff. The techniques of the single-session can be used with small groups and with large groups that break up into smaller units so that members can practice booktalking.

Again, the first part should be a demonstration of booktalks, either live or on tape, by at least two people, followed by detailed information on how to compose and present booktalks. This information should be tailored to the audience's needs. Perhaps these people don't need information on formal talks and presentations but want to know how to do short talks or low-key presentations in the classroom or on the library floor. They may also want lists of titles that are "just like" popular ones. (To develop such lists, the small groups could brainstorm and exchange results after all the members have finished their booktalks.) The demonstration should include various kinds of talks, but should emphasize the particular kind this group is interested in. Leave plenty of time for questions to make sure all the details are clear, since this will be the only formal information session.

The participants should then be given a one to one-and-a-half hour break so that they can prepare and practice their booktalks. When the workshop gets back together, the participants can form small groups of six to eight people for booktalking and brainstorming. Membership in the smaller groups could be based on either similarities or differences.

After the small-group interaction is over, entire workshops might reconvene for a brief discussion about what was accomplished. Copies of booktalks and any other material compiled by the small groups could be handed in for reproduction and distribution to all the participants, either immediately or after the workshop is over.

Lectures and Demonstrations

In a lecture situation, there is no chance for the audience to participate or practice what they're learning about. Nevertheless, information on how to do booktalks can be communicated. It is up to the individuals in the audience to use that information later. I have spoken at a variety of conferences and meetings and have found that the enthusiasm generated in the meeting is difficult to sustain afterwards. It is a classic problem, and I know of no real solution.

In a lecture as in a workshop, be sure to tailor your presentation to the needs of your audience, and vary the pace so your listeners don't go to sleep. One hour is about as long as your whole presentation should be. After that you will begin to lose your audience both mentally and physically (distracting, to say the least). Divide your presentation into three parts: a demonstration of booktalking, a lecture, and a question-and-answer period. The length of each section can vary, but the most successful combination seems to be fifteen minutes of booktalks, thirty minutes of lecture, and fifteen minutes of questions and answers. The pace should be lively, and the program should move rapidly until the question-and-answer session. The first question is sometimes a long time coming. No one wants to go first, so just wait till someone dares. Stay relaxed—the minute or so it takes to get the ball rolling seems longest to you.

The most common question, in my experience, is one asking what kind of books a particular group would like—and my response is always a perfectly clear and instantly blank mind, with nothing useful inscribed on it. I take along bibliographies like those in the last section to combat this reaction. Another favorite question is, "Can you recommend a book just like _____," which is also hard to answer. If I am temporarily stuck, I usually throw the question back to the audience, in the hope that someone will either jog my memory or provide the answer. If it's really impossible for me to answer immediately, I offer to let the questioner know later by phone or mail. Make sure as many questions as possible are answered before the program ends.

In all of these programs, the guidelines for dress, speech, and deportment that were discussed in Chapter 5 apply just as they do in a classroom situation. Relax and enjoy what you're doing. You know how to sell books, now you're selling how to sell books. Your presentation can be casual, flippant, or formal, whatever your personality and the audience dictate. Dress comfortably and appropriately. If possible, familiarize yourself with the room where you'll be speaking ahead of time. Make sure that all the props you'll need are there, and that the microphone is adjusted properly, so you can speak into it comfortably and still see your notes easily. If you need to set up a display of books and materials, see if there's a table you can use. If you are using any kind of audio or video equipment, check it ahead of time, so that all you'll have to do during the program is turn it on. If you don't know how to handle the equipment yourself, arrange for someone to help you, and make sure they will be there when you arrive. Take care of every possible problem ahead of time—plenty will come up at the last minute to keep you busy. (Murphy's Laws again!)

I have been asked more than once how to combat stage-fright when speaking to a large audience. I don't have the answer. I can control my nervousness in front of teenagers but find it very difficult to do so before an adult audience. Sometimes my nervousness goes away, but sometimes it doesn't, and my hands are shaking just as badly when I ask for questions as they were when I started to talk. My only defense is booktalks. I always start with booktalks, old friends that I could do in my sleep, ones that always work with any audience and help me calm down as well. *To Race the Wind* and *Bird on the Wing* are two I almost always use. I very, very seldom use new booktalks when making a presentation to a large group. If I'm nervous, there's no doubt about my blowing them. There are enough chances to make mistakes without asking for more with a new booktalk. So I make it easy on myself and my stage-fright, and probably do a better presentation as well.

You don't always have to teach booktalking to a group. You can work with just one other person, a much less formal situation. The same elements are involved, however.

Booktalking is not a static skill; you are constantly learning more and developing better techniques. New ideas and methods are tried and adopted or discarded. A partner or co-worker can help you decide what does or doesn't work. Carol Starr has the young adult services staff get together once or twice a year to exchange experiences, ideas, and actual booktalks. People who go out together should consult on how to improve their performances individually and as a team. This is probably one of the more valuable aids I have found—a colleague's candid appraisal:

"That was great!" or, "You really screwed up, don't try that again." Perceptions of the audience's reaction can vary—someone else can sometimes help you see more clearly when you've misjudged a response. This ongoing, inservice training is one of the most valuable assets a booktalker can have or give.

9

OTHER WAYS OF DOING IT

"Diff'rent Strokes"

BECAUSE BOOKTALKING is such an individual art, and there are so many ways of approaching it, I have tried to give a variety of examples as I've gone along. But I've centered everything around the classroom presentation to teenagers. Booktalking can work outside a classroom and with other ages as well.

Senior citizens in rest homes enjoy new ideas about books. Teachers in a faculty meeting can enjoy ten minutes of "books your students will be wanting to read soon." Librarians from both the children's and reference staffs need to know what books are being talked about in the schools, and what to recommend when all the copies of those are out. Many adult groups want to know what the latest books are like or what's on the best-seller list. Classes that visit the library will enjoy a few booktalks as part of their library orientation tour. And of course, reader's advisory work with any age is just short, informal booktalks.

And as far as methodology goes, whatever works for you, works. You may not be able to follow the methods I use, but that doesn't mean what either of us does is invalid. Elizabeth Talbot, a young adult librarian at Alameda County Library, uses a method that is totally different from the one I have described in this book. She doesn't write anything down, not even when planning, just picks out an incident and tells about it. That is her talk. Her method means both more and less work. She doesn't spend time writing and polishing, yet the night before every class visit she takes home all the books she's going to talk about the next day and reviews the scenes she's going to describe. She plans the "TV show" she plays in her head to help her remember what she's going to say. Her preparations do take time, and sometimes, especially if it's been a while since she gave a talk, she has to recreate it virtually from scratch. Elizabeth is the first one to admit that her way is harder than a more orthodox method: "It would be nice to have my talks written down and know which books I've got talks on already," she says, "but such a method is inhibiting to me. I would be utterly bored doing the same talk time after time." Her presentation varies according to the group she's addressing, the teacher, and her mood. Recently she has begun to keep a card file of *who, what*, and *when* information and the page numbers of exciting incidents, but she still doesn't write out the complete talk. Her method is similar to the one Sue Tait, the YA Coordinator at the Seattle Public Library, uses; she has many of the same comments. If you're most effective when you're improvising, and if the rules you make for yourself work, then you can get away with it. Elizabeth and Sue have—they do convince kids to read books, and that's the point.

Booklists can also be used in a variety of ways I have not mentioned before. Linda Lapides, YA Coordinator at Enoch Pratt Free Library in Philadelphia, told me about one list that is used there to let the kids themselves decide what books will be talked about. It's an unannotated list of about two hundred books, divided into broad subject categories. It's passed out to the class, and the kids are invited to choose any title they want to hear about. Obviously, someone is going to try to trip up the librarians, and according to Linda the class loves it when someone has to say, "I'm sorry, I haven't read that book." There's no way to prepare specific talks the night before; the situation calls for people who can think fast on their feet. My hair stands on end at the thought of trying this, but Linda reports that it's been done successfully for several years. Sue Tait uses a modified version of this same technique. Her list is shorter (only about thirty titles) but she finds that this method ensures a greater variety of talks. The same books are not always chosen, and the booktalkers don't get tired of giving the same presentation all the time.

Everyone has to do booktalking in his or her own way. The only real absolute is that kids have to be convinced to read. Although rules don't always hold true in every case, the ones I've outlined are as broad and basic as possible, and should work for most people. Seeing and hearing someone else do booktalks is of course the best way to learn what to do or not do. But don't be intimidated by someone better than you are. You may not know how good you really are—check the reserves on the books you talked about. If kids are reading what you talked about, you're good. You probably won't ever be good enough—no one is. Keep refining your art; don't let it get stale, or you'll lose your audience. Compare yourself to yourself—what you used to do and what you could do—and not so much to other people. Don't copy anyone else—be yourself, and keep trying to improve.

For other views of booktalking, some sources are: "Booktalking: You Can Do It," by Mary Kay Chelton, *School Library Journal*, April 1976, pp. 39–42; *The Fair Garden and the Swarm of Beasts*, by Margaret Edwards, Hawthorn, 1974; and "Easy YA Booktalking," the videotape produced by the Young Adult Coordinators of the Bay Area and available through the San Jose Public Library (see page 76).

Booktalking ends where it begins—with enjoying books and the various worlds, adventures, and escapes they offer. It's fun, even when your hands are shaking so much you're glad you have pockets, because if you can just keep on, one day you're *finally* going to capture the attention of that jock in the back row who won't stop talking, or the blasé intellectual in the front row who's so sure nothing you have today can possibly interest her. Books are fun; you know it, and you *can* convince every single member of that class of it, even the ones who never let you know you did.

So just relax, smile, stick those shaky hands in your pockets, and enjoy yourself. The kids will enjoy themselves too, whether they admit it or not. And in the final analysis, that's all booktalking is—holding a roomful of uncaged, untamed adolescents in the palm of *your* outstretched hand!

BOOKTALKS

AKU-AKU

By THOR HEYERDAHL

Easter Island is like many other hot Pacific islands, except for the huge stone statues dotted all over the place, stones many times the size of a man and each weighing many tons. How were they carved? How were they transported from their quarry to the places where they now are, miles away, by a primitive race possessing no mechanical or engineering skills? Each statue weighs over fifty tons, and all have been deeply carved. And what force has toppled most of them about like jackstraws?

Thor Heyerdahl went to Easter Island to find out, if he could, the answers to these questions. Instead of answers, he found many more questions. In dozens of secret caves were other strange objects—carvings of skulls and strange beasts and human masks, each giving clues about the people who had made them.

As the pieces slowly fall into place, you can follow Heyerdahl's explorations into the depths of the island, into the family caves of the natives, where no stranger had ever gone before.

This is a modern detective story, an exciting adventure about mysteries hundreds of years old.

Aku-Aku, by Thor Heyerdahl

THE ALFRED G. GRAEBNER MEMORIAL HIGH SCHOOL HANDBOOK OF RULES AND REGULATIONS

By ELLEN CONFORD

Alfred G. Graebner High will never be the same. During the summer the class scheduling has been taken over by a computer, and the chaos starts on the first day of school!

When Julie gets to her sophomore homeroom class, she finds out the computer has scheduled all the classes. Everyone gets a computer card with a schedule on it. Julie is horrified to discover she has *first* period phys ed. That means not only calisthenics (exercises) at 8:10 A.M. but a shower after class—her hair will look awful, every day, for her entire sophomore year! She's sitting there, contemplating this depressing prospect, when she suddenly notices the boy across the aisle. He is very carefully and methodically poking holes in his computer card with a pencil. Then he puts the pencil down, folds the card in half and creases it, folds it in half again, creases it, and keeps folding it until it's just a little square wad of paper. Then he unfolds it, and begins to tear it just a little around the edge, so it looks as if the card is fringed on all four sides. Julie can't stand it anymore, and so she says, "What *are* you doing?" He looks at her, grins, and says, "Revenge!" and hands her the card. By now it's pretty bedraggled, but Julie can just barely read it. This is what his schedule is: 1 Home Ec, 2 Lunch, 3 Home Ec, 4 Study Hall, 5 Home Ec, 6 Study Hall, 7 Lunch, 8 Wood Shop. And on top of *that*, he says, he is a junior and this is a sophomore homeroom!

Julie doesn't see her two best friends until after school. They look just as unhappy as she does, and don't seem at all impressed by her first-period gym. "That's nothing," says Natalie, "I have third-period lunch! Do you know what time third period starts? 9:30! Cafeteria chow mein is awful at noon, but at 9:30, it's obscene!"

"Neither of you has any hassles at all compared to what's happened to me!" replies Isabel. You know how, in every school, in every subject, there's a teacher that no one wants to get? Maybe it's 'cause they're strict, or hard, or boring, or whatever, but everyone avoids their classes like the plague. Isabel has gotten *every one* of them! Even for study hall! She says, "I kept thinking, it has to get better—but it only got worse!" But she's thought of a way out. She gets two books—an encyclopedia of religion and a medical dictionary. (At Alfred G. Graebner, you could get excused for illness or for a religious holiday.) Isabel figures she can change religions often enough and develop enough alarming symptoms to miss at least every other day of school. (And she isn't discovered for two months!)

Julie's sophomore year turns out to be quite something, what with the computer, a new English teacher who's better looking than Robert Redford, and a Home Ec teacher who tries to teach a unit on Human Sexuality but can't describe what sex is like.

And it's all a part of *The Alfred G. Graebner Memorial High School Handbook of Rules and Regulations*, by Ellen Conford.

ALL CREATURES GREAT AND SMALL

By JAMES HERRIOT

James Herriot is a vet in the Yorkshire Dales, farm country in the north of England. He began his practice in 1937, and the first thing he learned was that in real life, veterinary medicine was nothing like it was in the books. For instance, in the books, calves were born during the day, with few complications, from docile cows in warm, modern, lighted barns. Most of the calves James delivered were born on wet, cold, windy nights, in equally cold and windy pastures, from very uncooperative cows with many complications. And James's new boss, Sigmund Farnon, was about as far from a model vet as anyone could get!

The practice included small as well as large animals, and since James was the junior partner, he always got the cases Sigmund wanted to avoid. One of these cases involved Mrs. Pumfrey, a widow with a heart of gold. Someone had given her a small piglet that she named Nugent, and Dr. Herriot began making regular visits. One of these at least started as an emergency. [Read excerpt from book—Mrs. P's phone call to the end of Chapter 2—or tell the same scene.]

Mary James

THE AMITYVILLE HORROR

By JAY ANSON

This book appears to be true. The facts in it have been checked and confirmed. You can accept or reject what it says, but it seems to be a factual account of a house that is possessed. On December 18, 1975, George and Kathy Lutz moved into the beautiful three-story house at 112 Ocean Avenue, Amityville, New York. It was their dream house, perfect for them and their three children. Even though they'd spent every penny of their savings on it, they couldn't believe how lucky they were. Twenty-eight days later, on January 14, 1976, they fled, absolutely terrified of what was loose in the house. They left so suddenly they didn't even take a change of clothes, and within a few months had fled all the way to California, leaving everything they owned behind. They have never been back since they left at 7 A.M., on January 14, 1976. What happened during those twenty-eight days? First, their personalities began to change—the kids became brats and their parents angry and resentful, exploding about even minor things. Physical signs were next—foul odors, black stains in the toilet bowls that couldn't be scrubbed clean. In the sewing room on the second floor, they found hundreds of houseflies clinging to the inside of the screen. George woke up at the same time every night, about 3 A.M. And Missy, the youngest of the children, began talking about her new imaginary friend, Jody the pig. She was the only one who could actually see Jody—all the others could see were footprints in the snow and beady red eyes gleaming in the dark. George was out checking the lock on the boathouse door, after he'd waked up in the middle of the night as usual, and he turned to look back at the house and saw a pair of red gleaming eyes looking at him from Missy's window. He ran into the house and threw open his daughter's bedroom door. She was asleep, unharmed. Then George saw her rocking chair, by the window, slowly rocking back and forth, all by itself. Then, as he looked at it, it stopped.

But the woman who now lives in the house has a different point of view. She thinks *The Amityville Horror* is a hoax or a publicity stunt. In 1978, she appeared on *PM Magazine*, a syndicated TV program, and said, "We didn't know anything about the book when we moved in ... the book isn't true, it's unverified, I could tear it apart page by page.... The red room in the basement is part of a closet—I haven't even repainted it.... The sewing room on the second floor is my daughter's bedroom.... There's no sign of anything supernatural at all—except maybe the tourists that stand and stare at it!"

Still—I wouldn't live there. One of the most frightening books I've ever read: *The Amityville Horror*, by Jay Anson.

AMMIE, COME HOME

By BARBARA MICHAELS

When Ruth Bennett inherited an old house in Georgetown, a historic section of Washington, D.C., she thought that was all it was—an old house. Of course, there *was* the strange cold spot in the living room, but that was only a draft, even if the heavy drapes didn't seem to help much. Then Sara, Ruth's niece, came to live with her, and strange things began to happen. They kept hearing a voice call, "Ammie, come home, come home." Sometimes it even woke them up at night. Ruth thought Ammie must be a neighbor's lost pet, but neither the Siamese cat on one side nor the English bulldog on the other had names even close to Ammie. Then Sara brought home one of her professors, Pat, and he and Ruth started dating. At one of his mother's parties a conversation about psychic phenomena ended up with Ruth talking about the strange voice and the cold spot in her living room. Before she realized what she was doing, Ruth said she'd be glad to host a seance there. The night before the seance, Ruth had a dream, or what she thought was a dream. She dreamed she woke up, and saw a strange twisting black shadow hovering over her, choking her, until the sound of the voice outside, "Ammie, come home . . ." woke her up. Or had she been awake already? Had the shadow been real? At the seance the next night the medium wasn't the only one who spoke with someone else's voice. Sara did too—a low, evil, mumbling voice. When Ruth heard it, she knew that when the lights flashed on and she looked at Sara, someone else would be looking back—Sara's face, but without Sara inside it. It was as though someone else was wearing Sara's features. The effect lasted only a moment; then Sara was back. But Ruth remembered. She saw it again the next night. She woke up late, after midnight, and heard a noise in the hall. There it was again—Sara's long white nightgown and long black hair, but not Sara's face. When Ruth spoke to it, it said, "Not dead, not dead." And when Ruth reached out to touch it, it threw her down the stairs.

The spirits in that house had been waiting for the right people to come along and live in it. When Ruth and Pat and Sara and her friend Bruce were there together, the spirits reached out and took over.

AND I ALONE SURVIVED

By LAUREN ELDER

Jim shouted at her to hurry up and decide, and Lauren tried to make up her mind about going flying with his friends Jay and Jean that afternoon. Finally she decided to go—it would just be a short hop over the Sierras and back, and it was a beautiful day. Maybe she could get some good pictures. To celebrate the day, Lauren put on her favorite outfit—full skirt, short jacket, vest, and blouse, with high-heeled boots.

Not exactly the regulation outfit for a plane ride, but Lauren didn't care. She picked up her camera and her father's old flying helmet for luck, and was off. But Jay wasn't as good a pilot as he thought he was, and as they were going over the pass in the Sierras, they were caught in a downdraft and crashed on a mountainside, two miles up. When Lauren came to after the crash, she had a gash on her leg just above the top of her boot that went all the way to the bone, and her arm was broken. She spit out most of her teeth—but she was all right. She was alive. Jean died of massive head injuries and Jay of internal injuries during the first night. Lauren knew that search planes might not find the wreck—Jay hadn't filed a flight plan. If she stayed with the plane, she would surely freeze to death. So Lauren decided to walk down the mountain to the San Joaquin Valley. Even if she didn't make it, she'd be fighting to survive, not giving up. Her trip was to cover over twenty miles of some of the roughest terrain in the Sierras. She was alone, except for her hallucinations, and her only protection from the elements was the clothing she'd so optimistically put on the day before, for a brief flight on a beautiful afternoon. And she survived. This is her story.

A BAG OF MARBLES

By JOSEPH JOFFO

Jo Joffo and his brother Maurice live with their family in occupied Paris in 1941, and spend their after-school hours playing marbles and roaming the streets of their neighborhood. One night their mother sews yellow stars on their jackets, and suddenly their whole world changes. Jo's best friend thinks the star is neat, and offers to trade him a bag of marbles for it, but most of the other kids at school start picking on the brothers.

It soon becomes clear to their father that Hitler is planning to round up the French Jews, so one night he calls Jo and Maurice to him, gives them their knapsacks with a little food and money, and tells them to leave that night and make their way to the south of France, where their older brothers have gone. And he gives them one final very important piece of advice: to *never, ever*, under *any* circumstances admit to *anyone* that they're Jewish.

Traveling all the way across France with very little money and no permits, and with the Germans checking every train and bus, is pretty difficult, but Jo and his brother learn to be very resourceful. They learn to think really fast so that they aren't tripped up by unexpected questions, and, when they invent lies, to add details about real people and places so that their lies match and sound natural.

For instance, one time they have all day to wait for a train, so they spend the whole afternoon in a movie theatre seeing *The Adventures of Baron Munchausen* over and over. Then when Jo is questioned by police at the train station, he tells them that his papa owns the movie theatre in town and launches into a detailed description of the movie and how good it is, and he even finds a total stranger to talk to and tag after, pretending the man is his father.

The more outrageously and confidently Jo and Maurice lie, the better it seems to work, but they still have a lot of narrow escapes. They survive like this for three years. Then one day their luck runs out, and they are arrested and incarcerated in Gestapo headquarters, where following their father's advice becomes a matter of life or death.

Peggy Murray

BIRD ON THE WING

By WINIFRED MADISON

Elizabeth *hated* Lincoln, Nebraska! She didn't like Nebraska, she didn't like her high school or the kids she'd met, and she *particularly* didn't like her stepmother. She just couldn't understand why her father would marry someone like that.

Until her parents were divorced, her family had lived in Sacramento, and afterwards Elizabeth stayed there with her mother. But then her mother decided it was time for Elizabeth to live for a while with her father, who'd remarried and was living in Nebraska. So here she was, and she hated it!

The final straw was when Elizabeth had been promised she could go to a concert. She'd saved her money, got tickets, and was going to go with one of her few friends. But the afternoon before the concert, her stepmother said, "Oh, by the way, you're not going to be able to go to that concert. A party at church has come up, and your father and I have to be there." Elizabeth said, "What do you mean? You promised! Get a babysitter!" "It's too late, and everyone's going to be at the concert. You're just going to have to stay home!" Elizabeth said, "But, you promised!" And her stepmother said, "I don't want to discuss it any more. Speak to your father about it when he gets home!" So Elizabeth did. She was *sure* he'd understand, but he didn't. "Now Elizabeth, you're young. There'll be other concerts. This party's very important to Lorene. I'll make it up to you, I promise."

Elizabeth was really angry, but what could she do? She stayed home the next night and babysat. When her stepbrother and sister were asleep she went down to the basement, got her backpack, took it up to her room, and packed it. She remembered seeing her stepmother hide something in the floor of the closet, that looked like it might have been money. It was! Elizabeth decided her stepmother wouldn't miss some of it and took two or three hundred dollars. She started hitchhiking to California. The first man who picked her up was nice, and Elizabeth was sure it was all going to be easy. But the second man she rode with was a real weirdo! When he threw her and her backpack out on the road almost without stopping, Elizabeth was just glad she was *alive*!

She walked along the road till she came to a truck-stop, went inside, and huddled over a cup of coffee, trying to stop shaking. Then she noticed another young woman at the counter, and they started talking. Her name was Maya Hurdlka, she was eighteen (two years older than Elizabeth), and she'd been traveling all over Europe. She was a weaver, and had been learning old traditional European ways of weaving. Now she was on her way back to San Francisco. Maya asked Elizabeth if she'd like to travel with her, and Elizabeth jumped at the chance. They made it all the way back to California without any hassles. Maya seemed to know just which rides to accept and which to turn down. She gave Elizabeth her address and phone number in San Francisco, and Elizabeth went on to her mother's house.

Well, everything was great at first. Her mother was really glad to see her and made a big fuss over her. But that came to a screeching halt when the lady discovered her new husband making passes at Elizabeth; suddenly a beautiful sixteen-year-old daughter wasn't such an asset anymore. Elizabeth was finding out that she didn't fit in with other scenes, either. She went to a party with her old gang and discovered they were into things she wasn't into and didn't want to get into! Finally, her mother persuaded her to go back to Lincoln, but she didn't even care enough about Elizabeth to go see her off at the airport. She just handed her the bus fare to the airport and said, "See you next time you come out."

Elizabeth sat on the bus dreading getting back to Lincoln, especially since her stepmother would now know that she was the reason Elizabeth had run away. Things would be worse than ever! She didn't belong in Sacramento, she didn't belong in Lincoln. Then she remembered Maya, cashed in her plane ticket, and got a bus ticket for San Francisco. *Finally*, it looked like it might work out. Elizabeth began to learn how to weave, to get her head together, and then tragedy struck. It was sudden, horrible, and Elizabeth knew there was absolutely nothing she could do but just hang on and hope to survive.

BID TIME RETURN

By RICHARD MATHESON

Richard Collier has just learned he has only about six months to live. He decides he'll spend the rest of his life doing exactly what he wants—traveling around the country. So he converts everything he owns to cash, puts some clothes in the car, and sets out. The first night out of L.A., he decides to stay in an old Victorian hotel in San Diego—the Coronado Hotel (which really does exist). The atmosphere of the hotel affects Richard powerfully—the past actually seems to be alive here. Walking through the lobby, Richard sees a photograph of a beautiful woman and immediately falls in love. Her name is Elise McKenna, and she appeared in a play at the hotel in 1896. Richard tries to find out as much information about Elise as he can—he consults books, newspaper clippings, hotel records, anything he can get his hands on. The more he discovers about Elise, the more he begins to realize that he is truly in love with her, the real woman, not just the photograph. And he begins to believe that somehow, though he doesn't know how, he once met and loved Elise. He remembers that he read some place that "what you believe is your reality," and decides to go back to 1896 and Elise by letting that time become his reality. He has nothing to lose by leaving the present; he's going to die anyway. So he changes his room in the hotel to one that had been there in 1896, gets clothes, a watch, some money, everything from 1896. He puts on the antique clothes, lies down on the bed, and begins to tell himself, "When I open my eyes, it will be 1896, and I will be able to see Elise." It's not as far-fetched as it sounds—Richard knew he'd make it. You see, during his research he'd found an old hotel register, and on November 19, 1896, *he* had registered at the Coronado Hotel.

BLACK LIKE ME

By JOHN HOWARD GRIFFIN

The man who wrote this book is white, and yet he spent two months of his life as a black in the Deep South, in the late fifties, when segregation was the rule. Griffin, a writer, thought over the idea for several months before he asked George Levitan, owner of *Sepia* magazine, to foot the bill in exchange for a few articles for the magazine. Levitan agreed. Griffin underwent a course of medication under the care of a dermatologist. He shaved his head, and later he shaved his hands. One day he looked into the mirror and saw a middle-aged black staring out at him.

The things that struck him hardest were little things like not being able to go into any restroom, having to plan his day according to the placement of the segregated facilities. On the bus, an obviously tired white woman would stand rather than share his seat, and blacks would glare at him if he attempted to get up for her. White men came to the shoeshine place where Griffin worked, asking conspiratorily where they could get some black chicks.

The whole book was a revelation, too much of a revelation for the people of Mansfield, Texas, where Griffin lived. When the book came out, his neighbors burned him in effigy.

Mary James

THE BOYS FROM BRAZIL

By IRA LEVIN

Yakov Liebermann is a German Jew who has dedicated his life to bringing Nazi war criminals to justice. The one man he wants to find more than any other is Dr. Josef Mengele, the "Angel of Death," who performed atrocities on the Jews at Auschwitz. One night he gets a phone call from his contact in São Paulo, Brazil, who says that he has seen Mengele with a group of former SS officers, and that Mengele told them that ninety-four men must die at certain specific times during the next two-and-a-half years. Each of the officers received a list of people to kill, and the dates they were to die. The deaths are to seem like accidents, so that there will be no suspicion of murder. The first is only eighteen days away. Just as the contact is getting ready to play a tape recording of the meeting for Liebermann, there is the sound of a knock on the door and the noise of a brief scuffle. Then someone else picks up the phone. Liebermann can feel hatred and evil emanating from the receiver, just as clearly as words. Then the connection is broken. Liebermann knows only one person in the world is capable of such evil—Dr. Mengele is alive, in Brazil, and it was he who had picked up the phone. What Liebermann's contact had said, then, was true—and unless Liebermann can figure out the connection between them, ninety-four sixty-five-year-old men in government service will die, all over Europe and America, during the next two and one-half years. And Liebermann has only eighteen days before the first murder.

CALLAHAN'S CROSSTIME SALOON

By SPIDER ROBINSON

Have you ever known some place where you were sure anything could happen, and it usually did? Callahan's is one of those places. If you're there at the right time you can see all kinds of people—time travelers, aliens, telepaths—sooner or later, they'll all show up. It doesn't really look like any place out of the ordinary. It's outside town and doesn't even have a neon sign, just a wooden one with a light on it. And inside, it's about as bright as any room in your home. Callahan says people who like to drink in the dark are unstable. All drinks are the same price—fifty cents—with an option. The option goes like this: put a dollar on the bar (Callahan doesn't take anything but ones) and you can either take your change from the cigar box of quarters at the end of the bar, or, when you finish your drink, walk up to a chalk line in the middle of the room, announce a toast, and hurl your glass into the big brick fireplace at the end of the room. Callahan keeps your change. And if you feel like talking after your toast, you have the undivided attention and sympathy of everyone in the room. Callahan knows there are few hurts that can't be helped by the advice, concern, and sympathy of thirty or so people who really mean it. Callahan also believes a bar should be fun, and his place always is—fun of the loudest variety, most of the time. That's how it was the night the guy with the eyes walked in. Everybody shut up and looked at him. He was nearly seven feet tall, dressed all in black, and his toast was, "To my profession, advance scout for a race whose home is many light years away." And his story was even stranger. . . . Then there was the night the time traveler explained the Law of the Conservation of Pain. And the time Callahan sponsored the Third Annual Darts Championship of the Universe, open only to his customers, and a telekinetic arrived and cleaned up—until the regulars found him out, with somewhat regrettable results. Women didn't go into Callahan's very often, but one, who was obviously somebody special, became a regular. . . . And these are only a few of the unusual visitors you'll find in *Callahan's Crosstime Saloon.*

CARRIE

By STEPHEN KING

Carrie White was definitely different. She looked different: her mother, a religious fanatic, made her wear long, ugly dresses and fix her hair in an unbecoming style. And she had to carry a big King James Bible everywhere she went. Carrie acted different as well: her mother wouldn't let her go anywhere except to school and back—no extracurricular activities. Sports, clubs, dances, movies—everything was forbidden. The Whites didn't even go to church—Mrs. White thought that was sinful too, so they had their own church services at home, three or four times a week. And on top of it all, Carrie was the school scapegoat, the person everyone else laughed at, picked on, and mocked. She was the lowest of the low—*no one* was worse than Carrie White.

It had all started the first day of school in the first grade. Carrie had gotten her cafeteria tray of food at lunchtime, set it on a table, and knelt down on the floor to pray. Everyone had laughed, and she was marked.

Even kids who were younger than she was began to copy their brothers and sisters. Carrie's days were spent in a living hell. No matter what she did, she couldn't fit in. She just took it all until she was seventeen. Then one afternoon she was walking home from school after a big scene in gym class and the little brother of one of her tormentors rode by on his bike and called her a name he'd learned from his sister. Carrie turned around and looked at him and thought, "I wish you'd fall off your bike and *kill* yourself!" And he fell off his bike! He got up and stared at her, terrified, and then ran off screaming. Carrie thought about what had happened and realized her mind had flexed in a certain way. She tried to see if she could do it again, but she wasn't as angry at the plate glass window as she had been at the boy, so instead of breaking, the glass just wavered in the afternoon sunlight. Carrie went home and began to practice until she could move anything with her mind. She could stop your heart from beating just by thinking about it! Then, almost as a joke, she was asked to the Prom, where the ultimate horrible surprise was waiting for her and her date, the surprise Carrie decided *not* to accept. Carrie freaked out and took revenge on everyone who had ever done anything to her. That's why it was called the year of the Black Prom, and why, less than two years later, the town was all but deserted—no one wanted to live there any more with the memory of Carrie White's revenge.

THE CAT ATE MY GYMSUIT

By PAULA DANZIGER

Marcy is thirteen and a freshman at Dwight D. Eisenhower Junior High. She is fat and thinks she looks like a blimp. She hates her father, she hates Mr. Stone, the principal, and she hates gym. There's not much she can do about Mr. Stone or her father, but she can do something about gym—she refuses to change to her gymsuit. "The cat ate it," "My brother's using it for a security blanket," and "The Mafia stole it" are only some of her excuses.

But everything changes at Eisenhower Junior High when Ms. Finney starts to teach English. She's different—she looks different, she acts different, and she really cares. Maybe the way she teaches is unusual, but the kids in her classes begin to learn—not only English, but lots more besides. She even helps some kids start Smedley, an after-school club, where they can talk about all kinds of things that they want to discuss, but that don't fit into the English curriculum.

Unfortunately, Mr. Stone doesn't like Ms. Finney as much as her students do, and when he finds out she won't say the Pledge of Allegiance, he has her suspended. Suddenly, Marcy finds herself one of the ringleaders in the fight to get Ms. Finney back, and in even more hot water at home. She begins to realize she's got to do what's right for her, and not go along with what everyone else says is right.

CATTLE ANNIE AND LITTLE BRITCHES

By ROBERT WARD

Cattle Annie and Little Britches were two women who, in 1895, joined the Doolin-Dalton gang in Oklahoma. They met the gang at a barn dance, and discovered they were even more exciting than the dime paperback novels written about them. Annie fell for Big Bill Dalton right away. Even at fifteen, she was a woman who got what she wanted, and she decided she wanted Bill Dalton. Jennie, who was later nicknamed Little Britches, was fourteen, and fell in love just as fast as Annie had, but with Bittercreek Newcombe. Annie immediately decided they should join the gang, but Bill Doolin had other ideas, and he was the leader. No women in the gang! But Annie and Jennie were very persuasive, and Bittercreek and Dalton were in favor of having them in the gang as well. Finally Doolin gave in and said that if they could win a horse race with one of the gang members, they could join. Annie rode her pinto, Rex, against Bill Dalton. Annie was winning when Rex slipped on some loose pebbles and went down with a terrible scream. He'd broken his leg, and he would have to be shot. Bittercreek and Dalton were about to do it, when Doolin suddenly stopped them. "It's like this," he said to the two women. "You can ride, you got spunk, but you got to be able to shoot. Killing a horse is nothing like killing a man, but it'll give you an idea of what it's like. Shoot that horse and you can stay." He handed them each a gun and told them where to shoot. But Rex moved, and it took two tries to kill him. It was horrible. As both Annie and Jennie collapsed, Doolin said, "Congratulations, you're in the gang."

It's not easy to become a legend in your own lifetime, especially before you're twenty-one, but Cattle Annie and Little Britches did it, and this is their story.

THE CHILDREN OF HAM

By CLAUDE BROWN

A group of kids living together in the inner city—Claude Brown writes about them in his new nonfiction book, *Children of Ham*. Claude Brown, you'll remember, is the black man who wrote about his own childhood in *Manchild in the Promised Land* and described his struggle with Harlem, growing up in the fifties and early sixties. He became a lawyer and left Harlem, but not really. Here he tells the modern-day story of what it's like to grow up in the ghetto for a group of kids who have banded together and call themselves the Hammites. They live together in an apartment in an abandoned tenement in Harlem. They run electricity in from the light in the hall (that still works) and they do without hot water. They don't have many neighbors, 'cause the building's condemned. Only junkies would stay there, but Hebro ran them all away.

Hebro's one of the oldest ones and he has no use for junkies. His idea for solving the drug problem in Harlem is to give all the addicts, say, three months to clean up and after that declare war on them—let out all the convicted murderers from jail and tell them you'll give them a week off on their sentence for every doper they kill. Hebro agrees his plan is pretty cold, but he feels it *would* solve the problem, and he thinks junkies would be better off dead anyway. Those that didn't get killed would clean up pretty quick.

Mostly the Hammites' folks know where they are and don't care that much—it's one less mouth to feed. Forming a family of their own, they stick tight and expect everyone to speak up about what's right and wrong and stand by each other.

Salt-Noody, who likes to spray-paint the walls with his name—his territorial imperative, says Dujo—Salt-Noody also looks after the pigeons on the roof and fixes things. Jill is the big sister and mother to the Hammites. She's eighteen and she used to do everything—hustle, trick, cocaine, been busted and went into a detoxification program—swears off the stuff now.

Dujo is sixteen and though he's not the leader (the Hammites don't believe in leaders), his opinion is listened to and respected. He moved in when his mom went on a permanent nod. Dee Dee is fifteen and she has a thing going with Shaft—the only couple in the group. Dee Dee called the dime on her mother [story of dead junkie in bed with her younger brother and sister all day], so her folks were arrested. Her mother says she's gonna get Dee Dee when she gets out, but that's another two years.

They've all got dreams of escaping, mostly through college, and some are still in school trying to do well. They also dream of cars and clothes, and looking good, and some of the guys want to own a gun. Some of the younger guys think a lot about how to get their first lay. They dream about making it big in sports. They talk a lot about the life around them. And they're really street-wise: they know about heroin, unemployment, no hope, not enough food, pimping, hustling, running numbers, prostitution, having babies.

Do they realize their dreams? There must be an epilogue, Claude tells us, but time will have to write it for the *Children of Ham*.

Carol Starr

THE CRIME OF THE CENTURY

By HAL HIGDON

The "Crime of the Century" took place on May 21, 1924, in Chicago and was planned and carried out by two college students, seventeen and eighteen years old. Soon after Bobbie Franks, fourteen, heir to four million dollars, disappeared on his way home from school, his father received a ransom note demanding $10,000 for the return of his son. He was eager to pay the ransom, but before he could do so, Bobbie's naked body was found stuffed into a culvert near Wolf Lake, on the Illinois-Indiana border. The case made headlines across the country, especially when the two students were arrested and charged with the killing. They were Nathan Leopold Jr. and Richard Loeb, both sons of millionaires and near-geniuses. They felt no guilt about the murder—only chagrin that they had been caught, since they had planned what they thought would be the perfect crime. Bobbie's death was only a minor part of their plan, and they had felt no compunction about killing him. In fact they hadn't chosen him at all—they didn't pick out a specific victim, Bobbie had just been in the wrong place at the wrong time. Clarence Darrow agreed to defend Leopold and Loeb, and his reputation as a criminal lawyer is partly based on the fact that he won a sentence of life imprisonment for both of them, instead of the death sentence most people expected. Recently, after all the major participants in the case were dead, the author Hal Higdon went to Chicago and interviewed other people who had been involved. He did in-depth research on several aspects of the case that were too controversial to be made public in the 1920s and are revealed here for the first time. The question of who did the actual killing is raised, since Leopold and Loeb each accused the other and there were no witnesses. Their actual descriptions of what took place are horrifying [pp. 101-102, hardback edition].

If you liked *Helter-Skelter* or *Bonnie and Clyde*, you'll like *Crime of the Century: The Leopold and Loeb Case*, by Hal Higdon.

THE CRYSTAL CAVE
THE HOLLOW HILLS

By MARY STEWART

When someone mentions Merlin, you probably think of a very old, very strange man with magical powers, associated with King Arthur and his Knights of the Round Table. But who actually was Merlin? He wasn't an old man all his life—he must have been a boy sometime. Did he really resemble the traditional magician, white bearded, with a long black robe and pointed hat, and a staff or wand? Or is it true he was the illegitimate son of a king, or perhaps a "devil's spawn" condemned to death as a child? Mary Stewart has taken bits and pieces of legends and histories and woven them into a tale of Merlin's childhood and young manhood. She explains how he found the magical secret crystal cave that made him aware of his special powers, and who Merlin's teachers were. We first see him as a not-very-happy six-year-old boy, who doesn't have any idea what his destiny will be.

The Hollow Hills takes up the story and tells of Merlin as a young man, and of Arthur as a boy.

The life of Merlin the magician, a man who was and is a mystery.

DAUGHTER OF TIME

By JOSEPHINE TEY

Richard III: a villain incarnate, murderer of innocent children, one of England's most hated and wicked kings—true or false? This mystery tells of one man's search for the real Richard, not as Shakespeare described him, or as legends portray him, but as he really was. Inspector Grant of Scotland Yard was in the hospital, flat on his back from injuries received in his last case. Marta, one of his good friends, came to visit him and decided what he needed was a good mystery to take his mind off his problems—some unsolved historical mystery that he could work on while he was in the hospital, so he wouldn't have to run around looking for clues. Marta also brought a stack of portraits of famous and infamous people, past and present. Grant was a confirmed people-watcher, and she thought the portraits might keep him occupied until she could find a mystery for him. Grant wasn't really interested in any of them, but one picture caught his eye because he couldn't figure out who it showed—a man who looked as if he'd suffered a great deal, richly yet soberly dressed, a proud and gentle person. Grant turned the picture over and discovered it was the villainous Richard III. History's records of this king definitely did not fit that portrait! Who was right? Grant had his mystery, and when he began to investigate, he found some very unusual information. To learn what he found, and who Richard really was, read *Daughter of Time*, by Josephine Tey.

DEAR BILL, REMEMBER ME?

By NORMA FOX MAZER

This book is called *Dear Bill, Remember Me? and Other Stories*. It contains eight short stories by Norma Fox Mazer. The one I'd like to tell you about is called "Mimi the Fish." Mimi is not a fish; she's a teenager with a very active imagination. In her fantasies Robert Rovere is in love with her. He's the handsomest boy she's ever seen. Just being in the same classroom with him makes her heart beat faster. Too bad he doesn't even know she's alive. Or at least he probably didn't until Susan, Mimi's one and only friend, passed him a note in class. Susan figured it was time they found out what, if anything, Robert thought of Mimi. So she wrote him a note: "Robert, someone with the initials MH (that's for Mimi Holzer) likes you very much. How do you feel about her? Respondez s'il vous pleeze on the other side." Well, Robert responded, all right. He wrote back. "Tell her to go pluck a duck." Not a very romantic reply. With this Mimi went back to daydreaming.

Several days later, Robert called her and invited her to a dance. She was petrified that it was a prank. Maybe it wasn't even Robert on the phone. Maybe she'd get all dressed up and ready and then he wouldn't show. How disappointed she would be. How disappointed her mother would be! (Honestly, you'd think Robert had asked her mother out, she was so excited!)

Mimi was really surprised when there was a knock on the door that Friday night. Robert had shown up. She could hardly believe it. She tried to hurry him out as quickly as possible. She was embarrassed about the way their house looked; it was really just a couple of rooms behind the family butcher shop. And she certainly had no great desire for Robert to meet her parents. She and Robert were already out in the driveway free and clear when her mother came running from the house holding a package wrapped in white paper. She forced the package into Mimi's hands, all the while chitchatting with Robert. She told Mimi to deliver the package to Milly Tea. It was limburger cheese, and she had promised it to Milly for Milly's party that night. Do you know what limburger cheese smells like? It probably has the strongest odor of any cheese in the world. Even people who love it have to admit that it stinks. Mimi protested, but her mother was insistent. The cheese goes with Mimi.

Well, Robert didn't seem too put out about having to go out of their way on this errand, so they set out to Milly Tea's house. Mimi held the package in the hand away from Robert, but the smell seemed to be creeping right up her arm. At Milly's she rang the doorbell and a boy answered. She tried to offer him the cheese, explaining it was for Milly,

but all the boy said was, "Phew! That stinks. There's no Milly here.
You've got the wrong house."

Well, there was nothing left to do but take the cheese and go to the
dance. So Mimi goes on her first date ever, with a boy she's absolutely
wild about and also with a messy package of cheese that's smelling more
and more like somebody's dirty feet. It's called "Mimi the Fish" and it's
one of the stories in *Dear Bill, Remember Me?*

Rayme Gwen Meyer

A DEATH IN CANAAN

By JOAN BARTHEL

The justice system isn't perfect. It doesn't always work, and this is the
true story of one time when it didn't. On December 28, 1973, Peter Reilly
came home after a Methodist Youth Fellowship meeting to the three-
room house where he lived with his mother in Falls Village, Connecticut, and found the bloody and mutilated body of his mother lying on
the bedroom floor. He called an ambulance, his best friend, and the
police. Within an hour or so, Peter had been taken into custody and held
incommunicado for twenty-six hours. During that time he was questioned continuously, without let-up, by several shifts of policemen. He
was given no hot food and was never left alone, not even to go to the
bathroom. His friends, frantic about Peter, could get no information
about what was happening or even where he was being held. After
twenty-six hours, the interrogators persuaded Peter that he must have
killed his mother, even though he said he loved her and couldn't remember hurting her. They told him he must have blacked out and killed
her. They told him he had failed a lie detector test, and that showed he
must have really done it. (They didn't tell him the test was unreliable.)
They were very persuasive, and finally he signed a confession.

The police believed Peter had killed his mother in less than ten
minutes, without getting any blood on his body or his clothes. What he'd
done, they said, was undress, kill and mutilate his mother, wash the
blood off, get dressed again, and call the police. They didn't have any
explanation for the fact that no traces of blood were found in any of the
drains in the house, or for the county coroner's testimony that the

amount of damage done to Barbara's body could not have been accomplished in the three or four minutes Peter would have had to have done it in. Nevertheless, Peter was brought to trial.

The people of Falls Village were horrified—Peter wouldn't hurt anyone, much less kill his mother! They began to raise money for his bail and then for a lawyer. Yet in spite of evidence that indicated he was innocent, Peter was convicted of killing his mother. Even then, his friends didn't give up. They began to plan for an appeal.

As one judge involved in the case said, "When the system didn't work, the people did." But what if those people hadn't worked so hard for so many years? And what if *you* came home at 9:20 next Sunday night and found *your* mother dead on the bedroom floor, covered with blood—do you think the people of your town would band together and work for years to make sure you didn't go to jail?

The most frightening thing about this book is that it's *true*. It actually happened to Peter Reilly, and it *could* happen to anyone.

DEATHWATCH

By ROBB WHITE

Madec isn't the kind of person Ben usually takes on a hunting trip— he is cold and insensitive, and seems to enjoy hurting people. But it is nearly time for school to start, and Ben hasn't earned enough money guiding hunters in bighorn sheep country to pay for the next year of college. Madec has offered Ben more than enough money to pay his college expenses. Ben can't refuse, and since they'll only be gone for just over a week, he figures it'll be okay.

In order to hunt bighorn sheep, you have to have a license, and to get a license, you have to get on a waiting list, which can be *very* long. Once you have your license, it's good for only seven days, and for only *one* male sheep. If you don't get that sheep in seven days, it's just too bad, and you go back on the waiting list. You may never get to the top again.

Ben and Madec have been out for three days and haven't seen one sheep. By the fourth morning, Madec is getting impatient; he is sure Ben is deliberately taking him to the areas where there are no sheep. He decides to lead the way himself. He sees something moving up on a ridge and shoots it before Ben can check it out. Ben says, "Are you sure that was a male sheep? I didn't see any horns." But Madec is sure and goes up to get his sheep. Then he comes back down almost immediately and says he missed. When Ben gets up to the top of the ridge, he discovers that Madec has been lying—it isn't a male sheep. Madec has made a very bad mistake, because it isn't a sheep at all. It's an old prospector, and since Madec is a very good shot, the man is dead. Ben goes back down to bring the jeep to the foot of the ridge, put the body in it, take the body back to town, and report the shooting. When he gets back to Madec and explains what he's going to do, Madec is livid—"No! I'm not going to jail because of an old prospector that no one knows or cares about!" He tries to convince Ben to just bury the old man and offers him a bribe, but Ben refuses, saying only that a killing has been committed and he's going to report it. Finally, holding Ben at gunpoint with Ben's own rifle, Madec forces him to take off all his clothes and walk into the desert.

It's about forty-five miles to the highway and fifteen more back to town. Ben has no food, no water, no protection at all from the sun, and Madec is sure he will die in the desert. To make sure he does, Madec loads all the supplies into the jeep and follows Ben, keeping watch on him through the scope on his rifle, and staying far enough away to keep Ben from doubling back and ambushing him. And just in case Ben is rescued or survives all the way back to town, Madec has also altered the evidence to make it look as though *Ben* was the one who shot the old prospector, and not Madec. To see if Ben makes it back, and if Madec's plans succeed or fail, read *Deathwatch*, by Robb White.

THE DISTANT SUMMER

By SARAH PATTERSON

Kathie was only sixteen during that unforgettable summer of 1943—too young to get involved in the war, certainly too young to fall in love. At least, she was too young until the summer evening she walked into her father's church and found Johnny playing the organ. He was young, blond, handsome, and a gunner in the Royal Air Force. And suddenly

Kathie wasn't too young any more, and she was deeply, tragically involved. She was one of the people who watched and counted the big bombers, the Lancasters, as they flew out from the base near her home in southern England to bomb Germany. Kathie was also one of the many people who waited, watched, and prayed, and then counted as the big planes flew back in. Some flew in just as they flew out—those were the ones that hadn't been hit, and their crews were safe. Some limped back in slowly, maybe trailing black smoke—they'd been hit, and their crews might be wounded or even killed. Then there were the planes that didn't come back, the ones that had been shot down over Europe. Their crews might have been killed or captured. Or if they were lucky, they might have made contact with the underground and eventually get back to England safely. Kathie was lucky—Johnny's plane came back every time. One day he introduced her to Richie, an American who had entered the R.A.F. when the United States was so slow to get into the war. He was a pilot on another of the Lancasters, and he fell in love with Kathie too. So now she had two planes to look for and two men to love—*and* to decide between. Then one day, only one plane came back. . . .

Kathie looks back on that summer thirty years later, when she finds an old diary [read preface].

The summer when Kathie's whole life changed forever—*The Distant Summer*, by Sarah Patterson, who was only sixteen when she wrote it.

THE DOG DAYS OF ARTHUR CANE

By T. Ernesto Bethancourt

Arthur should never have made fun of James N'Gaweh's beliefs. It started out innocently enough with Arthur, James, and Lou sitting in Lou's living room in Manorsville, Long Island, celebrating the last day of high school and rapping about what they were going to do during the summer.

It is getting late, and the FM station starts playing a selection that James recognizes—an authentic African sacred chant used to cast out devils from a person who is possessed. James is a nineteen-year-old

African exchange student, and his father is shaman, witch doctor, of his village, a job that James intends to assume eventually.

Well, Arthur tells James right out that he thinks that stuff about witch doctors and spells is just superstition. James doesn't take it well—he doesn't say anything more, but his face gets all masklike. Nobody feels like partying anymore, and just as Arthur is about to leave, James reaches into the pouch at his waist, takes out some kind of powder, sprinkles it over Arthur, and starts to chant. It's just a little prayer to give Arthur some kind of understanding of other people's ways.

When Arthur wakes up the next morning, he tries to sit up but he keeps flopping over on his side. His head aches and there is a terrible smell in the room. He finally decides that if he rolls out of bed onto the floor he may be able to crawl as far as the bathroom for a drink of water. He feels as if his tongue is hanging out about six inches, and his vision is all blurry, and everything is in black and white instead of color. Well, Arthur finally makes it into the bathroom. Turning his head he finds himself face to face with the saddest, most raggedy-looking dog he has ever seen. What an ugly mutt, with a big head, large, evil-looking teeth, and matted, shaggy, dirty gray fur with black spots. He sure looks sick. Arthur's first impulse is to yell and scare the dog away, but his head hurts too much, and besides the mutt looks as if he weighs about sixty pounds and might bite. So Arthur decides to smile, the dog wags his tail; Arthur reaches out his hand, the dog reaches out his paw. But when Arthur reaches out his hand to shake the dog's paw his fingers bump into the mirror on the bathroom door. Arthur finally gets the message—*he* is that sad-ass mutt on his bathroom floor.

He keeps closing his eyes and then opening them, hoping to see good old Arthur Cane in the mirror, but no such luck. So Arthur has to learn to make it as a dog—no easy proposition, especially in Manorsville, where everybody has a pedigreed dog and Arthur certainly isn't that. He has several run-ins with the dog catcher, and problems with cars, subways, and even a crazy who poisons dogs, but life as a dog also has some rewards in store for Arthur. Is he destined to a be a mutt forever? Read *The Dog Days of Arthur Cane* to see.

Marianne Tait Pridemore

[Marianne takes only brief notes into the classroom with her. She copies the outline below onto three by five cards to make it easier to use.]

Arthur never should have made fun of James N'Gaweh's beliefs
Arthur, James, Lou—Manorsville, Long Island
Last day of school
Authentic African chant cast out devils "bunch of crap"
Pouch—powder—chant. "A little prayer to give Arthur some kind of understanding of other people's ways"
Next A.M.—tries to sit up—flopping over on his side
Headache—smell—tongue out 6"—black & white
Rolls out—crawls to bathroom
Ugly mutt—big head, large evil-looking teeth, matted shaggy dirty gray fur with black spots—looks sick
1st impulse—yell—head hurts too much, and a 60 lb. dog's bite
Arthur smiles—dog wags
Arthur—hand. Dog—paw
Arthur reaches out to shake hands—bumps into bathroom mirror
He's sad-ass mutt on bathroom floor—closing eyes, hoping . . .
Has to learn to make it as a dog in Manorsville—everyone has pedigreed dog
Run-ins: dog catcher—cars—subways—crazy who poisons dogs
Also rewards
Destined to be a mutt forever?

THE DRACULA ARCHIVES

By RAYMOND RUDORFF

This is supposed to be a novel, but I'm not sure it's fiction. It's made up of a number of documents that reveal the story of the Transylvanian nobleman who became history's most famous vampire—Count Dracula.

In the introduction, which is an excerpt from "A Manuscript in an Unknown Hand," the author tells how, after reading Bram Stoker's novel *Dracula*, he became fascinated by the life of the Count, his ancestry and origins, and his horrible career.

Indeed, the author claims that he was predestined for the task of investigating the story of Dracula. Haunting the British Museum and great European libraries, he finally discovered that what Bram Stoker presented to the world as fiction was actually fact.

Pouring his whole soul into the task, ignoring the scorn and jeers of those around, the author was able at last to travel to the Borgo Pass in the haunted Carpathian Mountains and search the deserted rooms of that towering, ruined castle which the guide books so strangely refrain from mentioning.

Here he presents the papers and proof of what he found there. Perhaps they are, like Bram Stoker's *Dracula*, fiction, but perhaps they are not—and what happens if they aren't? Read *The Dracula Archives* and decide for yourself!

THE DRAGON AND THE GEORGE

By GORDON DICKSON

Jim Eckert never meant to become a dragon—all he wanted to do was get his fiancée back. Angie had disappeared just as he'd burst into Grottwald's lab, and Grottwald said she'd "apported." He'd been trying out his new astral projection machine and had the power turned up too high, so Angie's body as well as her psyche disappeared. Jim was furious, and forced Grottwald to try to send him to the same place Angie went so he could bring her back. But, perhaps because Grottwald had changed the power output on his machine, only Jim's mind made the transition, and when he opened his eyes, he saw the roof of a cave, and then—a dragon! A genuine green, scaly, fire-breathing dragon, who was shouting at him irritably. Jim was in the body of a young dragon named Gorbash, and it was his uncle Smrgol who was demanding that he hurry up and come along. Smrgol was one of the oldest and most respected dragons and didn't have much use for his nephew Gorbash, whom he considered to be a somewhat retarded member of the species, not good for much.

One of the first things Jim discovered was that this *was* the world where Angie had gone, but not as a dragon. She was still a human female, called a *george*, as all humans were. She had fallen into the hands (or claws) of Smrgol's bitterest enemy, Bryagh. Jim only had a chance to see her for a minute before he had to leave with his uncle. He couldn't figure out how to rescue her, so he went to S. Carolinus, a wizard, for help. Carolinus told him Angie was no longer with Bryagh, but had been captured by the Black Powers and imprisoned in the Loathly Tower. Jim (or Gorbash, now) and Smrgol couldn't travel that far alone, so they decided to take others on their quest to help them along the way, and to fight with them to rescue Angie. There was Aragh, a large wolf, and his pack; Secoh, a mire-dragon (a smaller species than true dragons like Gorbash and Smrgol); Sir Brian Neville-Smythe, a knight; Dayfydd and Danielle, who were archers; and Giles of the Wold, leader of an outlaw band. Of course Carolinus came too. Together, they would travel across the barren lands, fight the Black Powers, rescue Angie, and restore balance to this world where science and magic were equally powerful.

DRAGONSONG

By ANNE McCAFFREY

Drummer, beat, and piper, blow.
Harper, strike, and soldier, go.
Free the flame and sear the grasses
Till the dawning Red Star passes

Menolly sang the deathsong solemnly, befitting the talent she had, for the old master-harper Petiron. He had been her only friend on Pern, the only one who encouraged her to sing and play musical instruments, for on Pern all music was controlled by Harpers, and to be a Harper one had to be male. Menolly had unusual talent, but girls had no future in music, and her folks, especially her father, the fisherman-leader, refused to allow her even to practice.

Life on Pern was largely agricultural. Farming and fishing were the main occupations. The constant danger from THREAD, a spore that fell to the ground and destroyed vegetation, made the inhabitants dependent upon the indigenous life form of dragons, to destroy THREAD and save the land. Dragons were awe-inspiring: When born, they formed an instant attachment to a human and the two had a symbiotic relationship, able to talk from mind to mind (human /animal) and able to travel through time, thus finding and fighting THREAD with little damage to themselves. There were even legends of small dragon-like animals— fire lizards—but none had ever been found.

Well, after Petiron passed on, a new Harpermaster came to Menolly's sea-hold, but her folks saw to it that she was kept constantly busy gathering food, working in the kitchen, and babysitting the elderly. Life grew more and more lonely, until one day Menolly wandered further down the coastline than usual and stumbled on a clutch of— miraculous!—fire lizard eggs, and a screeching mother lizard desper- ately trying to move the eggs off the beach, away from the incoming tide and up to a cave in the cliff. Menolly found herself trapped on the beach by the agitated fire lizard, and somehow understood that she was to help move the eggs.

After they were safely in the cave, Menolly was allowed to leave. Back in the sea-hold, telling no one about the fire lizard, she joined the others for dinner. Afterwards there was music for entertainment from the new Harpermaster. But when Menolly started to join in the song, her mother pinched her hard, warning her to be quiet. It's not fair, Menolly thought for the hundredth time, and I won't take it anymore. The next morning she sneaked out of the sea-hold and returned to the fire lizard cave to make a new life for herself. How she did it is the tune of *The Dragon- song.*

Carol Starr

DREAMSNAKE

By VONDA K. McINTYRE

Snake is a healer in a future world where there are no doctors, and healers use genetically altered snakes to cure people. She has just finished her training and is now traveling through the desert on her first journey. She has with her Mist, an albino cobra, Sand, a diamondback rattler, and Grass, a dreamsnake, a small green snake that looks like a little grass snake. Grass is not able to heal anyone; he can only give dreams and ease dying. Snake was a good student and her teachers had honored her when they named her Snake, but she is very young and trusting. The tribe of desert people she meets have never seen healers and are afraid of snakes, but they ask her to stop and heal a small boy named Stavin of a tumor. She agrees to do so. When Stavin asks to have Grass stay with him during the night while Snake gets Mist ready to cure him, she leaves Grass on his pillow. Mist has to be given a substance to alter her venom so that when she strikes the tumor, it will die and Stavin will live. Mist has convulsions all night as a result, and Arevin, one of the tribesmen, agrees to stay with Snake to help her stay awake and keep Mist from beating herself to death on the ground. In the morning, Snake goes to Stavin and finds Grass missing. Stavin's parents have killed him because they were afraid he would hurt the boy. Snake is bitter and angry, but she cures Stavin anyway, scorning his parents' fears that now she will kill their son. Arevin comes to her as she is preparing to leave and asks her to stay. She cannot, because of Grass's death. "What they did was my fault," Snake tells him; "I didn't understand their fear. Now I'm crippled without Grass and must return to my teachers and tell them I have lost my dreamsnake. They will be disappointed and they may cast me out." "Let me come with you," Arevin replies. Snake refuses, but she promises to try and return the next spring. "Look for me next year, and the year after that, but if I haven't come in two years, forget me, because wherever I am, if I am alive, I will have forgotten you." Arevin promises to wait, but not to forget her. Snake leaves, and soon hears of a place where there are hundreds of dreamsnakes, a place where they breed. None of Snake's people have ever been able to breed the snakes—this is a chance she can't miss. She has to go further than she ever has before, and, unknown to her, Arevin has begun to follow. He had only promised to wait for her, not to forget her, and now he's decided to find her. And so this isn't just a story of Snake's search for a dreamsnake, but the story of her and Arevin's love, as well.

DUNE

By FRANK HERBERT

Arrakis is the planet known as Dune—a desert world where water is as precious as jewels. Its only export is *melange*, an addictive spice that gives Spacing Guild navigators the prescience, or future vision, necessary to guide ships through the long wastes of space. Spice is necessary to the galaxy, and so Dune, its only source, is of major importance. Spice comes from the deserts of Dune and is mined by the Fremen, the free tribes of the desert.

To Dune come the Lady Jessica and her son Paul. Jessica is a Bene Gesserit, a member of a women's sect trained mentally and physically and dedicated to producing the Kwisatz Haderach—a male Bene Gesserit whose organic mental powers will bridge both time and space.

They had watched bloodlines for years and were within two generations of their goal when Lady Jessica produced, against orders, a son instead of a daughter—Paul. He becomes Muad'Dib, the leader of the Fremen of Dune and of the Bene Gesserit as well. His coming had been foretold in legends for centuries, and his power was unbeatable.

And the Guild navigators, their future vision made more acute by their addiction to spice, predict a great upheaval in the galaxy, one that will disturb the lives of everyone. Its source—Dune and Paul Muad'Dib.

FERAL

By BERTON ROUECHÉ

Have you ever seen a cat running across the street at night, its eyes shining in the headlights, or heard a cat howling on some black, windy night? I promise that whenever you see or hear a cat again, you won't be able to forget the horror of the wild cats in *Feral*, by Berton Roueche.

It starts innocently enough. A young couple, Jack and Amy, come to spend the summer at an island off the East Coast. They find a really nice small house out in the woods and settle down for the season. A man at the gas station gives Amy a kitten with white feet—they call it Sneakers. A couple of weeks later, they hear a horrible scream in the middle of the night. When they rush outside they see a cat—not Sneakers but a wild cat—with a baby rabbit in its mouth. They frighten the cat away, but the rabbit is dead. Next, people tell them how the indigenous wildlife seems to have disappeared. No coons or possum, no deer have been seen on the island in the last few years.

When it's time to leave, at the end of the summer, they decide they can't take Sneakers back to New York City, so they drop him off near a neighbor's house and hope he'll find a good home. That's what all the summer people do with their unwanted pets.

The next summer, Jack and Amy come back, but this time they decide to stay through the winter. Jack is a magazine writer and he is going to do his writing at home. They are only there for a short time when they find a half-grown mongrel hound in the woods. He's nearly starved, bitten and scratched, probably by cats, the vet says. They call him Sam.

Last summer the islanders noticed that there was no more wildlife in the area. This summer, even the birds have disappeared. A neighbor woman tries to feed one of the wild cats, is bitten and dies of the wound.

One day, Jack and Sam go out to cut some wood and Sam wanders off. When Jack hears a movement in the underbrush, he looks around thinking it's Sam coming back, but it isn't, it's a cat, just staring at Jack, then another cat and another. Jack counts eight cats, just crouching there, all watching him. He yells at them to get away, but they don't move. He yells again and they finally scatter.

Sam, the dog, doesn't come home that night, so Jack and Amy go looking for him. They find him, or rather what's left of him—the cats had found him first.

The terror grows until Jack and Amy find themselves beseiged in their house, surrounded by hundreds of wild, starving cats. *Feral*, by Berton Roueché.

Edith Czubiak

A FIVE-COLOR BUICK AND A BLUE-EYED CAT

By PHYLLIS ANDERSON WOOD

Fred and Randy are sitting outside the high-school counselor's office watching kids go in looking hopeful and come out looking very depressed. Finally there are only the two of them left. The counselor comes out and says, "Why don't you two come in together?" They go in and sit down and he says, "Well, you've seen everyone leaving—I just haven't been able to find jobs for anyone." Randy says, "Oh, no! I've gotta have a job! My mother won't buy gas for my car any more!" The counselor sits up and says, "Car? Car? You've got a car? I have just one job here. It's for two boys who are friends and have a car. Are you guys friends?" Fred and Randy have never seen each other before this afternoon, but they size each other up and say, "Yeah, yeah—we're friends."

The job turns out to be working for Palmer's Pets, a chain of pet stores in the Bay Area and the Valley, picking up pets at the airports and delivering them to the stores, changing pets from one shop to another, and delivering pets to airports and to their new owners. That sounds great to Fred and Randy, and they agree to go to an interview that afternoon.

But Randy's car is out of gas and neither he nor Fred has any money, so the counselor loans them two dollars for gas. They walk out of the school and Fred looks for Randy's car. It's a block or so away, up at the top of a hill—and when Fred sees it, he suddenly feels very depressed. It's an old fifties Buick—you know the kind—huge, built like a tank, low to the ground. And this particular Buick looks as if it's been in several wrecks. Almost every piece of it is a different color from every other piece—four different colors in all! And when Fred walks around to the back, he discovers it doesn't even have a trunk lid! But Randy says not to worry, he has it all under control. So Fred pushes and then hops into the open trunk to ride down the hill to the gas station. After they get gas, Randy peels out, leaving rubber for half a block. He drives really fast, screeching around corners on two wheels, and the engine sounds as though it's going to blow up any second. Fred thinks, as he hangs on for dear life, "If we had any animals in here, we'd scare them to death!"

They get to the interview and talk to Mr. Palmer, and he seems interested. Then he wants to see the car. Fred thinks, "Well, goodbye, job!" Mr. Palmer looks a bit taken aback when he sees the car, but Randy starts telling him what a great car it is, how they don't build cars like this any more . . . but then Mr. Palmer gets around to the back and says, "No trunk lid? How can you carry animals in the trunk without a lid?" Randy says, "Oh, we wouldn't think of putting your valuable animals in the trunk! I've taken the trunk lid off so I can take out the back seat and make a platform for the animals' cages behind the front seat. Your animals will ride in absolute safety and luxury *in*side the car. And you know, this car is safe. You could hit it with a Mack truck and not even dent it. Your animals will be well taken care of and protected." Mr. Palmer looks at Randy, then he looks at the car again, and then he says, "Okay, let me see how you're going to fix the car, and if it looks good enough for my animals, you've got a job. Be back here tomorrow morning." Then he stands outside his shop to watch them drive off. "Goodbye, job!" Fred thinks again, when he realizes Mr. Palmer is *not* going back inside. But Randy starts the car smoothly, quietly slips into gear, backs up, and then drives slowly away, the engine purring, just as if he were carrying a back seat full of raw eggs. Fred stares at him with his mouth open. Randy turns to him, laughs, and says, "See, I *can* drive when I have to. . . ."

And that's the start of a very exciting summer for both of them, and a very funny one, too. Especially when they meet a parrot that does nothing but yell cuss words and a Siamese cat that's allergic to the parrot! And wait till you see what happens when they get stuck in a traffic jam on a hot day with a carload of animals and a horn that won't quit honking!

Mary Moore and Joni Bodart

FIVE WERE MISSING

By LOIS DUNCAN

They weren't really aware that the bus driver was new until he missed one of the stops after school. Bruce volunteered to tell him where the rest of the stops were, and soon there were only five of them left on the bus, the five who usually got off at Valley Gardens, the last stop. There were Bruce and Glenn Kirtland—Glenn was a senior, student-body president and football team captain; Bruce was a freshman and as awkward as Glenn was smooth. He'd lived his whole life in his older brother's shadow. Marianne Paget rode the bus only because her step-father had come to pick her up, and she hated him! She knew he'd be hurt when she ostentatiously avoided his car. She was pretty, blonde, and popular, and she sat with Glenn. Jessie French wasn't kind of person who is a loner, anyway. Bruce sat down beside her when he got on the bus—it was the only seat left. Dexter Barton was one of the last ones on the bus. He had gym last period, and with his crippled arm, he didn't like to shower with the other guys. He hated to be laughed at. He was the one who noticed that the bus driver was a substitute.

But then the driver went by their stop, and kept on going, even when Bruce protested. Not too much further on, he stopped and picked up a guy in a leather jacket, who ordered them all to the front of the bus, so he could keep an eye on them. Suddenly they realized that they wouldn't be going home that afternoon. In fact, unless their parents could raise $15,000 ransom for each of them, they might never get home at all.

FOREVER

By JUDY BLUME

This is one of the most controversial books written for teenagers recently. That's because it's about Katherine and Michael, two high-school seniors who fall in love and have a love affair. And nothing bad happens to them—no one gets VD, or pregnant, or has to drop out of school. No one has a nervous breakdown, or an abortion, or a fatal accident, or anything else. They survive, and they handle it, and along the way they find out that even though sometimes love lasts forever, sometimes it doesn't. Katherine and Michael, two teenagers who might be real people, in a situation that's all *too* real—*Forever*, by Judy Blume.

THE FORGOTTEN BEASTS OF ELD

By PATRICIA McKILLIP

Sybel's father and grandfather were both great wizards, and she is a very powerful wizard, too. Her father raised her all alone in an isolated crystal house in the mountains, and then he died when she was sixteen. But she wasn't left completely alone then, because her father and grandfather had called several magical animals to live in the garden around the house, and they could all talk to her. There was a boar who always talked in riddles, an old dragon, a black cat, a savage falcon, a golden lion, and a gorgeous black swan. All these animals were larger than normal size, had magical powers over most humans, and were very wise (except the dragon, who was greedy and willful).

Because of the strange way she was brought up, Sybel is a coldly intellectual and emotionless sort of person, and spends most of her time poring over old wizards' tomes, trying to learn how to call more magical animals to her garden.

One day her concentration is broken by the arrival of a young man named Coren, bringing a baby for her to take care of. Coren is not a wizard himself, but he's the seventh son of a seventh son, which means that he has a lot of knowledge about magical things and a great appreciation of Sybel's power and beauty.

He says the baby belongs to Sybel's dead aunt and his own dead brother, so Sybel reluctantly agrees to take it. She's reluctant because she says the baby eats and sleeps and requires special care, and doesn't even think or talk to her like her animals do. But she raises the child for twelve years, and learns to love him more than any of her animals.

Then she finds out that the child is actually the son of a king, and so she's caught between warring political factions, because Coren, whom she's falling in love with, belongs to a family opposed to the king. The king and Coren's family each try to win her favor in order to use her powers against the other side, but she's determined to remain neutral.

In spite of her best intentions, one side does something to her that makes her embittered, and she becomes so trapped in a need for revenge that it threatens to destroy her relationship with Coren, and with her animals, and even her own magical powers.

Because of the child, she has discovered two of the most intense human emotions: love and hate. Now which one will win?

Peggy Murray

FRIENDLY FIRE

By C. D. B. BRYAN

On September 4, 1969, Sergeant Michael Mullen left the Waterloo, Iowa, airport on his way to Vietnam. His last words to his mother— "Don't worry yourself, now, okay? It will all be over March 1st." On March 1, 1970, Michael's body was returned to Waterloo in a silver-grey U.S. Army–issue casket, and the Mullens learned that their son's death was attributed to "nonbattle causes."

One year later, they were under FBI surveillance because they'd tried to find out just what that meant. They kept getting the runaround, and they got more and more upset and suspicious. They felt they had a right to know how their son had died, but the Army apparently didn't. Finally they discovered that Michael had been killed by "friendly fire"—that is, he had been killed accidently by U.S. bullets. The Army urged them to forget about it, now that they knew. "It's just one of those things." But Michael's parents, Peg and Gene Mullen, couldn't forget. This is the story of what they did, and of what an unnecessary death and a long string of lies did to them.

GHOSTS I HAVE BEEN

By RICHARD PECK

Blossom Culp, fourteen, comes from the wrong side of the tracks, lives by her wits, gets the Second Sight, and becomes the most famous girl on two continents.

It all began on Halloween night, 1913, when Blossom decided to teach Alexander Ormsworth and his friends a lesson. She knew that every year they tipped over Ol' Man Leverette's outhouse, so she hid inside it, in an old sheet with flour on her face and hair and a candle to light at the appropriate moment. But when Blossom opened the door, there was Ol' Man Leverette himself, caught, as it were, with his pants down! Blossom talked fast and explained her plan to scare the boys—Ol' Man Leverette thought it sounded like a good idea, and he had a few touches of his own to add. So Blossom hid in the outhouse, Ol' Man Leverette hid behind the compost heap, and just as the boys were about to tip the outhouse over, Blossom floated out, moaning in proper ghostly fashion. The boys scattered, but Les Dawson was last, and he was the one who got the rock salt Ol' Man Leverette had loaded in his shotgun—right in the seat of the pants! And over Les's screams of agony, the other boys heard Ol' Man Leverette shout "Guess we showed 'em, Letty!" Blossom, you see, had thought fast, and had not told him her real name.

There was only one girl in town named Letty—she was stuck-up and proper, and would never have been in someone else's outhouse on Halloween night, pretending to be a ghost. But Les didn't think about that when he found out about it the next day. He didn't get to school till noon, having spent a very painful morning having rock salt picked out of his rear end. He waited till afternoon recess and then jumped on Letty, and started grinding her face into the ground, screaming all the while. Blossom decided to put a stop to it, and who was in a better position to know just where to kick Les so it would hurt the most, and as she put it "be the most instructive"? Les nearly turned inside out with pain, dropped Letty, and began to strangle Blossom. Just before she passed out, Blossom saw the principal coming across the school yard with a paddle in her hand, which she applied very liberally to Les—also where it would be most instructive!

As a reward, Letty's mother gave Blossom some new clothes and told her daughter to be nice to Blossom. That meant asking her to the next meeting of Letty's club, "The Sunny Thoughts and Busy Fingers Sisterhood." Blossom came, but what happened that afternoon no one had expected. Blossom announced, more to annoy Letty than because it was true, that she had the Second Sight. No one really believed her, until she saw Letty's little brother get run over by a car five blocks away! After that, word got around pretty quickly, and Blossom's adventures began—she saw the sinking of the *Titanic*, she sneaked into Madame Tussaud's Wax Museum in London in the dead of night, she met the Queen, and lots more!

THE GIFT

By PETER DICKINSON

Davy Price has the ability to see the pictures that other people form in their minds. He can't do it all the time, only when he's bored or not thinking of anything else. It's funny, and sometimes embarrassing— once he picked up on the sexual fantasies of the men in the congregation during a boring sermon at church.

Evidently the gift has been a trait in Davy's family for many years. There is an old Welsh tale that portrays a legendary prince bestowing the gift on one of his captains. Davy's grandmother tells him the gift will bring him nothing but pain. Her first husband had the gift; he saw her picturing his partner as her lover. The next morning, at the slate quarry where they both worked with explosives, there was a blast that killed them both.

Davy himself finds out just how much of a burden the gift is when he starts picking up on a crazed mind that imagines gunning down schoolbuses full of children. Even more terrifying is the fact that his father is involved with this man; his father is not above illegal activities to make money.

Mary James

THE GIFT OF THE MAGI

By O. HENRY

O. Henry practically invented the surprise ending, the unexpected twist at the end of the story where the hero or villain gets what he or she deserves. ("Poetic justice," it's called.) His stories are short, often funny, and you can never be sure how he'll wind them up.

My favorite is a Christmas story, one that seems to express the very essence of the holiday. I've loved it from the time I first read it, which was when I was in high school—*eons ago!* It's called "The Gift of the Magi" and takes place on Christmas Eve. Della and Jim are young, very poor, and very much in love. They have only two things worth being proud of—Della's hair, which falls below her knees in gorgeous brown ripples and Jim's gold watch, which had been his father's and grandfather's. They have no money for presents, and Della decides to sell her hair to buy a watch fob for Jim, not knowing he has sold his watch to buy the tortoiseshell combs she wanted for her hair. They each had sacrificed their most precious possession to buy a present for the other. [Read last paragraph of story "The magi, as you know. . . ."]

THE GIRLS OF HUNTINGTON HOUSE

By BLOSSOM ELFMAN

Huntington House is a home for unmarried, pregnant teenagers. Just like other teenagers, they have to go to school, and this is what happened to one very idealistic English teacher who came to Huntington House with lots of ambitious ideas and ended up learning as much as her students did.

This is what she has to say about her first day there. [Read from pp. 1-2, paperback edition: "Huntington House is three stories of sooty grey stone ... And I'm tired of the joker who says 'What can you teach pregnant teenagers that they don't already know?' " and from pp. 8-9: "It was my intention on that optimistic afternoon .... but an unborn baby named Heather."]

For a book that'll make you laugh, and make you cry and laugh again, read Blossom Elfman's *The Girls of Huntington House*.

GLORY ROAD

By BRUCE CATTON

Bruce Catton is one of the very few historians I actually enjoy reading. He brings out the details of history, the human details that make his books read almost like novels. The Civil War era is his specialty, and the Army of the Potomac one of his favorite topics. He's written a trilogy about the activity of that particular army during the war, and this is how I first got acquainted with him. *Glory Road* is one of that trilogy—the second book—and it tells in detail how the Army of the Potomac changed the outcome of the Civil War, at Fredericksburg, at Chancellorsville, and finally at Gettysburg. You'll meet here the enlisted men, some volunteers, some bounty men, who fought like fiends during the battles and who swapped stories and coffee with the Rebels in between them. Catton introduces you to the three generals who commanded the army: Burnside, who meant so well, and did so badly; Hooker, who was a soldier's soldier, and Meade, who took over only three days before Gettysburg. Some of the less famous people you'll find here are the man who wrote "Taps," the laundress who took coffee and hardtack to men on the firing line, and a Union private who bodily seized and captured a Confederate general.

Bruce Catton looks at history first with a wide-angle lens and then with a microscope. For a glimpse of history that's as realistic as life today, try *Glory Road*, by Bruce Catton.

GUY DE MAUPASSANT'S SHORT STORIES

By GUY DE MAUPASSANT

De Maupassant is a past master of the art of suspense and the surprise ending. His stories are brief and to the point, wasting no words, often a little cynical or sardonic in tone.

My favorite is one called "The Necklace." It is the story of a beautiful but poor woman with high-flying dreams of wealth. She was married to a clerk, and one day he brought home an invitation to a ball, and they sacrificed until they could go. They spent all their savings on her dress, and borrowed a beautiful diamond necklace from a rich friend to complete her costume.

1. the ball—compliments, etc.
2. necklace's loss discovered
3. the search, the note to the friend
4. the new necklace
5. the struggle to pay the debt
6. after ten years. . . .

[Read excerpt from story beginning "And this life lasted ten years . . ." to end.]

HANGIN' OUT WITH CICI

By FRANCINE PASCAL

Fourteen-year-old Victoria has a reputation for being a troublemaker. It's partly deserved, but partly just rotten luck. She's *always* the one who gets caught, and sometimes the *only* one as well! Like this time— she got caught with a joint at her cousin's house-party. She was showing off, in the middle of comparing the merits of various kinds of grass (something she knew absolutely nothing about). Unfortunately, it didn't sound that way to her aunt, who called Victoria's parents and shipped her back to New York City on the next train. On the way back, Victoria thinks about how she dreads meeting her mother at the station. They haven't been getting along lately—her mother treats her as if she were about two years old, and doesn't understand how she feels at all.

It's like they're worlds apart, and can't communicate at all. Then, as the train goes through a tunnel, there's a sharp jerk, the lights go out, and Victoria hits her head on the window sill—hard! But then the train comes out of the tunnel and pulls into Penn Station. Victoria gets off and looks for her mother, who isn't there. Instead she meets Cici, who looks very familiar and offers to wait with her. They wait for over an hour, but Victoria's mother never comes, and the phone doesn't connect when Victoria tries to call home. She's beginning to feel strange, not only because her mother isn't there but also because everyone is dressed very strangely—the whole train station looks like a set for an old movie! Finally Cici suggests Victoria go home with her, and things get even stranger. Movies are 17¢, lunch 25¢, and shoes $2.99! Then Victoria sees a newspaper—dated May 9, 1944! That's when she suddenly realizes why it's all so strange—she has traveled, somehow, thirty years back in time. And when they get to Cici's, Victoria gets a shock that makes everything else look pale in comparison. They walk into the house and Cici's mother calls downstairs. Victoria would know that voice anywhere—it's her *grandmother*! And that means Cici isn't just Victoria's new friend who's fourteen years old and even wilder than Victoria's even *thought* of being—Cici is her own mother!

But that's only the beginning!

HAROLD AND MAUDE

By COLIN HIGGINS

Harold is eighteen and in love with death. Maude is seventy-nine and in love with life. This is their unique love story. Harold is making a career of suicide (he's done it fifteen times so far) because, he says, "I enjoy being dead." Maude spends her time looking for new experiences and enjoying the phenomena of life. They meet at a funeral—Maude goes because they're fun, Harold, because they're deathly. Maude doesn't own a car but she does have a set of skeleton keys, and when she needs a car, she borrows one. After the funeral she steals the Jaguar XKE hearse Harold drives, and offers him a ride home. When he tells her it's his hearse, she lets him drive her home. Harold is fascinated by the strange old lady, and they gradually become friends, the oddest of odd couples. Meanwhile, Harold's mother sets up three computer dates for Harold (she filled out the application herself), since it's high time he got married. Harold's agreeable—but he wants to marry Maude! He doesn't seem to be able to teach her much about death, but she's been teaching him a lot about life.

This is a comedy of life and love and freedom—almost everyone can identify with what it says. We're all Harolds, in one way or another, trying to become Maudes.

It's a beautiful—and hilarious—love story that you'll never forget!

HATTER FOX

By MARILYN HARRIS

Hatter Fox—Navajo, seventeen, pure spirit, anger, independence. She had no background, no family, no one to help her. She fought her battles alone, in silence, until Dr. Teague Summer decided to help her. The first time he saw her, she was directing traffic in her jail cell, making the other prisoners march back and forth. A boy who had committed suicide was lying in the corner of the cell, and when Summer went in to help him, Hatter looked at him with absolute terror in her eyes. As he walked past her, she stabbed him in the back. But he was still drawn to her, almost against his will, drawn by her aloneness, her pride, her regal bearing. The next time he saw her, Hatter was in isolation at the State Reformatory, her body little more than an emaciated husk for her almost totally submerged personality. Raped repeatedly by her keepers, Hatter was near death. Only her eyes were alive; they held the same fear and terror they had before when Summer approached. Slowly he worked with Hatter until she began to trust him and was pronounced cured, ready to become a productive member of white society. Or was she? And what about Teague Summer—what place did Hatter have in his life?

This is a strange and hauntingly beautiful story, but it is also brutal and harsh, just as life sometimes is. Meet Hatter and Summer, a most unusual couple, and one you won't soon forget.

THE HAWKLINE MONSTER

By RICHARD BRAUTIGAN

This is the story of two professional killers, Greer and Cameron, in the Old West of 1902. While they are both expert in the art of killing people, neither is prepared for what happens when they're hired by the two Misses Hawkline to murder the Hawkline Monster. The Monster, who lives in the ice caves under the family mansion in Eastern Oregon, is the creation of Professor Hawkline, a refugee scientist from Harvard. In addition to the two supercool killers, there is Magic Child, a fifteen-year-old Indian girl who looks so much like Miss Hawkline that she eventually becomes Miss Hawkline. (There is also a second Miss Hawkline, who is exactly like the first Miss Hawkline.) There is Mr. Morgan, the butler, who is seven feet tall and weighs three hundred pounds. There's also a large elephant foot full of black umbrellas, which turns out to be—guess who? And finally, there is the monster itself—evil, playful, and utterly unlike any other monster ever created!

In short, *The Hawkline Monster* is great for anyone who enjoys good writing and an offbeat imagination.

Larry Duckwall

HEAVEN AND HELL AND THE MEGAS FACTOR

By ROBERT NATHAN

In the firmament above the sky the Battle of Armageddon was being fought by the hosts of Heaven and Lucifer's fallen angels. But the battle was getting out of hand—it was too fierce and too bitter. Both sides fell back to reconsider, and each decided that the cause was the influence of the increased violence on earth. Something had to be done soon to counteract it, or the human race would destroy itself and, with its contagious violence, the rest of creation as well. So emissaries were sent from Heaven and from Hell, unknown to each other, to find the cause of this violence and to cure it.

Sophie was from Heaven, a gentle, rather old-fashioned woman, very slender and pretty. As she walked along the streets people were suddenly more happy, more aware of the goodness of life. She arrived in New York one warm spring evening, and went for a walk in Central Park. Buckthorne, Hell's emissary, also went to New York. He was a dark, saturnine man of indeterminate age with a confident air that made him rather unapproachable. People near him were suddenly more angry, envious, or greedy. He went to Central Park that evening too, and was just in time to chase off several muggers about to attack Sophie. They talked briefly and parted, each to begin his mission. But neither of them forgot the other, and both began to change because of that influence. They met again several weeks later at a rock concert, had a drink together, and shared an all-night carriage ride in the park. By morning, they were in love and wanted to get married. Of course, this created absolute chaos in both Heaven and Hell, and the lovers were told to stop the foolishness and get on with their missions!

However, Sophie and Buckthorne were made of sterner stuff, and they were very determined to get married. They began to plan how they might defy both God and Lucifer, and stay together forever.

THE HOBBIT

By J. R. R. TOLKIEN

"In a hole in the ground there lived a hobbit. Not a nasty, dirty, wet hole, filled with the ends of worms and an oozy smell, nor yet a dry, bare, sandy hole with nothing in it to sit down on or to eat: it was a hobbit-hole, and that means comfort. . . . [It had a round green door with a brass doorknob in the center. The hobbit who lived in this hole] was a very well-to-do hobbit, and his name was Baggins. The Bagginses had lived in the neighborhood of the Hill for time out of mind, and people considered them very respectable, not only because most of them were rich, but also because they never had any adventures or did anything unexpected. . . . [But] what is a hobbit? . . . . They are (or were) a little people, about half our height, and smaller than the bearded Dwarves. Hobbits have no beards. There is little or no magic about them, except the ordinary everyday sort which helps them to disappear quietly and quickly when large stupid folk like you and me come blundering along, making a noise like elephants which they can hear a mile off. They are inclined to be fat in the stomach; they dress in bright colours (chiefly green and yellow); wear no shoes, because their feet grow natural leathery soles and thick warm brown hair like the stuff on their heads (which is curly); have long clever brown fingers, good-natured faces, and laugh deep, fruity laughs, especially after dinner (which they have twice a day when they can get it)."

On this particularly beautiful sunny morning, Bilbo Baggins was standing in the doorway of his hobbit-hole, smoking his pipe, when a stranger came by. He invited Bilbo to share in an adventure he was going on, but Bilbo said, "We are plain quiet folk and have no use for adventures. Nasty disturbing things—make you late for dinner! I can't think what anybody sees in them!" And he began to blow smoke-rings again. However, when he realized just who the stranger was (it was Gandalf, a rather important wizard—Bilbo hadn't recognized him at first) he became quite embarrassed, invited the wizard to tea the next day to apologize, and popped back into his hole, slamming the door behind him. Gandalf just smiled and scratched a sign on Bilbo's door with his cane. The next day Gandalf came to tea, but thirteen dwarves came too and Bilbo's adventure began. The sign Gandalf had scratched on the door said, "Burglar wants a good job, plenty of excitement and reasonable reward." The dwarves were going back to the Lonely Mountains to rescue their treasure from Smaug, a dragon who had stolen it from their forefathers many years before. They needed a burglar, and Bilbo Baggins was it!

NOTE: This is one of the exceptions to the "never read" rule. I know of no other way to get the actual flavor of Tolkien's writing. Another scene to use is the riddle game scene with Gollum (pp. 79-93, paperback edition), especially if you can do voices well. Tolkien himself recorded it on a Caedmon record, and you can listen to his interpretation of the dialogue to get an idea of how each character ought to sound. This scene needs to be cut and paraphrased—uncut, it's about thirty minutes.

A HOUSE FOR JONNIE O.

By BLOSSOM ELFMAN

Jonnie O. was sixteen and pregnant ... she still went to school, though ... a special one for pregnant teenagers ... she rode with the other girls on the pregnant bus. School was really a waste. Then there was her mom, whom she fought with.... and maybe an icky new stepdad ... and her real father had stopped sending letters.

At school the nurse was always showing these dumb movies of little cartoon eggs falling out of cartoon Fallopian tubes, or a movie on the "terrible twos."

The English teacher was hung up on poetry, especially Robert Frost, and she flung out the words like a challenge: "Life can be a pathless wood where a branch cuts across your open eyes—what does that mean?" she would ask, as she tried desperately to relate English to life. But they would have none of her, and were caught up in soap operas, movie magazines, and their own boyfriends.

Jonnie O. was carrying Billy Veller's baby ... a brief summer romance ... when Jonnie got up the nerve to call him (by then she was six months pregnant), he did come back, but wanted her to give up the baby. Maryanne's boyfriend Arthur had a mother who refused to meet Maryanne, refused to acknowledge her son's involvement, just plain refused—and Arthur was tied to his mother's apron strings. Then there was Ada, an Indian, whose boyfriend was in jail ... and Antoinette, who was slightly retarded.

They all looked to Jonnie for leadership, 'cause even in the ghetto, on welfare, Jonnie O. had dreams of getting a house—a house for them all to live in and share—*A House for Jonnie O.*

Carol Starr

HOUSE OF STAIRS

By WILLIAM SLEATOR

Talk 1

[This is Mary's outline. She adds details when she presents the talk.]

Peter has been in an orphanage all his life and has decided that the best way to survive is to maintain a low profile. So he is rather upset and bewildered when he is called to the director's office. When he enters the office he is blindfolded and then led out, down the stairs, and into a car. No one speaks to him the whole time, and Peter, being the kind of guy he is, doesn't ask questions or try to tear off the blindfold.

He is led out of the car. He gets the feeling of going up in an elevator; then he is led out and left alone. Finally he takes off the blindfold and nearly collapses. He has to sit down—he sees he is in a place that is nothing but stairs. Tentatively Peter sets out to explore. He bumps down steps, he meets Lola who says this looks like a maze for rats, only it's for humans. They meet others and learn that all are sixteen, and from orphanages, and their parents are all dead. They conclude this is an experiment. They see Blossom kneeling on a landing sticking out her tongue at what looks like an electric eye—food appears. The rest try it, and learn that the machine doesn't always give food. They learn that some forms of violence can set it off. Lola and Peter can see where this is leading and decide to defy the food machine.

Mary Moore

Talk 2

In order to understand this book, you have to use your imagination. You have to imagine a place made up entirely of stairs. No ceiling, no floor, no walls, just stairs. In every direction you look, nothing but stairs. And if you try to go up, pretty soon all you find are stairs that go down. If you go down, all you find are stairs that go up. And if you try to go in any one direction, the stairs turn back on themselves, and you realize you're trapped in one section of this house of stairs. This is the situation that five teenagers, three girls and two boys, find themselves in. They get together and realize they have some things in common. They're all sixteen; they're all orphans, wards of the state; they all live in state orphanages; and none of them have any idea where they are, why they're here, or how they got here. But they do know that the two essentials are food and water, and they begin to explore. On a landing where two of the staircases come together, up nearly as high as you can go, they find a small indentation, like a bowl set down into the landing. It's full of water, fresh water. It's always fresh, and the water level never changes. So now they have water. Then on a landing further down, one of the girls finds a red light set into the landing. By now they've figured out that they've been put there by someone who's probably keeping an eye on them. The red light looks like the perfect place to hide a TV camera. So Blossom, who found it, starts to talk to it: "Let us out of here! I don't want to stay here—I want to go home!" and so on. But nothing happens. Pretty soon she gets mad and makes a face at it. And the light spits out a little pellet of food. She eats it, and it's *good*! So she tries it again—and it works again! Pretty soon she's making faces and eating as fast as she can. She isn't being very quiet about it, and when the other kids show up, Blossom explains what's going on and they try it too. But it doesn't work for anyone else, and when Blossom tries to get more food for the others, the food machine doesn't work for her either! So the group has begun to learn their first two lessons from the food machine: Everyone has to do something different to get food, and the food machine only gives food at certain times, not whenever you want it to.

Gradually the machine begins to teach them other lessons, to train them as you'd train an animal, by giving them food when they do the right thing and withholding food when they don't. Eventually they learn what they call a dance. It isn't really a dance, they just stand in a circle around the light and they each do what the light has taught them to do—snap their fingers, hop around, clap their hands—all nonsense motions, but when they did them at the right time, all together, the machine would produce enough food for one day. It was never enough to keep them from being hungry or to fill them up. It was just enough to keep them from starving to death. They were *always* hungry, and so they were also grouchy and nervous. Then one morning, they got up and did their dance and the food machine didn't give them any food. They tried it again and again—still nothing. The two boys began to shout at each other—"It's your fault." "No way! It's your fault!" And then one hit the other and the food machine suddenly began to produce more food than it ever had before. They all began to eat as fast as they could, but all of a sudden, one of the girls stopped—"Wait! Can't you see what they're doing to us? Can't you see what this means? From now on we'll have to *hit* each other, *hurt* each other, maybe eventually *kill* each other in order to get food!"

This is a story of survival—who survived after that, and how.

HUNTERS OF THE RED MOON

By MARION ZIMMER BRADLEY

All his life, Dane Marsh has liked solitary adventures—mountain climbing and other wilderness experiences—and he's on a solo sailing voyage around the world when an alien spaceship suddenly appears and kidnaps him. He finds out it's a slave ship, and he's locked up with lots of other creatures, some humanoid and some really exotic, like a giant lizard-man and a spider-man. Their captors, who are cat-men, have surgically implanted translator discs in the slaves so they can talk to each other, and pretty soon Dane has organized a conspiracy with two girls and the lizard-man to rush their guards and take over the ship.

Their attempt fails, but their captors are really pleased that they tried, because by proving their initiative and courage, they're now qualified to be sold as prey to a planet of hunters. These hunters make a religious ritual of the hunt, and they give Dane and his companions food and shelter, their choice of weapons, and time to practice. Dane has had some experience in the oriental martial arts, the lizard-man can defend himself pretty well by sheer strength and size, and one of the girls has had some judo training, but the other girl is a telepath, who is sort of frail and is deeply upset by violence around her, and the group is really worried about her chances for survival.

The hunt will last eleven days, from eclipse to eclipse of the planet's moon, and if they survive, they'll get their freedom and incredible riches. On the night before the hunt, there's a feast for the survivors of the last hunt, and they find out that of seventy-four creatures who were the prey, one survived.

No one has ever seen what the hunters look like, and Dane and his friends eventually figure out that they're shape-changers, so the hunt really turns out to be a game of wits. How do you survive for eleven days against creatures that can assume monster shapes, or can look exactly like one of your trusted companions?

Peggy Murray

I KNOW WHAT YOU DID LAST SUMMER

By LOIS DUNCAN

Julie, Ray, Helen, and Barry were juniors in high school when it happened. Helen was Homecoming Queen, Julie was a cheerleader, Barry was a football star, and Ray managed the football team. They double-dated a lot, and this particular time were having a picnic up in the mountains. They had a little bit to eat, a little bit to smoke, and a little bit to drink. It was dark by the time they left. Barry lost the toss and was driving—too fast, as usual. Julie and Ray weren't paying much attention (Barry always drove fast) until they heard Helen scream. They looked up, heard a thump, and saw a little boy on a bike sliding across the hood. And Barry didn't even slow down! "Stop! Stop!" Julie and Ray shouted. "It'll be a hit-and-run—stop!" But Barry said, "No—I hit him really hard, and it's miles to a hospital—we've got to get an ambulance up here as soon as possible—there's not time to stop." "Then at least slow down so I can jump out and stay with him," Julie begged. "A little boy shouldn't have to die alone in the dark like that. At least let me go back." But Barry wouldn't stop, and by that time, they were almost to town anyway. Barry said he'd stop at the first telephone, but when they saw the all-night diner with the pay phone, he went by. He said that phone was always busy, and if someone was using it, they'd just be delayed that much longer. Besides, there was another phone just a mile further on, in a roadside park, and no one ever used it—they'd stop there. Sure enough, a mile later, there was the phone booth. Ray was out of the car almost before Barry put the brakes on. He ran over to the phone, called the highway patrol, and reported the accident. He was just about to give his name when Barry reached over and broke the connection. "You don't really want to do that, do you?" he said. "What are you talking about?" Ray said. "Just think about it. We've had something to drink, something to smoke. We know we're not stoned, but do you think any cops are gonna believe us? Besides, I'm the only one that's eighteen, and I was driving. They'll take my license away at the very least, and I'll probably lose my football scholarship as well. My whole life will be down the drain—and for what? Just 'cause some stupid kid was riding down the middle of the road in the dark. He didn't even have on light clothes or a light. It's as much his fault as it is mine—and I'm not going to jail to pay for it!"

Barry talked and talked, and since Ray was his best friend, he agreed not to say anything. It was easy to convince Helen—she'd do anything for Barry. But Julie wasn't so easy—she refused to go along until the others said they'd all agree that she was lying, and no one would believe her. Finally Julie gave in, and they made a pact that they'd never tell anyone what had happened that night. But Julie still felt guilty, and she sent yellow roses to the little boy's funeral. He did die, on the way to the hospital—he never even made it to the emergency room. And it was

Julie who got the letter, about a year later, when she was just beginning to forget what had happened.

It came in the morning mail—a square white envelope with her name and address in square block printing. And when she opened it, there was just one line of writing, in those same square block letters: "I know what you did last summer." Julie was horrified, and called Helen. Helen found a little picture taped on her front door, a picture of a boy on a bike. And Barry got a strange phone call that told him to go to the football field after dark, where he got a bullet in his back.

Someone had found out that they had killed that little boy last summer, and now that someone was going to kill *them*.

Mary Moore and Joni Bodart

I NEVER LOVED YOUR MIND

By PAUL ZINDEL

Dewey Daniels feels (as many of you do, I'm sure) that he isn't learning anything valid in school. So he decides to drop out and concentrate on his major concern, SEX. He figures that the best place to get some action is in a job at the local hospital—lots of Candy Stripers and nurses' aides. . . .

During his first few minutes on the job he faints. He wakes to find himself laid out in the autopsy room in the care of Yvette Goethals, who offers him half of her broccoli sandwich. You could have offered him Lobster Cantonese and he would have turned it down in an autopsy room.

Yvette reminds him of an adolescent ghoul, with her white face, owl eyes, and straight brown hair, munching on her broccoli sandwich. But she does have what Dewey calls nice frontal insulation of the respiratory cage and he is reminded of his reason for getting a job in the first place—SEX.

Dewey and Yvette have one thing in common—they've both dropped out of school. But Yvette dropped out because she was sick of the middle-class hypocrisy that Dewey's very comfortable with. Their relationship seems doomed from the start, but Dewey isn't going to let that minor detail stop him—he has a *purpose* in mind!

by Mary James

I NEVER PROMISED YOU A ROSE GARDEN

By HANNAH GREEN

This is a look at what it's like to be insane, from inside the mind of a sixteen-year-old girl who's a schizophrenic. It's realistic because, although it's a novel, it's based on the author's life. Deborah lives in a mental institution when she's a part of the real world. When she's not, she lives in a world in her mind, called Yr, and is outwardly catatonic, not responding to anyone or anything. Deb has a brilliant mind—Yr is marvelously complete; its inhabitants have their own language and culture, and every detail is perfect. The people there comfort Deb when she goes to stay with them, when reality has become too hard for her to handle. But then these people begin to try to pull her into their world forever, and they torture her when she tries to leave. Soon life in either world is unbearable. Deb knows she's schizophrenic and tries to help herself, but the people of Yr are too strong for her, and she begins to realize she is in danger when she goes there.

Deb's encounters with the other patients in the institution are very revealing—the patients are shown as people, trying to help each other deal with a world they are not as well-equipped to handle as people on the outside.

As Deb fights to conquer her illness she learns many things, not the least of which is that no one was promised a thornless rose garden, and even the most fortunate have to deal with life and its problems.

I, ROBOT

By ISAAC ASIMOV

The Three Laws of Robotics, published in the *Handbook of Robotics*, 56th edition, 2058 A.D. #1 . . . [read from title page verso].

Dr. Susan Calvin, the first robo-psychologist, saw the development of robots from voiceless nursemaids to the great machines that stood between man and destruction. Cool, rational, seemingly emotionless herself, Dr. Calvin was fascinated by the machines' cold logic.

This collection of short stories is loosely grouped around her life, the robots she treated, and the development of the science of robotics.

The first story is about Robbie, a super-specialized silent robot who was a nursemaid and risked his life to save the child he loved—or *can* a mere machine love? How about one that gets drunk? Robot SPD13 (better known as "Speedy") was in exactly that state, but without the benefit of alcohol! "Runaround" tells how it happened. "Liar!" is about Herbie, a robot who could read minds because of a mistake that was made when he was assembled—a mistake with dire consequences. Stephen Bejerly was the first World Coordinator—and in the story "Evidence," Dr. Calvin intimates that even he, too, was a robot. For these stories and others, try *I, Robot*, by Isaac Asimov, and also *The Rest of the Robots*, his second collection of short stories and short novels about these machines with psy-onic brains.

ICE STATION ZEBRA

By ALISTAIR MacLEAN

When Ice Station Zebra, a meteorological outpost near the North Pole, reports a fire, a nuclear sub is sent to rescue the survivors. It's a difficult assignment, because the polar icecap shifts constantly and compasses are practically useless near the pole. Just before the ship sails, a British civilian, Dr. Carpenter, who has carte blanche clearance from the Secretary of the Navy, comes aboard and orders the captain to take him along. One of the men at the station is his brother; however, that's not the main reason he's going along. Dr. Carpenter hides his true identity behind one story after another, only revealing it at the final climax.

This is an adventure story of men against the sea, but it is also the story of men against each other, and of the tension that can build up when people are confined in a small space for weeks and months on end. Apparently the pressure of this confinement can affect people's minds, because no sooner is the sub under the icecap than a murder is committed, obviously by someone on board. For sheer excitement—*Ice Station Zebra*, by Alistair MacLean. It's not a book to read late at night. It's one of the ones you just can't put down till the last page, because only there will you find the solution!

IF BEALE STREET COULD TALK

By JAMES BALDWIN

If Beale Street Could Talk it would probably tell you a love story, but not a jive, everyone-lives-happily-ever-after love story. It would tell you of real love, of pain, of friendship, of struggle and hardship. It would talk of Tish and Fonny, who have been friends since she was six and he was nine. It would tell how, when he is twenty-two and she is nineteen, they decide to get married.

And that seems like a simple thing to do but it is not so simple when you're black and poor and live in Harlem, or if, like Fonny you find yourself in jail accused of rape. Fonny and Tish both know that he is innocent but they can't prove it because the woman who made the complaint has gone back to Puerto Rico and the cop who arrested Fonny has set him up and is out to get him.

So getting married isn't so easy and things don't look so good, and there is a good chance that Fonny may go to prison, and to complicate matters Tish is pregnant.

But if Beale Street Could Talk it would let you know that Tish and Fonny are real friends, and it is this friendship, Fonny's love of wood and stone, and his strong desire to be a sculptor that give them strength. They also have Tish's family, determined and willing to do anything to help them both.

Does Fonny make it out of jail? Is he proven innocent? Does he get to see his baby born? If Beale Street Could Talk it would tell you.

Karmann Reta

I'M DEBORAH SAMPSON

By PATRICIA CLAPP

Do you think that you could disguise yourself as a person of the opposite sex and get away with it for two years? It may have been possible during the Revolutionary War for a woman to pass as a soldier, but it wasn't easy. Deborah Sampson was a real person, and this is her story.

At eight years old Deb finds her mother has bound her out for ten years to the Thomases, as a serving girl. Heartbroken at her mother's lack of love, she discovers that the family she's been bound to is willing to accept her as one of their own. Still, she wants so badly to be loved and included that she learns to run and hunt and shoot as well as or better than any of the ten boys.

Discontent is beginning to spread throughout the colonies and several of the boys go off to war. Deb is fifteen and finds that she is falling in love with Robbie, the middle son, blond, gentle, kinder than the others. It turns out that the feeling is mutual, but Robbie has seen his younger brothers go off to war so he must go to prove to himself that he's not a coward.

You can guess what happens. Two years later Robbie is killed and Deb feels empty and purposeless. She's no longer the Thomas's servant, so she decides to join the colonial army. Bound across the breasts, dressed in men's clothing, she joins the line outside the house being used as the enlistment office. The men are joking and jostling, eager for the $40 bounty money. Feeling herself obviously female Deb tries to leave but the man behind her forces her back. She exits, newly enlisted as Tim Thayer, in the company of several boys who want to go celebrate. Friendly arms clasp her about the shoulders and she's forced to go along. Not used to strong drink, Deb opts for a glass of wine or cider, but nothing appears except ale. A few rounds later she hears a voice she vaguely recognizes as her own shouting, "I'm Timothy Thayer, I'm strong and I'm free." Then, after a few more rounds she's weeping into her beer about a golden-haired friend who will come home no more (which must have sounded strange). Her final recollection is of being violently ill by the doorway of the inn, supported by two disapproving acquaintances from the Baptist Church. The next day, with an awful hangover, Deb is visited by the Baptists, who want her to kneel and repent, and by the enlistment people, who want their $40 back. (Unfortunately it has been depleted by a whopping amount for the drink.)

Deb is even more determined to enlist now that she has shamed her foster family. She manages the second time without any slip-ups. Her story is funny, and filled with courage and close calls. To add a note that will pin it down and make it more real—years later, Paul Revere, her neighbor, suggested that she go on tour to tell about her adventures as a soldier in the revolutionary army, and she did, at age forty-two.

Mary James

INSIDE MOVES

By TODD WALTON

If you like basketball and San Francisco, and believe that sometimes even the craziest dreams really do come true, then Todd Walton's *Inside Moves* is the book for you. It's about Roary, who's a Vietnam vet. A land mine blew up in his back, and so now he holds his head to one side and he kind of shuffles when he walks. He's let his hair grow long and has grown a big bushy beard to hide the scars. Sometimes kids run when they see him, and even adults are nervous walking by him. They hold their kids close to them, as if Roary might hurt them. This makes him very sad, because he really likes kids. He's listed as totally disabled, but his pension still isn't very much, so he doesn't have a lot money for clothes, and since he knows he looks ugly anyhow, he doesn't always bother too much about the ones he has. If you saw him on the street in the city, you might think he was just a bum, drunk and stumbling down the street. Not many people are interested in looking behind the outside to the person Roary is within. But there is one place where people do just that—it's Max's, a bar down on Irving, near the Med Center. You probably wouldn't look at it twice, or even notice whether it was open or not. The guys who are regulars there are all cripples—freaks, Roary calls them—and he fits right in. One of the first people he meets is Jerry Maxwell, who's a part-time bartender there. One of Jerry's legs is shorter than the other; he was born that way. He and Roary get to be good friends. When Jerry isn't at the bar, he works nights in a box factory to help support his wife's drug habit (without his money, all she'd do is sleep around to raise the cash herself). Days, he plays basketball with a bunch of guys at Edison Park. That's when he really comes alive—basketball is the most important thing in Jerry's life. Whenever the Golden State Warriors are in town, Jerry's right there, on the front row, the best seats in the house, and usually with Roary, since he hates to go anywhere alone. He does a lot of shouting at games, especially at the rookies, when they're not doing too well. The guys on the team notice him—they call him "The Mouth." One night the Warriors are playing a championship game with the Bullets, and Alvin Martin, the rookie Jerry most identifies with, misses a clear shot. He freezes on the court with the Warriors behind one point and seconds to go in the game. Jerry screams at him, Martin comes to life, but by then there are guys all over him, and he misses the shot. Jerry can't stand it. He's absolutely beside himself, and fights his way into the dressing room after the game, Roary right behind him, saying, "Hey, wait, Jerry! You can't go in there! *Wait!*" Jerry ends up right in front of Alvin Martin and starts to tell him off. Martin doesn't appreciate this one bit, and before Jerry realizes what's happening, he's challenged Martin to a one-on-one game the next afternoon at two o'clock. It's so crowded in the dressing room that Martin hasn't noticed his limp.

That's when Jerry's dream starts coming true—the next day at two o'clock. As he says, "Playgrounds don't turn into Madison Square Garden, whores don't turn into virgin pompom girls, and cripples don't play for the pros," except *sometimes*, when even the craziest dreams really *do* come true.

INTERVIEW WITH THE VAMPIRE

By ANNE RICE

If Louis is a vampire, he is two hundred years old. This is the story of his life, the way he told it to a boy he met in a bar in San Francisco. After two hundred years, Louis was at last ready to tell his story.

"But how much tape do you have with you?" the vampire asked. "Enough for the story of a life?" "Sure, if it's a good life." The boy got his tape recorder ready. "I'm really anxious to hear why you believe this, why you. . . ."

"No," said the vampire abruptly. "We can't begin that way . . . I'm going to turn on the overhead light." "But I thought vampires didn't like light," said the boy. "If you think the dark adds to the atmosphere. . . ." The vampire said nothing, just reached for the light cord. [Read from Part I, p. 3, paperback edition, from "At once the room . . ." to "Just start the tape."]

It took the boy a moment to collect himself, then he turned on his tape recorder and began. "You weren't always a vampire, were you?"

"No," replied the vampire. "I was a twenty-five-year-old man when I became a vampire, and the year was 1791. . . ."

THE INTRUDERS

By PAT MONTANDON

This is a ghost story, one that's scary because its true. It took place in San Francisco, on Lombard Street, the crookedest street in the world. Pat Montandon was a TV talk-show hostess and one of the city's best-known party-givers. Lots of celebrities came to her parties, as well as the cream of San Francisco society. Each party was centered around a theme, and she chose an occult theme for her first party in her new townhouse on Lombard Street. All kinds of people were invited to come and entertain her guests—palm readers, astrologers, tarot card readers, fortune tellers. The party was in full swing when Pat realized the tarot card reader wasn't there. But then the door crashed open, and there he was—a huge man with a fiery red beard and a long black cape. He swept into the room with his entourage following, set up a table, and began to read the cards. He was rude to everyone, and when Pat came over to make sure everything was okay, he demanded a drink. She went off to get it for him, but she got sidetracked taking care of her other guests and then forgot. When she next saw him, he was *livid*! "I've never been so insulted in my life!" he screamed, and gathered up his stuff and marched out. But he turned in the doorway and said, "I lay a curse upon you, you and this house. I do not forgive and I do not forget!"

The party went on, but from that day strange things began to happen—the house stayed cold, no matter how high up Pat turned the thermostat. People were very uncomfortable in the house, and Pat's friends began to refuse to visit her at home and arrange to meet her somewhere else. Pat began hearing eerie music and footsteps when there was no one else in the house. Her dog cowered in corners, afraid of things Pat couldn't see, and finally became so neurotic it began to bite itself, and she had to give it away. Finally, she decided to have the whole place redecorated and throw another party. Surely that would take care of all the problems! But in the middle of the party, a fire mysteriously broke out, and although no one was hurt, Pat decided to give up and leave. But that wasn't the end. One of Pat's good friends persuaded Pat to let her stay in the house while her daughter and son-in-law were honeymooning in her own apartment. The first night she was in the house, another fire broke out, and she was killed. The police had to break down the outside doors and the bedroom door to get in—they were all locked from the inside. They found the woman dead, lying face down on the bed, but it didn't look as if she had fallen there—more as if she had been dragged. The autopsy showed she was dead before the fire started, and yet the doors were locked and she was alone. Who had started the fire, killed her, and then dragged her across the floor and thrown her on the bed? In addition, the fire had started in the closet, and had burned in a perfect V-shape pattern, with the point ending in the middle of her back!

No one was ever able to find any answers—not even Pat Montandon, who went back to the house only once more. She had a psychic medium with her, who said that the house was indeed possessed by evil beings, and that Pat was in danger every minute she was inside. If she returned to the house again, he could not guarantee her safety, or even that she would leave alive.

It's a true story, documents in the back of the book support it, and it may not be over yet. One of the rumors I've heard is that the house was purchased by Anton Le Vey, head of the Church of Satan in San Francisco....

THE KILLING GIFT

By BARI WOOD

It was true—there *was* something strange about Jennifer, something that made people afraid of her, and kept her apart from the rest of the world. She'd been born that way, changed because her mother was x-rayed only a day or so after Jennifer had been conceived. It had been an imperfect, newly developed, and defective machine, and it had irrevocably changed the tiny mass of cells that became Jennifer.

Jennifer Gilbert killed people. Not just *any* people, though, only the ones she *wanted* dead—three of them over the years. Hal Kearney was the first. Jennifer was only eight or nine at the time. He was a bully, bigger and older than she was, and he'd already beaten up on her once. When he tried it again, she pushed him. He hit his head on a stone wall and died with his skull broken in five places—"smashed to pieces" is what Jennifer had wanted for him. The second time, Jennifer was older, in college, and in love with Marvin Ross, but when he jeered at her and called her a freak and a monster, she stopped his heart from beating.

The third man Jennifer killed was Amos Roberts, a burglar and a totally evil man who deserved to die. But this time the detectives weren't persuaded by a young girl's innocent air to drop the investigation, nor could they be bought off. David Stavitsky, instead of giving up when faced with an "impossible" murder, began to dig, and Jennifer's life began to crumble around her.

Stavitsky was determined to find the answers. How could Jennifer kill without touching the victim? How could she do something the chief pathologist said was completely impossible—kill a man the size of Roberts, when she was much smaller and weaker?

One answer Stavitsky must find is the reason for his own fascination with this woman, the reason he is increasingly drawn to her, even while he's trying to prove she's a killer, a killer who murders with her mind, nothing more. . . .

KILLING MR. GRIFFIN

By LOIS DUNCAN

It was easy to hate Mr. Griffin. He was the hardest, coldest, most arrogant teacher at school. There was no such thing as an A in his class—that would mean perfection, and to Mr. Griffin, no one was perfect. He'd taught college English before he'd transferred to teaching high school, and his memory was excellent. So when Mark turned in a brilliant paper for his senior English class, Mr. Griffin recognized it as a college paper turned into him several years previously. Mark failed the class and had to repeat his senior year. So he had a particular reason to hate Mr. Griffin, and to want to see him humbled and broken. It started as a private joke between Mark and Jeff, the idea of killing Mr. Griffin, but soon it was a fully-planned kidnapping plot, involving not only them but also three other kids. They put it into action, and it worked! They blindfolded Mr. Griffin and took him up in the mountains to a secret place Mark knew about, and tried to force him to beg to be let go. But he stayed as cold and hard and arrogant as ever, even when they smashed his nitroglycerin pills to see if they would explode. They didn't—and when the kids read the label, "For Angina," Mr. Griffin didn't tell them that it meant he had heart problems. But maybe it wouldn't have made any difference if he had. They decided to leave him there, tied up on the ground until after the game that night. It would be several hours, he'd be cold, frightened, and *then* would certainly beg to be released. But two of them got scared and went back earlier, about nine o'clock, only to find him dead. He'd had a heart attack, and without his pills he'd died. Now it was real—it wasn't a joke any longer. It certainly wasn't a joke to Kathy Griffin, Brian's wife, about to have their first child. She didn't believe the story the kids told about her husband, and began to investigate on her own. She couldn't believe anyone would hate Brian so much that they'd kill him. She knew, too, that the cold, controlled person he was in the classroom wasn't the real Brian Griffin at all, but it was a long time before any of his students (and murderers) began to realize that.

LANDLADY

By CONSTANCE RAUCHER

Watch out when you rent your first house or apartment that you don't end up with a landlady like Mrs. Falconer. Sometimes you can't tell, of course, but Jessica and Sam Porter had some suspicions even before they moved into their new apartment that there might be some problems.

It seemed to be the perfect apartment in the perfect New York suburb, Wimbledon-on-Hudson. And they were the perfect family, with their adorable little two-year-old daughter Patience. They did wonder, however, if Mrs. Falconer would be a source of anxiety and in fact, their move there had some not-so-perfect consequences. Mrs. Falconer's constant interference in their lives, her sudden appearances in their apartment, her extreme changes of mood, the clumping of her cane as she moved about in her apartment overhead, were all annoyances, to be sure, but they only took on sinister overtones when considered along with some other events. For example, there was a murder in the tranquil village the very night the Porters moved in.

It was the first act of violence in Wimbledon-on-Hudson that anyone there could remember. And there were warnings by their new neighbors that Mrs. Falconer had harassed every previous tenant. Not only that, but she had driven every single couple to divorce.

The neighbors were actually afraid to enter the Porter apartment—they were afraid to visit Jessica and Sam there. But most frightening of all was a mysterious occurrence in their daughter Patience's bedroom one night, something that totally traumatized the child and caused a regression in her behavior, so that the Porters feared she might have suffered a deep psychological wound. When Jessica learned the truth about the clandestine visitor to her baby's crib—when the unknown became known—it was almost too late to save herself. A very menacing landlady and a very bizarre tale.

Rayme Gwen Meyer

LAST BUTTERFLY

By MICHAEL JACOT

Of the 140,000 people who passed through Terezin, a Nazi concentration camp during World War II, *15,000 were children*. Only a hundred of these children survived. Terezin was supposed to be a "model" camp where the world could see how well the prisoners were treated, but in fact it was a way-station on the road to Auschwitz, and most of the inmates knew this.

Antonin, an aging clown who has poked fun at Hitler once too often, has been sent to Terezin to entertain the children before a Red Cross visit. They are to look well and happy when the officials come around. Antonin is a Jew like most of the other prisoners, and he's frightened, but he's also stubborn and brave. He is horrified at what the children must endure. When a trainload of children from Poland arrives, the mere sight of showerheads sends them into hysterics—they have seen their parents gassed in the showers of a death camp.

With the help of a Red Cross nurse, Antonin sets out to give these children a new hold on life, to restore their ability to laugh.

The changes that occur in Antonin's character and philosophy when he confronts the depravity and horror of Terezin are astounding. In helping the children to live, he gives himself new hope too.

Last Butterfly, by Michael Jacot.

THE LEFT HAND OF DARKNESS

By URSULA K. LE GUIN

Genly Ai has been sent to Gethen, or Winter, to persuade the inhabitants of that planet to join with the other planets in a galaxy-wide federation. However, it isn't as easy as it might seem—the Gethians are not interested in forming alliances, and their unique sexual orientation makes them different from all the other races in the galaxy. Gethians are androgynous; that is, they are both male and female, each one of them. When the time of mating, or "kemmering," occurs, then one partner becomes male and one female, for that time. They don't always become the same sex, and one person may be mother to several children and father to several others. The rest of the time except during kemmering they are neuter, neither sex, and sex is not a motivating factor in their society. Life on Winter is strikingly different from life on other planets, since all other planets, whether hetero-, homo-, or bi-sexual, have sexually constant societies.

This is an excerpt from a report by one of the First Investigators, who went to the planet long before Genly Ai. [Read from pp. 93-94, paperback edition.]

Ursula Le Guin has taken psychology, mythology, and poetry, and woven them together with suspense, intrigue, and politics. She has created in Winter a society totally foreign to human experience, and she has done this so skillfully that in spite of its strangeness, Winter is believable. It becomes almost more natural to Genly Ai and to the reader than the society that we call natural today.

LISA, BRIGHT AND DARK

By JOHN NEUFELD

Lisa is sixteen years old, and she's going crazy. She tells her parents she needs to go to a psychiatrist, and they don't believe her. "Oh that's just a fad! This year shrinks, next year something else—we're not going to spend money on your keeping up with everyone else!" Three of Lisa's friends do believe her and they try to help, but they're only sixteen too and can't really do much. So Lisa's bright days get further and further apart, and her dark days get darker and darker, and come more and more frequently. Finally Lisa knows she has to have help or she's not going to be able to survive. She's *got* to catch someone's attention, she's *got* to make someone listen to her. And when she finds someone she thinks will listen, she does catch their attention—*she walks through a plate glass door.*

Carol Starr and Joni Bodart

LOGAN'S RUN

By WILLIAM F. NOLAN and GEORGE C. JOHNSON

Logan's Run—society of youth—in future age—totally computerized—flowers on palm at birth hooked to a computer—first seven years blue—certain rules and duties; second seven years orange—more places to go, more things to do. Then red for next seven years—even more privileges; blink black—do anything; black, turn yourself in for extermination. A society of youth. But there were rumors spread mostly by poets and folksingers of a distant "safe place" where people grew to be older than twenty-one. But if you tried to run—hooked to computer, special force (Runners) hunt you down.

Logan's Run is the story of Logan, a Runner going after a person who's over twenty-one, trying to escape—but Logan catches up with him. The guy, dying, hands him a ticket to Haven and instructions on how to get to the rendezvous point. More important, Logan's own flower starts to blink black.

Carol Starr

LOOSE CHIPPINGS

By THOMAS WHEELER

Destiny waits for all of us, our ultimate fate, good or bad. For Bob Vickery, a California professor, destiny waited in England in a small village called Loose Chippings. The decision to visit England was a sudden one—Bob's wife had died two years before and he'd never recovered from his grief. Then one day, he couldn't stand Santa Cruz any longer, so he left for London the same day. But London wasn't the place he wanted to be. He rented a car and began to explore the backcountry byways.

Seeing the "Loose Chippings—¼ mile" sign on a narrow road, Bob decided to see the town that had such an interesting name. Just as he came into view of the valley where it was, he hit a pothole in the road, burst a tire, and bent an axle. Getting out, he walked into the village, and his great adventure began.

The people and village itself all seemed unreal somehow—mysterious and occasionally, vaguely hostile. Then a whispered half-heard conversation helped Bob begin to put the pieces together, to form a very strange picture indeed. To learn where Loose Chippings is, and how Bob got there although it was not on any map or in any guidebook, read *Loose Chippings*.

LUCIFER'S HAMMER

By LARRY NIVEN and JERRY POURNELLE

When they first found the comet, it was a great scientific discovery—it would pass closer to Earth than any other comet ever had. Then someone said, "What if it comes so close it hits Earth?" The chance that it would was one in a million, then one in a thousand, then a hundred, then ten—and then it did hit, and earth and its inhabitants were all but destroyed. The lucky ones went first. They didn't have to struggle desperately for survival, fighting not only the dangerous new environment but the others who had been left. For this disaster seemed to bring out the worst in people, and survivors spent a lot of time fighting each other.

Civilization was all but wiped out, modern society completely gone. Life went back to what it had been thousands of years before. An Ice Age began; the climate and the entire face of the earth were completely changed. Suddenly the human race was an endangered species! [You may wish to add a description of the changes in climate and geography in your own area. I used to say, "What was once the California coast no longer existed, and the San Joaquin Valley became the San Joaquin Sea."]

MARY JANE HARPER CRIED LAST NIGHT

By JOANNA LEE

Mary Jane Harper was three years old—beautiful, big dark eyes, high cheekbones, dark hair. You knew, just looking at her, that she'd be even more beautiful when she grew up. But life wasn't beautiful for Mary Jane—you could tell from the way she talked to her kitty. "You be a good girl now, Kitty, or Mommy spank." That was the problem—Mommy spanked all too often and too hard.

It wasn't really Mommy's fault. Rowena Harper had gotten married before she was even out of high school—just one mistake one night down by the lake—and her whole life seemed to be out of her control. Especially since she'd had a miscarriage just a few weeks after she and Bill had gotten married. Then drinking, running around—and she got pregnant again. But by this time, Bill had had enough. Not long after Mary Jane was born, he left. Rowena tried, but that just wasn't enough.

Mary Jane went to the emergency ward with a broken arm—an arm that had been twisted until it broke. But Rowena didn't remember, and wouldn't have dared to confess if she had. "She fell out of her crib...." (But there was a thick plush carpet in Mary Jane's bedroom.) One of the doctors noticed, but Rowena's father was well known in town, and his influence was stronger than a newly-hired doctor's.

And then one night Rowena needed help. She knew, deep inside, she'd been hurting her child, and she had to get out of the house—now, right away! She ran out, got into her car and drove away, leaving Mary Jane standing in her crib crying, "Mommy, Mommy! Dark, Mommy!" And a forgotten cigarette burning in the living room. . . .

THE MAUDE REED TALE

By NORAH LOFTS

"I don't want to be a lady. I want to be a wool merchant." But in fifteenth-century England, young girls like Maude Reed didn't have any real choice about what they were going to be. So Maude was packed off to Beauclaire Castle to learn to be a lady. Maude lived with the other children in the Children's Dorter, a wing of the castle set aside for them, but she worked harder at playing knight with the boys than she did at her needlework. And although Maude didn't mention it to many people, she had not given up her dream of becoming a wool merchant.

Maude learned many things at Beauclaire—the hardest lesson was that life had to be lived by a strict set of rules that nothing could alter. Those who broke the rules suffered for it. When Melusine, beautiful but poor, and Geoffry, Maude's handsome but poor uncle, fell in love, their romance was doomed from the start. Geoffry married Madge FitzHugh, awkward, retarded, and very rich. Melusine committed suicide and was not even given a Christian burial.

After that, Maude couldn't bear to stay at Beauclaire any longer, and so she started home. Little did she realize that the chance for her dream to come true was waiting for her there.

MINDFOGGER

By MICHAEL ROGERS

Talk 1

Mindfogger is about a young man named Niles Spindrift, who is fleeing from the police and the FBI. He goes to stay with an old friend in L.A., who is now a big-time dope dealer, and meets and falls in love with a girl named Lila. When the house is raided, they escape the bust together and head for her sister's house, where they plan to hide out for awhile.

Niles is a genius at electronics, and though he ostensibly is wanted for drugs and draft evasion, he is really being pursued for a device he is working on, called the Mindfogger, which makes it impossible to concentrate on anything. The government agents who are after Niles intend to turn the Mindfogger into a mind-control weapon, if they can get their hands on it.

While he and Lila are staying with her sister, Niles completes the Mindfogger and decides to try it out on a nearby defense plant. Production comes to a complete halt, because the workers feel totally stoned whenever they enter the building—they're unable to do any work, but they're enjoying coming to the factory for the first time in their lives!

The Mindfogger is a success, but then an old boyfriend of Lila's tracks them down, and Niles knows it is only a matter of time before the police find them, too. But now, of course, he has the Mindfogger. ...

Richard Russo

Talk 2

Niles Spindrift is a very special person. He's a twenty-two-year-old electronics wizard—one who wants nothing to do with war, with killing, or with the government men who keep trying to persuade him to make bombs and to turn over his new device to them. All Niles wants to do is perfect his new device, the Mindfogger—an invention that can control the human brain. And every so often he's able to get away from his pursuers and work in quiet, but after a few weeks or months, there'll be a knock on the door and a smiling, well-dressed man will say, "I'd like to speak to Niles Spindrift, please. It's very important." And Niles will be on the run again.

He meets Lila in Southern California, and when he has to run again, she goes with him. She helps him hide, and Niles finally finds time to perfect his Mindfogger, and to use it in a way that only he would think of. But he stays too long to enjoy the effects, and the police and FBI catch up with him and Lila. But as the two turn to face their enemies, they discover that they have crossed a new frontier, creating strange new possibilities, and that nothing will ever be the same again.

To find out what that threshold is, and how they discovered it, read *Mindfogger*, by Michael Rogers.

MR. AND MRS. BOJO JONES

By ANN HEAD

Talk 1

Respect and a sense of responsibility—not much to build a marriage on, is it? Especially when the marriage is between two crazy, mixed-up kids who have to get married. And July and BoJo not only have to contend with their own personal problems in working out a relationship satisfactory to both of them but also have to cope with alienation from their friends (since they've both dropped out of high school), two sets of overprotective and feuding parents, and the problems of making a living. BoJo has a football scholarship for college next year, but that's out of question now. How BoJo and July meet these problems and how they handle an experience that would break up even a settled couple is the story told here. Dating and marriage are very different, as July and BoJo find out, and it takes more than sharing an apartment to make a marriage work.

To find out if the Jones's made theirs a success, read *Mr. and Mrs. BoJo Jones*, by Ann Head.

Talk 2

Marriage was the farthest thing from July and BoJo's minds when they started dating. But then July got pregnant, and marriage was suddenly a reality. July and BoJo had to learn the hard way that marriage solves no problems, only creates new ones. After the wedding, July's grandmother gave her a set of four bracelets, chained together, each bearing an engraved reminder—*Faith, Humor, Forgiveness,* and *Eternal Vigilance.* When July asked why she hadn't given those bracelets to July's mother, her grandmother's reply was, "Your mother had love." And so they began—with a marriage, an apartment, and soon a baby, instead of high school, college, parties, friends. . . . But July and BoJo discovered something more important to them than what they'd lost. To learn what that was, read *Mr. and Mrs. BoJo Jones*, by Ann Head.

MY DARLING, MY HAMBURGER

By PAUL ZINDEL

Told in the form of notes passed back and forth in class, plus diary entries, essays, and such, this is the story of what happened to Maggie and Liz and Sean and Dennis.... This first note tells about what happened in health class—the gym teacher was having a session on sex for the girls in her class. Afterwards she invited questions—well, one hesitant girl asked what to do, etc., etc.... well, what do you *do*? "Suggest going out for a hamburger," was the teacher's brilliant reply! Yes, well, the class members thought about the same thing of that answer as you do—it's not really helpful, to say the least. Face an endless stream of hamburgers or end up in the same situation as before. The rest of *My Darling, My Hamburger* tells the story of how Liz handled that "situation" in *her* way.

Carol Starr

NIGHT SHIFT

By STEPHEN KING

Talk 1

In the worlds Stephen King writes about strange and horrifying things are almost commonplace, and most often happen at night. In these stories, he takes ordinary situations and twists them just slightly—with terrifying results!

If you've read *'Salem's Lot*, King's second novel, about the New England town that's taken over by vampires, you'll be interested in "Jerusalem's Lot," a story that gives some of that town's horrible history.

Basements are notorious for being full of slimy, ugly things that hide in the corners among the junk. "Graveyard Shift" has a basement too, but the dark creatures in it aren't content just to hide in the corners.

The Blue Ribbon Laundry's pressing machine was completely reliable until Adelle Frawley got caught and dragged into it—after that none of the women wanted to work on it. It was as if the machine had tasted blood and decided it liked it . . . "The Mangler."

Boogeymen who hide in closets to frighten little children at night aren't real, except in the story, "Boogeyman."

These stories sneak up behind you, turn out the light, and slam the door when you least expect it, leaving you alone in the dark, with IT waiting for you. Don't read this at night, unless you're ready to take the chance. . .!

Talk 2

"The Mangler" is about an industrial accident that Officer Hunton has been assigned to investigate. A death has occurred at the Blue Ribbon Laundry. The culprit is the speed ironer. [Read description of the ironer, paperback edition p. 76, "It formed . . . the worst." Draw a sketch of the mangler.] Officer Hunton is relating the incident to his friend Professor Mark Jackson. "It tried to fold everything," he says to Jackson, tasting bile in his throat. "But a person isn't a sheet, Mark. What I saw . . . what was left of her . . . they took her out in a basket," he says softly.

The safety bar at the feeder end of the machine was supposed to snap up automatically and stop the machine if anything other than laundry went underneath it. Nevertheless, Adelle Frawley was sucked right in. It seemed a clear case of equipment malfunction. But when the state inspectors went over the machine, piece by piece, meticulously, they found it to be in perfect working condition—including the safety bar mechanism. In other words, the accident was impossible. It couldn't have happened.

But it did!

The following week Mark Jackson shows Officer Hunton an article he noticed in the newspaper which mentions another accident at the Blue Ribbon Laundry. The story says that a steam line had let go on the speed ironer, burning three of the six women working at the feeder end. Hunton goes to visit one of the women in the hospital—Mrs. Gillian, who suffered second-degree burns in the accident. Mrs. Gillian tells him that there has never been a problem with the mangler (they called the speed ironer that even before the grisly death) until recently. Lately all sorts of things have been going on—bolts have come loose, another worker's dress was caught in the drive chain, sheets were caught in the folder. It's as if the mangler has a curse on it. Ever since Sherry Ouelette cut her finger on the clamps. Sherry, a new employee just recently out of high school, was adjusting the clamps to tighten the feeder belt when she cut herself and bled all over everything. Before that the mangler had never been a problem. A week later it took Adelle Frawley's life. Mrs. Gillian may be more correct than she thinks when she tells Officer Hunton, "It's as if the machine had tasted blood and found it liked it."

Rayme Gwen Meyer

NO LANGUAGE BUT A CRY

By RICHARD D'AMBROSIO

[Read Tennyson quote.]

This is a true story. It is the story of a girl the author calls Laura. Laura was an abused child, a battered child; and the experience she went through as an infant left scars not only on her body but also on her mind. She didn't talk for the first twelve years of her life. Richard D'Ambrosio is the psychologist who persuaded her that the world was not the completely hostile place she thought it must be.

Laura's parents were alcoholics. They lived in a cheap apartment over a bakery, and the neighbors complained frequently about Laura's crying. In fact, her father (who went in for killing cats when he was drunk—once he even poured gasoline on one and set it alight) said the reason they did to Laura what they did was that "she cried too much." She was brought into the hospital emergency ward by a police ambulance with second-degree burns on more than fifty percent of her body. She was barely a year old. Her parents had gotten drunk and put her in a frying pan over an open flame.

Today Laura is a nurse, and she is well. This is a story of a doctor who wouldn't give up, and who finally convinced Laura that she *did* have a life worth living.

NONE OF THE ABOVE

By ROSEMARY WELLS

When Marsha's father remarried, she suddenly discovered she was a misfit. Her stepmother was slim, intelligent, sophisticated, and ambitious—so were her two children, Chrissy and John. Marsha didn't know about things like putting tarragon in blue cheese salad dressing, or puns, or skiing, or studying French, and she did like Day-glow pink angora sweaters, bubblegum, and David Cassidy. But she was happy being who she was until her stepmother decided to make Marsha into someone she wasn't. No matter how Marsha tried, she couldn't be another Chrissy.

She worked hard at school and got into the college prep sections, and even got accepted at an exclusive college; she lost weight. She learned a lot of ways to fake it, but she refused to compromise in one area. She insisted on dating Raymond, who wasn't the sort of person the new Marsha should have been dating at all. He liked cars, planned to be a mechanic, and sometimes rode a motorcycle. And he wanted to marry Marsha—now, just as soon as she got out of high school.

Finally Marsha realized she had to decide—who was she? The old Marsha or the new one?

NOT COMIN' HOME TO YOU

By PAUL KAVANAGH

When Jimmie John Hall and Betty Dienhardt found each other, all the lonely corners of their young lives were filled with love and hope. As a result, fourteen innocent people were murdered. This novel is based on the Starkweather Case of January, 1958, when two teenagers on a wild killing spree terrorized Nebraska and Wyoming.

Jimmie John is adrift and feeling good. He lives for the moment, taking what he needs when he needs it—whether it's legal or not. And when he's feeling on top, things just seem to work out right. Like passing up a ride in a beat-up old Ford and getting picked up by Walter P. Harris, in a new Toronado, complete with a gun and a handful of credit cards. Of course he has to get rid of Harris, who is soon lying naked, dead in a cornfield in the middle of nowhere. Things are still going great when he meets fifteen-year-old Betty Dienhardt in Grand Island. She comes out of the movie theatre and there he is, waiting just for her. For both of them, there is an immediate reaction that they call love at first sight. They plan to go away together, just the two of them. They'll never be alone again, and they've got everything to live for.

The first victim of their romance is the gas station attendant whom Jimmie John murders to get some cash. The second, third and fourth are Betty's parents and her senile grandmother, whom Jimmie John shoots in cold blood while Betty watches. Then they run, across the

Southwest on back roads, talking, sharing, loving, and trying to believe in their future. They play out their chance at happiness in a few short days, as Jimmie John stops only to kill, change cars, and replenish supplies, keeping just ahead of the police, and the future they *won't* be spending together.

OF LOVE AND DEATH AND OTHER JOURNEYS

By ISABELLE HOLLAND

"I met my father for the first time when I was fifteen," Meg Grant's story begins. Her parents had been divorced before she was born, and she, her mother, her stepfather, and a young painter nicknamed Cotton had traveled all over Europe. Everywhere was home, and the only reason to stay in one place was to earn enough money to move on to the next.

Meg helped guide tourists and could speak five languages. But the summer she was fifteen, life began to change suddenly and alarmingly. Meg's mother went into the hospital for a cancer operation, and almost as soon as she was out, Meg's father arrived. Apparently her mother had never told him about Meg. She had left him rather suddenly—she didn't fit in with his extremely proper family—and had run off with another man. Until Meg was born, she wasn't even sure whose child she was carrying, but Meg's "gray Grant eyes" were unmistakable. Before Meg's mother went into the hospital for the cancer operation, she had written to Meg's father, to let him know he had a fifteen-year-old daughter "just in case anything happens." Her premonitions were right—things did happen, and Meg was horrified to discover that her world was falling apart around her, and she could do *nothing* about it.

OLD GLORY AND THE REAL-TIME FREAKS

By RALPH BLUM

This book begins, "I'm 17, fighting a case of the munchies, and trying to crank out an opening page to someone who won't read it for a hundred years. Quintus Ells here. Call me 'Fiver.' Just about everybody else does. My outstanding feature is my hair, red gold wire. Six foot six, counting the hair. Some people would call me a freak. I call me a rich happy intelligent freak. Also I just happen to be your grandfather. And grandson, I want you to know how really weird it feels, sitting in my room a hundred years away from you, and thinking of you sitting here, just 17, reading what I am writing now. It's enough to blow my meager mind with some left over for years. I mean it's weird! No kidding, how do you start? There's really a lot happening now, so here I am, typing away in my jockey shorts, trying to put it all together in a loving letter. So that when you reach my age you can know what it was like to be 17 during one summer, a century ago.... I am addressing you through a hole in my coffin."

That's how Quintus, one of the foremost citizens of American Freakdom, begins his letter to his grandson—his map, made the summer before he turned 18, while he was still a member of the "privileged minority." He talks about his girl, Laura, and his grandfather, Bebe, who are his two favorite people in the world, the only two he's chosen to love. He's almost always stoned, so he talks a lot about that, and about how he and Bebe are into all kinds of mystical experiences—and how he turns Bebe on to more than Carlos Castaneda.

Quintus is a thoroughly likeable sort of person—fun, sensitive, loving, a freak. Meet one of the world's outstanding (if not upstanding) people.

ORPHAN JIM

By LONNIE COLEMAN

Trudy and her brother Jim are two kids on their own in Alabama during the Depression in 1932. Their mother died, their father ran off, and they're forced to live by their wits—mostly Trudy's. They decide not to go to the Orphans' Home but to run away to their Uncle Earl, who lives in Montgomery and who once said if they ever needed any help, come to him. However, his wife and family don't feel the same way—they hate Trudy and Jim, and soon they are back on their own. They only get as far as the edge of Montgomery, where they stop for a rest in the lumberyard. A bum there rapes Trudy, and then beats up both of the kids before he leaves. Trudy spends the following day crying, but the second day she and Jim go back into town to beg for food. They ask in the white part of town and in the black, but no one will help. Then a bunch of girls on the way to school tell them to go to the white house—"the whore's house"—and that's how they meet Hazel Fay, a retired prostitute with a heart of gold and enough love to go round with some left over. They move in to live with her, and she takes care of them.

One day, they go on a picnic and then decide to go to the movies. But Hazel's black, and in Montgomery, in 1932, blacks don't go to the nicest movie in town—except that Hazel has a plan.

This book makes you laugh, but it can also make you cry at the cruelty of the people in it. Just the same I think you'll enjoy meeting Trudy, Hazel, and, of course, Orphan Jim.

ORPHAN TRAIN

By JAMES MAGNUSON and DOROTHEA PETRIE

In 1853, there were thousands of homeless children in New York City, deserted by the immigrant families who had brought them to America. They were homeless, lost, abandoned—they slept in the street, begged, sold papers or apples, shined shoes, and survived. The Reverend Edward Symes had a plan for these children—out West, children were valuable commodities, needed to help settle the land. So why not take children from the streets of New York and ship them to the West where they could be adopted by families who wanted them? This was the purpose of the Children's Aid Society.

The first train carried twenty-seven orphans, and was to go from New York City to Rock Springs, Illinois. Emma Symes, 28, a spinster, went with the children when her uncle wasn't able to go at the last minute. It was she who herded the group along, kept them together, rejoiced when some were chosen to stay at a stop along the way, and comforted the ones who were left, the ones no one wanted.

Emma found her home too—because Frank Carlin was on that train. A young daguerreotypist on his way west to join a surveying team, he delayed his journey because of Emma and her charges.

Based on facts, *Orphan Train* will make you laugh and leave you with a lump in your throat.

THE OTHERWISE GIRL

By KEITH CLAIRE

Matt is fifteen and wants to be an artist, so he goes to Elverly to stay with Dockhurst and study drawing with him. But when he arrives at the Elverly station at midnight, Dock isn't there. Suddenly a voice behind him says, "You must be Matt," and he turns around to see a girl sitting on the churchyard wall. She's about his age, barefooted, and is wearing a T-shirt and short skirt, and has long red hair. She says her name is Chloe and that she can show him the way to Dock's house. He accepts, and off they go through the fields, since Dock lives a little way out of the village in an old barn.

When they get there, Matt turns around to say thank you, but Chloe is gone so quickly it's as if she'd never been there at all. When he goes in and tells Dock how he got there, Dock acts very strange but doesn't explain why.

Chloe shows up again in his bedroom, just as he's about to go to bed, snitches his pajama jacket, and tells him to meet her in the village the next morning. Matt finds out the next day that everyone acts strange around Chloe, and then Dock tells him why—she's his daughter, and she drowned eight years ago. And then Matt confronts Chloe with what Dock told him. And Matt learns that Chloe desperately wants to stop being half and half, to cross over and be "otherwise" completely. And when he agrees to help her, he realizes that her release will be his most bitter loss.

THE OUTSIDERS

By S. E. HINTON

Ponyboy's a greaser, from the wrong side of the tracks; he has long hair and sometimes carries a switchblade, but he's a dreamer too. He lives with his older brothers, Darry and Sodapop. Their parents are dead.

Ponyboy's best and only friends are the boys in his gang—Dallas, wild, restless, hard; Steve, whose specialty is cars, both stealing and fixing; Two-Bit, a wisecracker, famous for shoplifting and his long, black-handled switchblade; and Johnny, the youngest, who looks a little like a small, dark puppy lost in a crowd.

Johnny's the gentlest and the most vulnerable of the gang, but he is the one their enemies, the Socs, the rich kids with Mustangs, choose to beat up, one night when they find him alone. From then on, Johnny carries a huge switchblade, and swears that he'll kill the next guy who tries to mess with him. Not long after that, the same gang of Socs in a nasty mood find Johnny and Ponyboy alone, and Johnny gets a chance to use his blade. Then they have to split just ahead of the police.

To find out what happens next, read *The Outsiders*, by S. E. Hinton.

THE PAST THROUGH TOMORROW

By ROBERT HEINLEIN

Some science fiction authors write many unconnected stories. Heinlein, on the other hand, has written many stories that fit together, forming a "Future History" series. They are collected in this book. In fact, Heinlein has drawn up a huge chart of "Future History" which includes main events and important technological advances, starting in the late 1980s and going into the twenty-second century.

These stories are among the most famous of his works, and are where some of his best known and most durable characters originated. For instance, there's Lazarus Long, the oldest person in the world, who also has a leading role in several of Heinlein's later books. And D. D. Harriman, "the man who sold the Moon," in the story by the same name. In "Requiem," Harriman finally does get to go to the Moon. Johnny Dahlquist, in "The Long Watch," can make a Geiger counter go crazy just by blowing cigarette smoke at it. Holly Jones, at fifteen, realizes that she has to deal with "The Menace From Earth" or she'll lose her best friend and business partner, Jeff, to a sexy blonde bombshell. Andrew Jackson Libby, a mathematical genius, has the title role in "Misfit," but discovers he has his own niche too.

My favorite character is Rhysling, the Blind Singer of the Spaceways, in "The Green Hills of Earth." Rhysling is blinded by a leaking jet and spends the rest of his life cadging rides on the jets that shuttle around the solar system, writing hauntingly beautiful poetry about the sights he will never see again. Finally he decides to go back to Earth one more time and loses his life because of yet another faulty jet. This is how some of his poetry goes. . . . [Read "Green Hills of Earth" and other poems. Leonard Nimoy reads the story "Green Hills of Earth" on a Caedmon record of the same title, and you might get some good hints about effective recitation from it.]

PATRIOT'S DREAM

By BARBARA MICHAELS

Jan wasn't all that wild about spending the summer with her elderly aunt and uncle in their restored house in old Williamsburg. But she didn't want to spend the summer with her mother either, so she went. It turned out to be the most incredible three months of her life.

Not long after she arrived in Williamsburg, she began to dream—a continuing series of dreams centered around two men: her ancestor Charles Wilde and his friend Jonathan. She thought Jonathan might be a family member, because his portrait hung in her bedroom. But her aunt said no one in the family had ever figured out exactly who he was.

The first dream was set in May, 1774, and the ones afterward continued through the Revolutionary War, as the two men grew up and put their beliefs into action. Charles became a soldier, and an aide to General Washington. Jonathan, a pacifist, stayed home and worked underground, helping slaves to freedom.

Meanwhile, during the day, Jan, increasingly fascinated by what she was dreaming about, began to research the time period, only to discover that her dreams seemed to be historically accurate. But she still couldn't identify Jonathan. And she also began to date two men: Richard—handsome, charming, gentle, interested in antiques; and Alan—brusque, abrupt, homely, and yet surprisingly understanding about people, including Jan herself. And when things suddenly became confused, and the two worlds Jan had been living in began to merge in a terrifying way, even she was surprised to see who stood by her and who couldn't take it.

An unusual love story with a psychic twist—*Patriot's Dream*.

PORTRAIT OF JENNIE

By ROBERT NATHAN

This is a love story, but not a typical one at all. Eben first meets Jennie when he is a struggling, discouraged young artist (complete with an unheated garret room) in New York City. She comes up to talk to him while he's sitting in the park one day, and he notices she has on a rather old-fashioned-looking black dress. She says her parents work as jugglers in the Hammerstein Music Hall, and suddenly Eben realizes that the building was torn down years ago, when he was a boy. As she leaves, Jennie tells him to wait for her to grow up, and she sings him a little tuneless song—"Where I come from Nobody knows, /And where I'm going Everything goes. /The wind blows, /The sea flows, /And nobody knows."

Each time Eben sees her after that, she's a little older than she should be, and she always asks him to wait for her, and says she's hurrying as fast as she can.

There is something elusive and haunting about Jennie, and when she is a young woman, Eben manages to capture this quality in a portrait of her. Almost overnight he's a huge success—he sells all his pictures, even the ones he painted years earlier.

And then he realizes that Jennie comes less and less often, but now Eben's in love with her, and so he still waits for her.

PRINCES OF EARTH

By MICHAEL KURLAND

Adam Warrington had his future all planned out—he would go to college on his home planet, Jasper, and join his father's business afterwards. But he didn't include the results of his reputation for practical jokes in his plans. Someone vandalized the high school just before graduation; Adam was blamed and not allowed to graduate.

That ended his plans for staying on Jasper for the rest of his life—he couldn't go to college without a high school diploma, and that was unattainable now. So he took a scholarship exam for the University of Sol, on Mars, and even he was surprised when he passed with honors and was offered a full scholarship. It was the highest honor a student could receive—a chance to go to the top school in the best university system in the Imperium. Adam's parents didn't see it that way, though.

Jasper was the most conservative of the 1,423 planets in the Imperium, and its citizens usually stayed on their own world. Adam's parents felt he should remain on the home planet. But Jasper held nothing for Adam now. He accepted the scholarship and left almost immediately.

As soon as he was on board the ship, he discovered just how provincial Jasper really was—and how lucky he was to be a scholarship student at the University of Sol, Mars. He was a celebrity, entitled to sit at the captain's table the first night out and allowed to space-walk outside the ship.

Some things may have been different on board, but Adam's ability to get into trouble was not one of them—he could do it even more easily on the ship. Soon he was involved with Michael, one of the Princes of Earth, an heir to the throne of the Imperium. Even before the ship reached Mars, Adam's adventures had begun.

PSYCHIC SUMMER

By ARNOLD COPPER and CORALEE LEON

Talk 1

By now, most of you have heard about people who have communicated with the spirits of the dead. Some of you believe those stories to be true, and some of you do not. If you haven't yet been convinced that it is possible to communicate with the spirit world, then *Psychic Summer*, by Arnold Copper and Coralee Leon, might just be the book to convince you.

In the summer of 1967, Arnold Copper and three of his friends, Michael, François and Howard, rented a beach house on Fire Island. The four friends planned to use the house as a place to escape to on weekends.

After dinner the first evening, the four men were discussing *Rosemary's Baby*. The discussion led farther and farther afield until finally Michael suggested that they try to have their own seance. François was sure that it wasn't a good idea to try and communicate with the dead—

he said that he'd heard of evil spirits wanting to take over the souls of live people, and that it was too dangerous. Arnold and Howard convinced François to try it while Michael got out a Magic Marker and drew on the surface of the round pine dining table. Michael drew a circle and wrote out all the letters of the alphabet around the edge. Inside the circle he wrote the numbers 0 through 9, and below them the words Yes and No. He smoothed the surface of the table with olive oil, added an upside-down juice glass, and they were ready to go. The four touched their fingertips to the glass and waited. Nothing happened.

Arnold went outside and invited the spirits in. He then returned to the table and joined with the others in placing his fingertips on the edge of the glass. It moved. The glass began to move faster and faster. At last Arnold asked, "To whom do you wish to speak?" The glass moved from letter to letter, forming the words ALL CONCERNED. Arnold, Michael, François, and Howard were all silent, surprised. Arnold continued, "Who are you?" ZENA was spelled out, letter by letter. The glass continued, VERY UNUSUAL TO BE AS LONELY SO LONG BY MYSELF REST FOR TEN.

Arnold, Michael, François, and Howard were speechless. What could this mean? Howard was convinced that it meant that it would take ten minutes for whoever was pushing the glass to get the game going again. But no one was pushing the glass, and it wasn't a game.

Over the course of the summer, Arnold, Michael, François, and Howard were to be trusted with the secrets that Zena had carried to her grave almost one hundred years before. Zena, her sister Bethlene, and Higgins, Bethlene's lover, were to use Arnold, Michael, François and Howard to air the arguments that they had suppressed since 1873. This was to be a summer that would change all their lives. As you read it, remember, there really was a Psychic Summer.

Ilene Injelmo

Talk 2

The night Zena died on that fiery ship she had her sister Beth's baby with her. Zena had taken the baby as her own—an act of compassion which shielded Beth from the shame of having an illegitimate child and allowed Beth the freedom to carry on her love affair with Captain Higgins. The captain and Beth did nothing to save Zena and the baby from drowning that night.

It sounds sort of like a soap opera, but according to Arnold Copper, one of the authors of *Psychic Summer*, these people did live once, about a century ago, and their spirits still haunt the site of their deaths. How does Copper know this? Well, he says he and several of his friends, both believers in the astral world and total skeptics, were in contact with the spirits of Zena, Beth and Captain Higgins during the summer of 1967.

Copper and three other rather well-off and respectable young Manhattanites rented a house on Fire Island that summer, intending to escape New York City on the weekends and relax on the beach, socialize with friends, and visit the Island's discos. But this carefree attitude changed sharply when, on the very first weekend, on a pure whim, they decided to hold a seance. They sketched an improvised Ouija board on the table, and Arnold made up a dramatic invocation, welcoming any spirit that happened to be around and inviting it to communicate with them. They were totally astonished by the results of this invitation, and on the ensuing weekends they were drawn deeper and deeper into the spirit world. But it wasn't just light-hearted summer fun. Arousing the spirits also had some dangerous consequences for the participants in the seances.

Each chapter of the book relates an encounter with the spirit world and events of the past. *Psychic Summer* may or may not change your opinions but it certainly is a fascinating tale.

Rayme Gwen Meyer

Talk 3

It had all begun as a result of a relaxed, after-dinner conversation one lazy summer evening. Three of the men in the room were in favor of walking down to a nearby disco while the fourth preferred to stay at their beach house and read *Rosemary's Baby*. Arnold was caught up in the story, although he felt skeptical about the existence of spirits. Howard, a young motion-picture distributor and a practical individual, had also read the book and shook his head over the ridiculous plot. François, on the other hand, was totally convinced of the reality of devils, evil beings, and threatening spirits who could possess people and send them straight to eternal damnation. He wouldn't even open a book like *Rosemary's Baby*. The fourth member of the household, Michael, was an imaginative sculptor whose grandmother had certain unexplainable powers, such as the ability to identify a playing card over the telephone!

It was Michael who suggested that they set up their own Ouija board and attempt to contact the spirit world. At the time it seemed like fun. Four bachelor professional men, all in their mid-twenties, renting a beautiful house for the summer on Fire Island . . . playing a game with a homemade Ouija board. Michael got a black Magic Marker from his room while the others cleared the surface of the round pine dining table. He drew a circle of letters, all the letters of the alphabet, evenly spaced, and across the diameter of the circle he wrote the numbers 1 2 3 4 5 6 7 8 9 0, and below them, also inside the circle of letters, YES and NO. The guys settled on a small glass as a marker, and placed it upside-down at the center of the board. Armed with a legal pad and a pencil for note-taking, the group was ready.

François felt they were trafficking with evil and became more and more agitated as the minutes passed. Howard, slightly amused, agreed to participate in order to observe the reactions of his friends. Only Michael and Arnold were serious about going on with the seance. The lights were turned out and a single candle lit. Arnold slid open the glass doors which faced the ocean and quietly spoke into the night air, inviting any listening spirit to enter the room. Returning to the table, he felt a strong gust of wind envelop him. Incredibly, when fingers touched the glass, it began to circle the board furiously, and eventually responded to Arnold's question, "Whom do you want to speak to?", spelling out ALL CONCERNED.

Thus began their communication with loving Zena and malevolent Beth, two sisters who had drowned over a hundred years ago. Only now that the summer house has burned to the ground is it possible for Arnold to describe what the Ouija board told them.

[Items needed: Small, lightweight jelly glass, black Magic Marker, wooden board or stiff sheet of paper approximately 18″ square. See p. 29 in paperback edition.]

Elizabeth Talbot

Talk 4

Today Arnold Copper doesn't try to contact the spirit world. He doesn't go to seances or use Ouija boards. He was cured of any desire to meddle with such things during the summer of 1967.

This book is about that summer and the author says it is all true. [Read from the prologue, from "For a long time . . ." to "I was free to tell my story."] The psychic summer began when Arnold and three friends rented a beach house on Fire Island for the season. They planned relaxing weekends with friends (none of which ever took place).

The first night they were there, they decided to experiment and drew a Ouija board on the dining room table to see if they could contact any spirits. They immediately reached two sisters: Zena—warm, loving, eager to tell her story, and Beth—cold, evil, trying to control her hosts' actions as well as what they learned. They had died in a shipwreck off Fire Island in 1873.

As the summer went on, the four men became more and more deeply involved, and strange things began to happen, as the evil power they had released grew stronger and stronger, even reaching beyond the island.

Arnold's new Mercedes was wrenched from his control and totalled on a New York City street, although he walked away from the crash without a scratch. He went swimming one weekend at the island and nearly drowned when something (someone?) clutched at his legs and tried to pull him down. The ashtray with a lighted candle in it that they used during their seances was hurled across the room at Melissa, a neighbor who was watching, while Beth, who was in control of the board at the time, spat obscenities at her. Then there was the night when the glass went spinning around the board, spelling out THIS NIGHT ZENA CAN APPEAR. YOU CAN SEE ZENA AND BETH TONIGHT.

Perhaps if they'd known what was going to happen, they would never have started—or perhaps it wouldn't have made any difference. In any case, it happened, and this book tells how.

Except for a few names, it is completely true—including the fact that Arnold Copper has never tried to contact the spirit world again.

RAISE THE *TITANIC*!

By CLIVE CUSSLER

In 1911 French industrialists discovered a rare metal, byzanium, in rich mines in an uninhabited area of Russia. Miners from the Rocky Mountains were smuggled into the area, and the mines were stripped secretly. The ore was supposed to be shipped back to France, but the American miners sent it home instead. But the ship it was on sank midway, so nobody made any profit after all.

Now it's 1988, seventy-seven years later, and the world is in desperate need of byzanium. The only source has been mined, but the ore is missing. The U.S. government begins to trace it and finds it's not *really* missing—just hard to get to.

It's been in the same place since the ship carrying it sank in April, 1912—in the hold of the ship where the expedition's leader put it. So the U.S. government decides to bring that ship up to the surface and retrieve the byzanium. And the Americans begin to plan to raise the *Titanic*!

One of the things I like about this book is that it really does keep you in suspense till the last page! About the time you decide you've got it all figured out, Cussler lays on another layer of mystery, and you're back at the beginning again!

RED SKY AT MORNING

By RICHARD BRADFORD

After Pearl Harbor, Josh Arnold's father decides to send his family someplace safe. Safe is Sagrado, New Mexico, a little town up in the mountains, about as far from Atlanta's shipbuilding yards as you can get. It's the kind of place that has a population of six cows, four dogs, seventeen chickens, and almost no people. Josh has to get used to a whole new way of life, and he gets into trouble his very first day at school.

He's watching this beautiful girl walk down the hall and notices that no one else is looking at her. It's as if she doesn't even exist. Just at that moment, Josh feels a knife stick in the back of his neck, and a voice growls in his ear, "You look at my sister like that, I cut your ear off!" It is Chango, the town bully, and that's why no one is looking at his sister. Then Josh hears, "Oh, lay off, Chango, he's new—let him go," and Chango skulks off down the hall, muttering under his breath. Josh turns to his rescuer. It's Steenie, the local doctor's son. Steenie decides that Josh needs some lessons on how to survive in Sagrado. He enlists the help of Marcia, the daughter of the local minister. They are without doubt the two best people in town to teach Josh how to survive in Sagrado. Steenie read all his father's medical books and knows all the Latin and Greek medical terms for all the parts of the body. He can cuss you out for ten minutes, and you'll never have any idea what he really said—and what's better, neither will his teachers! Marcia, on the other hand, is a typical "preacher's kid"; she specializes in dirty jokes. Every year she goes to church camp and comes back with a whole year's supply—the *worst* ones in town! Marcia and Steenie decide that the first thing Josh needs to learn is how to play "Chicken," Sagrado-style.

On Saturday, they take him out to lunch: the greasiest, hottest tacos and burritos they can find—as many as Josh can eat, and really more than he wants. (Remember, Josh is from Atlanta, and his stomach isn't used to Mexican food.) Then they go for a walk. Josh isn't used to the high altitude, and he's lagging behind, panting for breath, his stomach feeling worse by the minute, when he notices that Steenie and Marcia have stopped and are talking. They're at the top of this little rise and are pointing to something below them, and saying things like, "Boy, this is gonna be a great game of Chicken—the best we've had in a long time!" "Yeah, Josh is really gonna learn to play the right way!" "He's one lucky fellow—it wasn't this good when I learned to play," and so on. Josh is really wondering what's going on, till he gets to the place where they're standing and looks down. There in front of him is the town dump, and in the middle of the dump is a dead horse, a *very* dead horse—bloated, covered with maggots, and smelling *horrible*. The object of the game is to walk, or run, up to the horse, touch it, and walk, or run, back to the starting point, which is back just far enough that you can take a deep breath without throwing up. If you walk up, you have to walk back, which takes longer, but you aren't so likely to get out of breath. If you run up, you run back, which won't take as long, but you may lose your breath, and have to take another. Marcia says, "Ladies first!" Marcia is a walker. She walks up to the horse, touches it—"nice horsie"—and walks back. Steenie is a runner. He dashes up to the horse, gives it a kick—"Hey horse"—and runs back. Josh just can't *believe* this stupid game! And he's so busy thinking about these small-town kids and their dumb games that he doesn't see the empty beer bottle lying right in front of the horse—the bottle Steenie and Marcia have very carefully avoided. He trips and falls and slides right into home plate, which is, of course, the horse.

Now, what do you do when you fall down suddenly? You lose your breath. And what do you have to do when you lose your breath? Take another one. Well, that's what Josh does, he can't stop himself, and that's when Josh loses both his lunch and the game of Chicken. When he gets back to where Steenie and Marcia are, they're still howling with laughter, hardly able to talk. But when she gets her breath back, Marcia says,

"You know, Josh, we've been playing the game wrong all these years. You're not supposed to just *touch* the horse—you've got to get in there and hug him like a *brother!*"

And that's only the first of many lessons that Josh learns about how to survive in Sagrado, New Mexico!

REPRESENTING SUPERDOLL

By RICHARD PECK

They seemed an unlikely pair—Verna, fresh off the farm, and Darlene, the beauty-contest winner. In fact, they didn't want to be together really but Darlene's mother had decided what would be best and she'd swept them all along, just the way she always did. It had started the year before, when Darlene had won her first beauty contest. And, with Darlene's looks, it wasn't hard—blonde hair, baby blue eyes, and gorgeous! The kind of person who comes out in beauty marks instead of pimples. And she was just as dumb as she was beautiful—maybe that's why she let her mother keep her under her thumb the way she did. She just didn't know any better. But she did know how to look beautiful, and won one contest after another. Finally she'd won the Central United States Teen Superdoll contest, and would go to Las Vegas for the national contest. But first there was a trip to New York and a chance to appear on *Spot the Frauds*, a TV contest show like *To Tell the Truth*. Since Darlene's mother couldn't go, she had decided that Verna, the most presentable of Darlene's friends, would be superdoll's companion, and before they knew what was going on, the two girls were on their way to New York. The morning they were supposed to film the show, one of the two frauds that were to appear with Darlene got sick, and Verna got drafted to fill in! They rehearsed her lines, fixed her hair and face, and pinned her into the long white gown with a ribbon over her shoulder. Then Verna got a chance to look into the mirror and saw a stranger staring back at her—a stranger who looked almost pretty.

And then they were on stage, and as Verna said, "My name is Darlene Hoffmeister," suddenly she knew that nothing would ever be the same again!

RICHIE

By THOMAS THOMPSON

This is a true story, about a boy who turned from nature to drugs and about his father who followed him to try to bring him back.

At Richie's funeral, the mourners were divided into two groups. The older ones were George Deiner's allies; dressed in black, they clustered around his wife, Carol. Further back were Richie's friends—young, longhaired, dressed in bright colors, even their glasses tinted. When the ceremony ended, the older people left in their sober, serious, straight automobiles, while the young ones hurried to brightly painted psychedelic cars, and rock music filled the air as they rushed to get away from the place of death, blotting out its cold silence.

This is the story behind that funeral. It's a heavy story, about a father and son who were at one time very close, and who were first separated, then hostile, and finally bitter enemies. And as with most enemies, they fought a war, a war that ended in death, when George Deiner shot his son.

There's no blame laid in this book—you can decide for yourself which group of mourners to stand with. You can mourn only for Richie, or you can mourn for both him and his father.

RITE OF PASSAGE

By ALEXEI PANSHIN

Mia Havero lives on one of the seven giant spaceships that are all that's left of earth's civilization. There are a few primitive colony-planets that the spaceships visit to get raw materials, but the ships are the real centers of science and culture. With so little room on the ships, the population has to be strictly limited, so one of the things the people do is make all teenagers go through a thirty-day period of trial, where they are put down on a primitive planet with some simple weapons and equipment, and have to survive on their own. After thirty days the spaceship comes back to pick them up, and if they've survived, they're considered adults, with all rights and privileges. If they haven't, the ship doesn't have to worry about them anymore.

At the beginning of this story, Mia has two years to go before her trial. She's a pretty shy, meek person, and her father is afraid she won't make it, so he moves to a different section of the ship, where she gets a new tutor and meets Jimmy, a guy who has the same tutor. Now Jimmy is far from meek, and pretty soon they get to be friends and start doing things together, like exploring the outside of the ship where they aren't supposed to go, and getting into trouble, but all their activities really increase Mia's confidence in herself.

A year and a half before trial, they start survival class together, where they learn things like how to build shelters in the wilderness and how to stalk and kill wild animals with their bare hands. By this time, they have become romantically interested in each other, and they plan to go down for trial as a team, which increases Mia's confidence still more. Then, three days before trial, Mia has a big fight with Jimmy, and they decide to go down separately. So if you want to find out if they make it and ever get back together, read *Rite of Passage*, by Alexei Panshin.

Peggy Murray

ROAD TO MANY A WONDER

By DAVID WAGONER

In March 1859, Ike Bender, twenty, sets off for the Pike's Peak Gold Rush with all his possessions in a wheelbarrow christened "The Millicent Slater." He'd been thinking about leaving for a while, but he decided to do it the evening he heard Pa cuss out the farm. [Read Pa's curses from pp. 4-5, hardback edition.] But Ike hadn't gotten very far when the real Millicent Slater, aged fifteen, caught up with him and told him she was coming along. They were married by a drunken minister at Ft. Kearny—he was too drunk to ask awkward questions about Millicent's age, which made things a lot less complicated! They were accompanied on their adventures by a rather unusual mule named Mr. Blue, and on the way to their fortune they met any number of hilarious people, all guaranteed to have you rolling on the floor! But no one is more surprised than Ike himself when they do find their fortune and their fate!

RUN SHELLEY RUN

By GERTRUDE SAMUELS

Shelley started running when she was ten years old. Her alcoholic mother decided she didn't want to take care of her anymore and made Shelley a ward of the court. Every time she was sent to a foster home, Shelley ran away, back to her mother. But her mother only turned her over to the court again. Then when Shelley was almost sixteen, she ran home to her mother only to find her mother had remarried. Cal, her new stepfather, began to make passes at her. When Shelley told her mother about it, her mother said she was lying, and so Shelley ran again. She was too afraid of Cal to do anything else. But before, Shelley'd always been running *to* something—home. Now she was just running. Anywhere. Away.

A year or so later, she ended up at the Rip Van Winkle Center, the state training center for girls—girls who ran away, slept around, did drugs of various kinds, and refused to go to school. They were called PINS— persons in need of supervision. And by the time Shelley got there, she was one of them. She'd learned a lot in her time on the street—about rape, sex, crime, drugs, and how people of all ages can be cruel beyond belief. She'd survived, but she still needed to learn more—about herself and about her mother. She kept on running until she found the answers, because Shelley was different—she had a spirit that wouldn't quit, even when she was threatened with a mental institution.

'SALEM'S LOT

By STEPHEN KING

Talk 1

Jerusalem's Lot, or 'Salem's Lot as the locals call it, is a small town about twenty miles from Portland in Northeastern Maine. It's not the first town in American history to dry up and blow away, and it won't be the last, but it is one of the strangest. In the Southwest, towns sprang up around the lure of gold and silver and then once the veins ran out were left deserted to crumble in the desert silence, but 'Salem's Lot was not one of these; it was an established New England community with over a century of history—in the 1970 census the town claimed 1,344 persons, a gain of 67 over the 1960 count.

But then just a few years ago in September 1975 strange things began to happen. First, some people moved into the old Marsten Place, a mansion that sits on a hill above the town like an evil idol. The house had been vacant for over twenty years since its original owner and builder, Herbert Marsten, had butchered his wife and hanged himself in the bedroom.

And then after that, people began to disappear. At first only a few, but then more and more, until in just a few weeks everyone was gone.

No one shops at Spencer's store any more, even though there is merchandise on the shelves and money in the cash register.

No one attends the new brick and glass tri-city high school any more. Not the students and not the teachers.

No one goes to any of the three churches, and no one is locked in the jail. Everyone is gone.

Of course a lot of people didn't really disappear. Parkins Gillespie, the town constable, is living with his sister in another part of the state, and Charlie James, who ran the gas station, has a repair shop over in Cumberland, just a few miles away, and Pauline Dickens is living in Los Angeles, but what is mystifying about this is that if you track these people down they won't talk to you about 'Salem's Lot at all. Some of them were born there, and yet they refuse to say anything at all about it or about the other people who used to live there.

And then there is another list, a list of people who really are missing. People who can't be found—not by the police or FBI or anyone. People like John Groggins, the pastor of the Methodist church, and Father Callahan from St. Andrew's and Mabel Wert, a widow who was active in social affairs. These people and others like them are gone, and nobody wants to talk about it.

Nobody except a writer named Ben Mears and a young boy named Mark Petrie, whose parents are among the missing, and the story they tell is almost unbelievable.

They say it all began after the new people moved into the Marsten Place and Danny Glick and his kid brother Ralph went for a walk one night with strict orders to be in by nine. When they were a little late nobody was too worried, but then Danny showed up alone, so scared he couldn't talk, and nobody ever saw Ralph again. He was the first to disappear.

They say there wasn't very much wrong with Danny except shock, but he was dead within two days anyway and nobody really knew why.

And then at the funeral everybody commented on how lifelike Danny seemed, and some of the people say he opened his eyes and looked around.

And on the night after the funeral Mark Petrie says he woke up to find Danny Glick knocking on his window asking to be let in, and he looked just fine except he had two new teeth, just like something you'd see in an old movie on Saturday night.

And they say that after that lots of people began to disappear, and maybe it really did start right after the new people moved into the Marsten Place, and maybe they aren't people at all, but something a lot older and a lot stranger—something you have to kill with a stake through the heart.

And if that's true, then 'Salem's Lot could be a dangerous place to be, and maybe that's why no one lives there anymore.

Larry Duckwall

Talk 2

Ben Mears, a writer, returns to his home town of 'Salem's Lot after twenty-five years and before long strange things begin to happen. The old Marsten house, which has stood vacant since its owner killed his wife and committed suicide thirty-six years ago, is rented to a very mysterious stranger. A dead dog is found hanged, head down, from the stakes on the cemetery gate. A little boy disappears and shortly afterward his brother, who had been with him when he disappeared, dies of severe anemia, as if all the blood had been drained from his body.

Being a writer and naturally curious, Ben does a little research and finds that the last time the Marsten house was occupied four children had disappeared from the area without a trace. When he discusses what he has learned with other people, he becomes increasingly alarmed by the strange things they tell him about. Small scratches on the neck of the boy who died of anemia. Townspeople who have disappeared. Corpses that get up off the slabs in the morgue at night.

Twelve-year-old Mark Petrie doesn't need any research or discussion to figure out what is going on. One night his friend, the boy who died of anemia, appeared outside Mark's second-story bedroom window begging to be let in. Mark knew there was nothing to stand on outside that window. There could be only one explanation for his friend's presence.

'Salem's Lot, by Stephen King.

Gloria Hanson

THE SANTA CLAUS BANK ROBBERY

By A. C. GREENE

Just before Christmas, 1927, Santa Claus and three helpers robbed the First National Bank of Cisco, Texas. They were so sure they'd succeed that they laughed and sang carols all the way to the bank. But the robbery quickly turned into a comedy of errors—the bandits had even forgotten to buy gas for the getaway car! (Maybe they should have used reindeer.)

The four robbers were Marshall Ratcliff, who wore the Santa Claus suit because he was well known in Cisco and didn't want to be recognized, Louis Davis, Henry Helms, and Robert Hill. Davis was the only one who wasn't an ex-con—the other three had met in Huntsville Prison. They all were sure that there'd be no problem—after all, the bank didn't really need the money, and they counted on no one objecting. However, they had forgotten that the state had recently gotten tired of all the bank robberies and had offered a five thousand dollar reward for any bank robber brought in, alive or dead. But the men of Cisco remembered, and the news of a bank robbery had them all running for their guns and the bank, in that order. The news spread like wildfire, and Santa Claus and his helpers stepped out of the door of the bank into an unexpected hail of bullets!

Fortunately, the townspeople were just as discombobulated as the robbers, and the gang escaped. A high-speed (for the twenties) chase ensued. But eventually the robbers were caught. Davis died of gunshot wounds, Ratcliff was lynched, Helms died in the electric chair, and Bob Hill went to prison and was granted parole in the 1940s. He changed his name and moved to another part of Texas, where he still lives today.

Although it's a little slow at first, as soon as the robbery takes place, this story is off and running. A. C. Greene talked to as many of the witnesses as he could, so it's as accurate as it is unusual. For a fascinating tale that sounds more like fiction than fact, read *The Santa Claus Bank Robbery*, by A. C. Greene.

SCIENCE FICTION FOR PEOPLE WHO HATE SCIENCE FICTION

By TERRY CARR

Do you hate science fiction? Have you ever said, "Oh, no, I *never* read that stuff!" If so, this book is for you—and the title says it all. Science fiction doesn't have to be about imaginary places and bug-eyed monsters, so full of futuristic machinery that it's incomprehensible to the average nonscientific person. This book proves it!

The first story in the book is one of the most powerful I have ever read—"The Star," by Arthur C. Clarke. It records the thoughts of a priest-astronomer on a spaceship many light-years from earth. The crew's mission: to study the Phoenix Nebula, the remains of a star that became a supernova (grew incredibly hot and exploded), to reconstruct the events that led up to the explosion, and to find the cause. On a small planet, almost an asteroid, they discover the vault. The people of that solar system had known what was about to happen to them, and that they could not escape. They left in the vault the records of their civilization, the fruits of their genius, visual and written records of a beautiful people, disturbingly human-like.

The men on the expedition found it difficult to reconcile the idea of an omnipotent, loving God with the evidence of a civilization carelessly destroyed in full flower. The priest began to trace back to see if he could find out exactly when the supernova had occurred, yet when he had pinpointed the time, he was afraid to reveal it to his colleagues. [Read last three paragraphs, starting with "We could not tell, before we reached the nebula...."]

"A Sound of Thunder" by Ray Bradbury is about time travel, and how injuring even one small butterfly in the time of the dinosaurs can change the whole face of the world today, as a group of dinosaur hunters discover to their horror when they come back from one of their trips in time.

These stories deal with ideas we all have to stop and think about, no matter what kind of setting they're in, "science fiction" or not.

THE SEARCH FOR JOSEPH TULLY

By WILLIAM HALLAHAN

Peter Richardson is living in a condemned building in Brooklyn. One by one, all the other tenants, his friends, are moving out. He is almost alone in the building, and the winter is particularly harsh this year. He begins hearing strange noises, like a golf club being swung in the middle of his living-room, yet no one is there.

At a party, a young woman who reads Tarot cards in a nightclub act turns up cards that indicate a violent death for Richardson. She is sure she has misdealt. She lays out the cards again and gathers them up in consternation, without giving the reading.

Richardson has a recurring dream of being pursued by a faceless monk with a flaming sword.

He is sure that he only needs rest and some time off from work to banish the apparitions. When this doesn't work, Richardson thinks Clabber must have something to do with it. Clabber is one of his ex-neighbors, a defrocked priest who believes in occult phenomena. Richardson is sure that Clabber must have planted microphones in his appartment to frighten him into believing his supernatural garbage.

At the same time in another part of Brooklyn a man named Matthew Willow is searching for a descendant of Joseph Tully, an eighteenth-century wine merchant, whose four sons had come to America to make their fortune. Using all the tricks of the geneological detective, he has make a very thorough search, but he seems curiously relieved each time he comes to a dead end: No issue. Finally he chances upon a diary that reveals the last descendant of Joseph Tully.

Mary James

SEAL-WOMAN

By RONALD LOCKLEY

Talk 1

While on a naval intelligence mission along Ireland's coast during World War II, the author, Ronald Lockley, caught a glimpse of a dark-haired woman swimming in the ocean with a group of seals. Not believing his eyes he asked questions of the local people and learned that there was a legend about a newborn child found in a cave who grew up among the seals.

After the war he returned to Ireland to do a two-year study of the seals. He searched continually for the seal woman, and though he never found her, he became convinced that she really existed.

The story grew in his imagination, and a few years ago, using his diary notes as a basis, he wrote a novel that blends reality and fantasy in an enchanting way.

He called her Shian; she was the last of the O'Malleys of Kilcalla, descendants of Irish rulers and Vikings. A born naturalist, intuitive and intelligent, Shian could swim long distances with the seals (she had thin webs between her fingers and toes) and she talked with and even tamed wild animals.

From early childhood Shian had been told by her grandparents that she was a sea-child, born in a cave, and that one day a prince would come from the sea and return with her to her own kingdom over the horizon.

Obsessed with these strange tales Shian chose to give up her heritage and await her destiny by the sea. And for awhile the prophecy seemed near fulfillment, when she and a young man who had come journeying down the Irish coast fell in love. In her mind he became the prince.

They had one good summer together, swimming with the seals and sleeping on the sand, but as the summer drew to an end, the young man became restless and eager to return to a more normal life on the land. At the same time, Shian became more certain than ever that her life belonged to the sea.

Larry Duckwall

Talk 2

Seal Woman is a love story, but it is perhaps the strangest and saddest one you'll ever read.

Shian's parents had died when she and her brother Brendan were too young to remember. Raised on the Irish Coast by their elderly grandparents, Shian was allowed to do pretty much what she wanted. Her grandmother told her tales based on the Irish legends of the Sea Folk; she even went so far as to call Shian a sea princess, telling her that she had been found, newborn, in a cave by the sea and that someday a sea prince would come out of the sea to take her off to a far island, the home of her people.

Then the grandmother had a stroke and after she recovered she no longer recognized Shian nor would have anything to do with her. Shian became wild, swimming for hours in the sea and relating better to the animals than to people.

Ronald had come to the coast of Ireland on an intelligence mission. There he met Brendan and heard Shian's strange tale. He was impressed with Brendan's capabilities and asked that he be assigned to an intelligence mission on the English Channel. There Brendan was mortally wounded. Dying, he asked Ronald to see to the welfare of his sister.

Ronald goes back to Kilcalla with a wound in his throat that makes it impossible for him to speak. He hears that Shian had become almost a creature of the sea. He decides that the best way to get to Shian will be from the sea. He buys a boat which he knows will shatter in the rough surf, and sets out to the cove. When the boat breaks up, he begins to swim toward the shore. He sees a bunch of seals feeding; he sees a wounded fish thrashing on the top of the water, and realizing that he is hungry he takes out his knife and cuts off a bit of fish. Too late he realizes that he has taken food from a large bull seal. A huge body comes crashing down on him and sharp teeth tear into his shoulder. After a life-and-death battle Ronald is in such pain and so weary that he loses consciousness. The seal is dead, but Ronald is washed onto the shore unconscious. He wakes in the arms of Shian, who thinks she's found her Sea Prince, and he cannot or will not tell her otherwise.

Mary James

SERPICO

By PETER MAAS

Serpico is a true story, the story of an honest cop who, having solemnly sworn to uphold the law, chose to do just that—to enforce it against everybody, and not (in the tradition of even honest policemen) against everybody *except* other cops. What it got him was a bullet in the head, *not* from the gun of one of his fellow officers, though by and large, they hated him enough to have done it. But a twenty-four-year-old heroin addict and pusher beat them to it.

Frank Serpico had wanted to be a cop ever since he was a boy playing in the streets of Brooklyn. In March of 1960 his dream came true—he reported for duty as a patrolman in the Eighty-first Precinct, an area in eastern Brooklyn with a high crime rate—auto thefts, burglaries, robberies, rapes, homicides. It didn't take him long to learn the ways of the precinct, or to discover the places where cops could eat free in return for some special kind of treatment. Serpico started paying for his lunches because he liked to eat well and the restaurant owners always fed the cops all the leftovers from the previous day or items on the menu that weren't moving. As soon as Serpico started paying for his meals he got a lot of respect from the restaurant people.

One night Serpico and his partner arrested a young black for raping a black woman in a schoolyard. Four men had attacked her, but the others got away. The woman was taken to the hospital and Serpico had to turn his prisoner over to the precinct detectives for questioning. One of the detectives was nicknamed "Blackjack" because he liked to use one in questioning. He kept ramming it into the rapist's stomach, his kidneys, the back of his neck. The kid passed out and was revived with a pitcher of water; then they proceeded to whack him on the ears with the telephone book, but the kid wouldn't talk. It seemed to Serpico that the detectives were more interested in beating the prisoner than in getting any information from him. Frank had an idea. The next day, when he had to pick up his prisoner to take him for mug shots and to court, Serpico took off the handcuffs and took the boy across the street for something to eat. The boy was in bad shape—he couldn't eat, but he did have some coffee and a smoke. Then instead of taking his prisoner to the detention house in the wagon, Serpico drove him in his car. On the way, he tried talking to the boy like a human being instead of beating him, and got the names of his three accomplices. Serpico tried to give the information to "Blackjack," the detective handling the case, but he was on vacation and none of the other detectives could handle it because it wasn't "their" case. So Serpico tracked down two of the other rapists and arrested them, but he didn't get the "collar," credit for the arrest, because it wouldn't look good for a patrolman to have made the arrests when it was a detective's job. At first Serpico wasn't willing to hand over the collar; after all he had alerted the detectives and they'd refused to move; he'd done all the detective work and made the arrests. But when he was threatened with a departmental trial (like a court martial) he gave up on the collar.

Frank Serpico had many more encounters with the absurdity of police regulations and with cops breaking the law and taking bribes. But it wasn't until he had made it into the plainsclothes division that he felt morally obligated to do more than just be a fair and honest cop himself. One day a black cop handed him an envelope containing three hundred dollars in small bills from Jewish Max, a well-known local gambler. Serpico began a search for someone in the police department or local government who would be willing to get involved in cleaning up the New York City Police Department. Finally, three years later, in desperation, Serpico took his story to the *New York Times*. On April 25, 1970, the *Times* ran the story under a front-page headline that said, "Graft Paid to Police Here Said to Run into Millions."

This is a fascinating true story of one honest cop who tried to do the impossible—fight crime in the streets and in the police department as well.

Marianne Tait Pridemore

[Marianne takes only brief notes into the classroom with her. She copies the outline below onto three by five cards to make it easier to use.]

True story—honest cop solemnly sworn to uphold the law against everybody.

Got him a bullet in the head

Not from the gun of another police officer—a 24 year old heroin pusher and addict beat them to it

Wanted to be a cop—March 1960—81st eastern Brooklyn.

Ways of precinct—restaurants

One night young black arrested for raping a white woman—four others got away—"Blackjack"

Next day Frank had to pick up his prisoner to take him for mug shots and to court—took handcuffs off

Got names of the three accomplices

Attempts to give information to "Blackjack"—on vacation

Tracks down the other two rapists—doesn't get collar—departmental trial

Many more encounters—absurdities of police regulations and cops breaking the law and taking bribes

Plainclothes—morally obligated to do more than just be a fair and honest cop

Black cop—envelope—$300—Jewish Max

Search for someone in the police department or government who will get involved in cleaning up the NYPD

Three years later, in desperation—*New York Times*—April 25, 1970

"Graft Paid To Police Here Said To Run Into Millions"

Fascinating true story of one honest cop who tried to do the impossible—fight crime in the streets and in the police department as well

---

THE SHERWOOD RING

By ELIZABETH POPE

Peggy had never been happy in her life, and she didn't think things would get better when her father died and she went to live with her only living relative, her uncle Enos, at the ancestral home, called Rest-and-Be-Thankful. Once, before he died, Peggy's father had told her that the house might be haunted, and that made the trip seem a bit more interesting.

When Peggy got off the train, there was no one to meet her, and she had a long walk before she got to the house. But before she'd gone too far, the path split into two, and she didn't know which one to take. She was nearly in tears when suddenly, silently, a girl in a long scarlet cape on a black horse came up behind her and said if she took the lefthand fork, she'd find a man who could tell her the way to Rest-and-Be-Thankful. She found him, and he told her the way to the house and gave her a ride as well. But Peggy met her uncle, who reacted very strangely to her new friend. She had meant to ask him about the girl she met on the road, but she didn't have a chance to—her uncle nearly had a heart attack when he saw Pat, the man who had given Peggy a ride to the house. Peggy found out when she started upstairs. On the landing there was a full-length portrait of the girl she'd seen—red cape, black horse, just as she'd been that afternoon. And the plaque beneath the picture read, "Barbara Grahame, painted at the age of 16, by John Singleton Copely, 1773," and Peggy knew that she'd seen her first ghost.

THE SHINING

By STEPHEN KING

This is the story of the Overlook Hotel, high up in the mountains of Colorado. It's also the story of Wendy and Jack and their six-year-old son Danny. Jack was all but an alcoholic, and their marriage was about to break up because of it. So when they learned that the Overlook needed a caretaker over the winter, they decided to take the job. The hotel would be snowed in for four months; their only communication with the outside would be a CB radio and a snowmobile. By the time they left, their marriage would either be a success or a failure. The decision about divorce would be clear. What Wendy and Jack didn't know was that Danny had been having dreams about the hotel and what they would find there. Danny sometimes knew things and saw things that no one else could. And when he thought about the hotel he could hear voices shouting at him, and a word, written on walls or on mirrors—REDRUM. He didn't know what a redrum was, but he knew it was dangerous. When they got to the hotel, Halloran, the cook, could see right away that Danny had the same ability that he himself had—Halloran called it "shining." It meant he and Danny could see things that had left an impression on the place where they'd happened, rather like a psychic photograph. They could also see and feel things no one else could, and Halloran was sure they could also communicate telepathically over long distances. He explained to Danny that the things he'd see at the hotel couldn't hurt him—just like seeing something on TV. But if Danny ever needed him, he could call Halloran mentally, and Halloran would come immediately. And he told Danny never to go into one of the rooms in the hotel—*never*. Of course, since Danny was a normal boy, as soon as Halloran had left and he could get hold of the key, he opened that door and walked in. When he did, Danny realized why Halloran had told him not to. The hotel had been owned by the Mafia at one time and because of its isolation was the scene of many Mafia executions. This room was where some of them had taken place, and to Danny's eyes, it was as if they had happened only minutes before. The floor and walls were covered with blood and gore. Danny fled, followed by the voice chanting, "Redrum . . . redrum . . . redrum. . . ." Danny began to notice strange things after that. His parents were changing, especially his father, who didn't do anything any more except sit in the basement and look at the old hotel scrapbooks. His mother was different too. Then Danny saw the most frightening thing of all—the topiary animals on the lawn were changing! They were just carved out of shrubbery, but they were moving closer and closer to the house, and looking more and more dangerous.

Danny began to understand that Halloran had been wrong when he told Danny that the things he saw and heard couldn't hurt him—it wasn't like TV after all. The forces that possessed the hotel were real, and so were the things Danny saw. They *could* hurt him and his parents. But by now they were snowed in. The snowmobile had crashed, and the radio was broken beyond repair, and his father was getting worse and worse. They were trapped—there was no way to escape.

THE SHOOTIST

By GLENDON SWARTHOUT

J.B. Books is the last survivor of the famous gunfighters, and he rides into El Paso in 1901 with a terrible pain in his groin. He's looking for the doctor who operated on him the only time he was ever shot in a gunfight, because Books knows he can trust him. If the doctors tells him what he wants to hear, he's going to turn the town upside down! Wine, women, and song, and lots of all of them! But this doctor tells him just what other doctors have told him—he has an advanced cancer of the prostate and only has about two months to live. He will die a slow and incredibly painful death, and nothing the doctor can give him will help the pain at the end. And the more morphia he uses now to kill the pain, the less effective it will be at the end. Most men in this situation have only two choices: suicide or a slow death from natural causes. As Books thinks about this, he realizes that because he is who he is—the last of the really good gunfighters—he has a third choice other men don't have. There are many people who would like to say, "I'm the man who shot J.B. Books." He can arrange a fight and let himself be killed, and die without the stigma of suicide. He picks out of three men: a flashy card sharp, a cattle rustler, and a pimply-faced kid. One of them will be his killer. And then Books begins to plan his own death, using these three—how, where, and when he will die, and, finally, who will kill him.

Mary James and Joni Bodart

SLAVE DANCER

By PAULA FOX

Most of us don't associate the slave trade with music, and Jessie Bollier certainly didn't until the night he was kidnapped and taken to play his pipe aboard a slave ship. Jessie had been sent on an errand by his mother that night and found himself trapped in a canvas bag, destined for the slave ship *The Moonlight*.

Jessie usually made spare change playing his pipe on the New Orleans docks where the ships from every part of the world loaded and unloaded their cargo, and he had seen the slave ships with their human freight.

One of these ships needed someone to dance the blacks that were bought in Africa for rum or tobacco, or a price of $10 a head. The ship's captain, Captain Cawthorne, wanted to be able to deliver a shipload of muscular young blacks to the Portuguese in São Paulo, and he needed some way to encourage them to exercise. Jessie's pipe-playing seemed just what he needed, so he kidnapped the boy.

On the ship, Jessie got used to the stench, the bugs, and the constant thirst, and he learned how the slavers avoided the law with such tricks as changing flags, presenting Spanish papers, or forcing the slaves off the boat and into the water as the inspection party boarded on the other side.

He came into contact with cruel men such as Ben Stout, who claimed to be Jessie's friend and then stole his fife and threw it down into the hold. Jessie had to retrieve it frcm among the packed bodies, his stomach retching from the stench.

This story is built around an incident that really occurred in 1840—a slave ship was wrecked in the Gulf of Mexico on June 3. There were two survivors, a white boy and a young black.

Mary James

A SLIPPING-DOWN LIFE

By ANNE TYLER

Evie says that this might be the best thing she's ever done. Something out of character. Definite. Not covered by insurance. She's sure it will all work out well. What Evie has done is really out of character. She has just

cut letters in her forehead with fingernail scissors. The letters are
C A S E Y, for Drumsticks Casey, a rock-and-roll singer.

Even being in the dump where Casey plays is out of character for a
girl like Evie. Evie is seventeen, plump, drab, and a loner. She isn't even
a music fan. She has lived alone with her father all her life, since her
mother died when she was born. She has led a very sheltered life. Casey
is tough, hard, and cool, but he's a loner, too. And he can hardly ignore
the girl sitting in the front row with his name carved on her forehead.

Something about Casey has attracted Evie, but he seems so indiffer-
ent to her that she laughs the night he suggests that they get married.
Evie had wanted a courtship, double-dates, dances, romance, but she's
not going to get it. She tells Casey, "Oh, well, why not?"

A *Slipping-Down Life* is the story of Evie and Casey's life together.
They are very different people from different backgrounds. Casey has
his music, which is the most important thing in his life. Evie has never
had or wanted anything except Casey.

Kay Roberts

SONG OF THE SHAGGY CANARY

By PHYLLIS ANDERSON WOOD

Sandi changed roles every day at 2:30 P.M. She changed from a
high-school senior to the mother of a ten-month-old little boy named
Chuckie. His father had decided that a wife and son were more that he
wanted and split when Sandi got pregnant. It wasn't easy for her to play
both roles, and in ten months she hadn't been anywhere without
Chuckie, except school. Then she met John, who'd known her when
they were in the same class two years before. He'd been hurt too—his
girlfriend jilted him when he was in Vietnam. He offered to help Sandi
get into an evening sewing class so she could learn to make some clothes
for Chuckie, and that was the beginning. They were both scared of
commitment and of being hurt again. For a long time it seemed that
every time one of them advanced, the other retreated. Their relationship seesawed back and forth, back and forth. And just as they were
starting to really get things together, John's old girlfriend came back
and decided she wanted him after all. Sandi was left with a ruined
dinner and a graduation present, and no one to give it to. To see if John
ever came back, and why a small, shaggy, orange canary meant so much
to Sandi, read *Song of the Shaggy Canary*, by Phyllis Anderson Wood.

A SPECIAL KIND OF COURAGE

By GERALDO RIVERA

In his job as a reporter for ABC, Geraldo Rivera has met a lot of people in varied circumstances. The eleven people in this book have two characteristics in common: all of them are young, and all of them are very special. What makes them special is the way they have handled difficult situations. These profiles include the only survivor of a mid-air collision that killed 132 people, the first black child to attend a previously all-white elementary school, an explorer scout who saved the lives of two deputy sheriffs in a shootout, a teenager who was brutally murdered by other teenagers when he tried to help a small child recover a stolen bike, the first girl to play Little League baseball, and a eleven-year-old boy who had leukemia. But the profile that affected me the most was the description of Bernard Carabello's sixteen years of internment in an institution for mentally retarded children.

Willowbrook, one of the world's largest and most notorious institutions for the retarded, was the only home that Bernard could remember. He was placed at Willowbrook because his non-English-speaking parents had been convinced by social workers that he could best be taken care of in an institution. They were told that their son was retarded, and that he was a hopeless case. Because of their own extreme poverty, Bernard's family could not afford the care that he would need to stay at home, so the public institution seemed the only solution.

Bernard spent most of his childhood there. He lived most of the time as one of sixty to eighty patients squeezed into a small room. The patients were often left naked or partially clothed, because that was more convenient for the attendant. They were left to urinate anywhere. Often only one attendant was left to supervise a room. It is a wonder that anyone grew up under these conditions, but Bernard did.

Reading Bernard's profile I found myself getting very angry. The fact that Willowbrook was a tax-supported institution and yet treated Bernard and the other patients in such an unhealthy and demeaning manner made me angry. The fact that Willowbrook did not have nearly enough staff to care for the patients and teach them basic skills made me angry. Most of all, the fact that Bernard, like many other Willowbrook patients, was labeled retarded when he was *not* retarded at all made me angry.

Bernard finally got out of Willowbrook. His family signed him out after a doctor, who was fired from the Willowbrook staff, took the time to explain to them, as no one had bothered to before, Bernard's real situation and his needs.

Bernard's is just one of eleven lives profiled in *A Special Kind of Courage*.

Ilene Injelmo

THE SPIRIT

By THOMAS PAGE

The Sasquatch is heading home and whatever gets in its way will be destroyed. Two men are following it—one Indian, one white. To the Indian the Sasquatch is a spirit, a mythical creature to be protected at all costs, but to the white man the Sasquatch is a savage killer that must be exterminated.

The Indian is John Moon, a Vietnam war veteran who has come home to the mountains of Montana in search of his Indian name. It is a tradition in his tribe that a young warrior's name must be given him by a spirit, a sort of guardian angel. If John Moon cannot learn his name, he will die.

When he sees the Bigfoot, John Moon is certain that it is his spirit. Neither man nor beast, it stands seven feet tall, weighs close to eight hundred pounds, and is covered with a coat of thick black fur. John Moon begins to trail the Sasquatch, his spirit, waiting for it to tell him his new name, and when it leaves the Montana mountains, he follows.

When the Sasquatch reaches the Canadian Rockies, it comes in contact with an animal survey group. They get in its way and the Sasquatch kills two of them. The Indian follower kills another of the men by shooting down their helicopter. As the last survivor, Raymond Jason, lies waiting to shoot this thing that has killed his three companions, he is surprised by the Indian, who hits him with a rifle butt, leaving him for dead. But Jason survives, and when he leaves the hospital three weeks later, he is a man obsessed with revenge.

But this is no normal Bigfoot that Jason is pursuing and the Indian is protecting. It is a sick and starving survivor of a band of creatures that had once been numerous in the deep forests of the Northwest. One of the last of its kind, it is fighting for survival and killing anything that gets in its way.

What will happen when the Bigfoot reaches home and finds a ski resort full of innocent people on its mountain? A savage tale of pursuit and terror—*The Spirit*, by Thomas Page.

Marianne Tait Pridemore

[Marianne takes only brief notes into the classroom with her. She condenses her talks into the outline below and copies it onto 3x5 cards to make it easier to handle.]

Sasquatch—heading home—whatever gets in the way—destroyed

Two men—1 Indian, 1 white

To Indian, Sasquatch = spirit, mythical creature to be protected at all costs—but to white man, savage killer—kill.

Indian, John Moon, Vietnam—home to mts. Montana—search for Indian name

Tradition of tribe—young warrior's name must be given—spirit—sort of guardian angel

If cannot learn name—will die

When sees Bigfoot—spirit—neither man nor beast—stands 7 ft.—800 lbs.—coat thick black fur

John Moon begins to follow Sasq., his spirit—waiting for it to tell him his new name—leaves Mont. mts., he follows.

When reaches Canadian Rockies—contact survey group

Get in way—Sasq. kills 2

Indian follower kills 1—shooting down helicopter

As last survivor Raymand Jason is waiting to kill thing—killed 3—surprised by Indian—rifle butt—leaving for dead—survives—hospital—3 weks. later—obsessed—revenge

But no normal Bigfoot—Jason pursuing and Indian protecting—sick, starving survivor—band of creatures—once numerous—deep forests Northwest—one last of its kind—fighting for survival—killing

What happens—home—ski resort—innocent people on its mt. Savage tale of pursuit and terror.

STAYING ALIVE!

By MAURICE and MARALYN BAILEY

Maurice and Maralyn Bailey dreamed for years of having their own boat. But on their small salaries as printer's clerk and tax officer, it was impossible to pay for both a house and a boat. So Maralyn suggested they sell the house to pay for the boat and make it their home until they could leave their jobs and sail to New Zealand. So that's what they did. They named her *Auralyn*, a combination of both their names, and set sail for New Zealand in June 1972. By early 1973 they were nearly a week out of Panama and heading southwest, toward the Galapagos Islands. Their trip so far had been marvelous, the ship was responding beautifully, and the Baileys had met many new people and made many friends.

Just after 7 A.M. on March 4, 1973, the ship was struck by a whale. Maurice described what happened [excerpts from pp. 2-4, hardcover edition]. These are pictures of the *Auralyn* as she sank [show pictures]. These are pictures of the Baileys, before and after [show pictures]. They had been slender when they started, 158 and 118 pounds, and they each lost about 40 pounds on the voyage. When they were picked up, Maralyn, at 5'7", weighed only 78 pounds, and Maurice only 118.

On June 30, 1973, they were picked up by a Korean fishing vessel, and as they sipped their hot milk after being pulled from the sea, their first words to each other were: *Maurice*: "We made it!" *Maralyn*: "Now for *Auralyn II* and Patagonia!" This from a woman who'd just spent 118½ days adrift on the Pacific in a rubber raft—and she didn't even know how to swim!

STICKS AND STONES

By LYNN HALL

Tom Naylor is new to Buck Creek, Iowa, and though the small town has a certain charm of its own, there is only one other boy Tom's age—and they do not get along well with each other. Tom finds relief from his isolation when Ward Alexander returns home from the Air Force and begins working on a small cottage outside of town. At last there is someone who shares Tom's interest in music and art and what life is all about, someone that Tom can talk to.

But Tom Naylor isn't the only one who feels isolated in Buck Creek. There is Floyd, the class dunce, who longs for Tom's friendship and feels hurt and rejected when Ward Alexander arrives on the scene. Floyd starts the rumor: *Tom Naylor is queer!* Then there is Amber. In a senior class of twenty girls and only fifteen boys, Amber is one of the girls left without a boyfriend. She longs for Tom's attention, and when she doesn't get it, she too feels rejected and hurt. Amber passes the rumor on.

Before long, everyone in Buck Creek knows "the truth" about Tom. The other students giggle behind his back at school. The basketball coach tells him to keep his hands off the other boys. At first, Tom can't understand what's happening—but then his own doubts begin to gnaw away at him. "Maybe there *is* something wrong with me.... It's not normal to be so interested in music. And why *was* Ward Alexander discharged from the Air Force?"

"Sticks and stones may break my bones but names will never hurt me!"

Is that really true? In Tom Naylor's case, one ugly rumor almost destroyed his life.

Richard Russo

SURVIVE THE SAVAGE SEA

By DOUGAL ROBERTSON

In January 1971, a Scottish farmer, Dougal Robertson, his wife Lyn, and their four children, Douglas, Anne, Neil, and Sandy, set sail around the world. They started from England and went westward across the Atlantic. In Nassau Anne left, and in Panama they picked up a student, Robin, and set out across the Pacific to New Zealand. At 10 A.M., on June 15, 1973, their forty-three-foot schooner *Lucette* was attacked by killer whales and sank in sixty seconds. They were set adrift in an inflatable raft, towed by a nine-foot dinghy, with three days' supply of food and water and a handful of things grabbed as the ship sank—some oranges and lemons, a bag of onions, and Lyn's sewing kit. They had no compasses or instruments and no shelter from the elements. They could have died easily. But these six people were determined to survive. Steering by the sun and stars, they set sail for Costa Rica in Central America, a thousand miles away. On the seventeenth day their raft sank, and they were left with only the dinghy, but they didn't die. They learned how to get along, and how to help each other, and they survived. They were rescued after thirty-seven days on the Pacific Ocean, with only two hundred and ninety miles to go to land. And when the seamen on the fishing boat that picked them up started to abandon the dinghy, they couldn't bear to leave it, so they brought it back with them.

This is an almost unbelievable, but absolutely true and very real story of a family that decided not to die.

THE SWORD OF SHANNARA

By TERRY BROOKS

Two thousand years into the future, and one thousand years after the last of the Great Wars, the world is slowly rebuilding. But this is a much different world from the one we know today.

For one thing, humans are no longer the dominant race on earth but must now share the planet with others, such as dwarves, elves, gnomes, and trolls. For another thing, the huge, centralized nations of our world have now given way to small, separate communities, made up of people who travel little and know even less of life beyond the boundaries of their territory.

In one of these communities, the Shady Vale, two brothers, Shea and Flick Ohmsford, live with their father, the innkeeper. Shea, the older of the two brothers, is an adopted son and is half human and half elf. Unknown to him, he is also a descendant of Jerle Shannara, the greatest of the Elven kings who, a thousand years before, vanquished Brona, the Warlock Lord who ruled the evil Northern Kingdom. But Shea knows nothing of this and feels that his beloved Shady Vale is a haven of undisturbed peace.

Then a stranger comes into the Vale. He is the huge and forbidding wizard/historian Allanon, and he reveals to Shea that the Warlock Lord, long thought to be dead, is alive and once again plotting to destroy the world. Against his power the only effective weapon is the Sword of Shannara, which can only be used by a true descendant of Jerle Shannara. Shea is the last heir, and upon him all the hopes of the people rest.

At first Shea and his brother Flick try to convince each other than Allanon is only a faker and that the Warlock Lord and the Sword are merely myths, but before long a Skull Bearer, the dreaded messenger of the Warlock, comes into the village seeking to destroy the heir. Shea and Flick are forced to run for their lives.

Realizing that Shea will never be safe as long as the Warlock Lord is in power, the two brothers decide to search for the only thing that can defeat him, the Sword of Shannara.

And so begins an almost hopeless journey, on which the brothers cross many strange lands, face many dangers, and make many friends and enemies. Through it all, they know that eventually they alone will have to make a stand against the greatest evil the world has ever known.

Larry Duckwall

TAMSIN

By TAMSIN FITZGERALD

Talk 1

This is a poem Tamsin Fitzgerald wrote:
> Uncertainty,
> Hope and despair
> Striping my days
> Like the bars.

At that time, Tamsin was nineteen, terribly in love with a young man named Michael, and in prison for her part in a comic attempt to hijack a plane.

Her story begins in 1969. Michael decides that he does not want to go to Vietnam and kill people, but he does not want to go to Canada either, because it might be too cold. He thinks Cuba might be a good place. So he decides to hijack a plane. He tells Tamsin that if she does not want to go, it's okay, he will understand. But Tamsin loves Michael and wants to go with him.

They buy plane tickets from New York to Florida, and while they are landing in Florida, Michael pulls out a kitchen knife and orders the stewardess to let him into the cockpit. She doesn't take him very seriously, but she does what he says.

In the meantime, the plane has landed and the passengers have been evacuated, and Tamsin is sitting very nervously in her seat waiting to hear from Michael. The stewardess comes to tell her that Michael wants to see her. When she gets to the cockpit, the place is swarming with FBI men. They grab Michael and Tamsin and haul them off to jail.

Tamsin and Michael are tried and found guilty of a crime against society and are sentenced to many years in prison. Tamsin is taken to a women's federal prison in West Virginia, and Michael is taken somewhere else. While Tamsin is in prison, she keeps a journal and writes letters to her family and special friends, and it is from this journal and those letters that most of this book is composed. Through her journal and her letters, Tamsin shares with us what it is like to be nineteen years old, so young and in prison, and very much in love with someone she will not be able to see for a long, long time.

Karmann Reta

Talk 2

In 1969, Tamsin was eighteen and her boyfriend Michael was about to be drafted. Michael thought it was pretty stupid to go into the army and kill a lot of people he didn't even know, so he and Tamsin decided to hijack a plane to Cuba. They were serious, but it was a comically naive attempt and a complete failure. Tamsin wrote this book during her almost two years in federal prison—it's a prison journal, the diary of a young girl, a poetic love story. It's angry and bitter and sad. It will probably make you cry, but if you've ever been in love, it will also make you smile.

Joan Ariel

A TEACUP FULL OF ROSES

By SHARON BELL MATHIS

This is a story about three brothers: Paul, who painted like a god and who took drugs to forget he hadn't made it with his art; Davey, the youngest, smartest, and tallest, who was a natural athlete with a brain that wouldn't stop working; and Joey, who wasn't anyone special, except to his girl Ellie. But Joey could tell beautiful stories. He promised Ellie they'd be happy and live in a teacup full of roses, and he promised Davey he'd help him go to college. This is also a story about being black and living in a ghetto, when your father can't work and your mother's working too hard and nobody's ever *really* happy.

When this story begins, Paul has just gotten back, clean, from a drug rehab center. Joey is about to graduate from night school, after going for two years with a full-time job during the day, and he and Ellie want to be married soon. And Davey has been chosen as one of nine high-school juniors to participate in a special academic program the next year. Everything looks good.

Then, in one week, it all falls apart. Joey realizes that Paul's hooked again, that Davey's caught, and that he and Ellie may never have their happiness, their teacup full of roses, after all.

THE TESTING OF CHARLIE HAMMELMAN

By JEROME BROOKS

Charlie woke up one morning at the end of his junior year in high school to really bad news—Charlotte Kaplan, the only decent teacher at Shaw High School, had died. She was only forty. Charlie was really devastated. She was the only adult he could really talk to. (He certainly couldn't talk to his parents. His mother watched soap operas and his father was usually away on a sales trip.) What would he do without Charlotte's advice? He crawled right back into bed and didn't get out again until his best friend Hicks came over to see what was up. Well, in addition to his unexpressible grief over Ms. Kaplan, he was worried about a few other little things, like his lack of *action* with girlfriend Shirl, and his problem, and especially the swimming test he had to pass before graduating from high school. To avoid the locker room scene, where he knew he'd be tormented unmercifully, he had skipped high school gym for ROTC, but there was no way he could graduate without passing that swimming test and there was no way, he thought, that he was going to undress down to swimming trunks and learn to swim. *The Testing of Charlie Hammelman* is the story of getting through that summer: a visit to the cemetery, a visit to Shirl's camp for the weekend, even a take-your-heart-in-your-hands visit to a psychiatrist to overcome the fear of being Charlie Hammelman.

Carol Starr

THEY CAME TO STAY

By MARJORIE MARGOLIES and RUTH GRUBER

Marjorie Margolies was twenty-five when she first thought of adopting a child. She was a TV reporter, and had just finished a special on interracial adoption when she decided that although she wasn't ready for marriage, she was ready to be a mother. Lots of adoption agencies won't allow single women to adopt, and she ran into many hassles. But thirty months and miles of red tape later, she became a mother. Lee Heh, a beautiful seven-year-old Korean girl, became Marjorie's first daughter. And two years later, Marjorie decided to adopt a Vietnamese child, and Holly arrived. Lee Heh and Marjorie were in for a shock— Lee Heh had been, and still was, a perfect little girl in every way— pretty, smart, minding and adjusting well, never any problem. Holly was just the opposite. She not only had severe health problems but, after the seven years she had spent growing up in war-torn Vietnam, severe emotional problems as well. Adjusting wasn't easy for her, and that meant it wasn't easy for Lee Heh or Marjorie, either. But in this case, love did conquer all. This is the story of how it did, and how these three strangers became a family.

THROUGH A BRIEF DARKNESS

By RICHARD PECK

When Karen was twelve years old, she walked into the girls' restroom at school and saw this rhyme written on the mirror:

> Andreas daddys a fireman
> Carmens fathers a cook
> Rachels dad is a doctor
> But Karen's old man is a CROOK.

Her father was away on a business trip, but when he got home, she told him about it. He was livid! He took her out of public school immediately—"I don't want my little girl going to school with trash like that!"—and put her in a very expensive private school. She expected to go back there the next fall, but one afternoon, when she got home from a shopping trip with her father's secretary (her mother was dead), she found a letter on the floor of her father's office. It was full of long sentences that didn't say anything clearly—"illegal connections of any parent of a student... responsibility to other students and their parents ... Karen is no longer a suitable classmate... I am returning your check for the fall semester's tuition." On the floor by the desk was a little pile of paper scraps—the check. So Karen went to a boarding school that fall, a school a long way from New York, where no one knew about her father. And to another school the next fall, and the next. She spent her summers at camps and hardly saw her father, even on holidays—he was always off on a business trip somewhere.

But when she was in the eighth grade, Karen met Bea, who finally explained to Karen why she kept changing schools—it was dirty money that was sending her there. As Bea put it, "Your Dad practically *is* the New York operation—he can work both sides of the street and still come out looking like Mr. Clean!" Karen didn't believe her—almost. It seemed to answer so many questions, but the *Mafia*? Her *father*?

Karen was sixteen, daydreaming through English class at yet another boarding school, when she was called to the principal's office and told that her father wanted her to meet him in London for the Easter holidays. But when she got to the meeting place in New York, neither her father nor his secretary were there. Instead, she was met by a girl from his office whom she'd never seen before and put on a non-stop jet to London. About midway in their flight, there was an announcement that they would have to land at Shannon, Ireland, because of a bomb threat. They landed and the plane was searched, but there was no bomb. But when Karen started to get back on the plane, a man in an overcoat who said he was from the airlines tried to pull her away. When someone else saw what he was doing, he let go of her and ran. But

Karen's cousins were there to meet her, just as they were supposed to be, and Karen thought it would be all right after all. But it wasn't—the big dark house seemed more like a hotel than a home, and the maid and chauffeur were sinister-looking. And then Karen overheard a conversation that let her know that the uneasy feelings she'd had all along were right—these people weren't her cousins, this wasn't their old family home, and the chauffeur wasn't a chauffeur, and the maid was only hired by the week, just like the house. And her father hadn't been delayed on business, he wouldn't be arriving in just a day or so. "They might have killed him and then where would we be? . . . Hired to give him a scare . . . but he's been in a coma for a week—some scare!" And suddenly Karen knew who her cousins were—they were her father's enemies, and she'd been kidnapped. Her father was hurt, maybe dying. But what can you do when you're all alone in London? Who's going to believe you when you tell them you've been kidnapped? Karen didn't dare go to the police, but there was one other person. It wasn't really much of a chance, but it might work, and it was her *only* chance.

TO MY BROTHER WHO DID A CRIME

By BARBARA HABENSTREIT

Do you ever wonder what it will really be like to go to college? Does it ever seem a little scary sometimes, though you might not want to admit it? The fourteen students in this book, *To My Brother Who Did a Crime*, by Barbara Habenstreit, would probably answer those questions much the same way you would. In fact, in many ways they probably *are* very much like you would be, if you were beginning college at Long Island University. With one very critical difference: they have just come from doing time in prison. Twelve boys and two girls in all, they are taking part in an experimental parole program from New York prisons. To qualify for the Long Island University program they had to be thirty-five or younger, and to have shown a particular interest in continuing their education. If they didn't have a high school diploma, they could take classes to prepare for the equivalency test. But in order to be chosen, they also had to be without a home they could go back to or have a very strained home situation. Most of them had been addicted to drugs and their parents had kicked them out or they had just sort of wandered out.

Mickey, Derrick, Smitty, Brenda, and the others tell their stories in their own words—what it is like to grow up in the pressure-cooker world of busts, trials, jails, and prisons. Smitty talks about doing drugs on the street, about homosexuality in prison, and about reading every book in the prison library to prepare for the high-school equivalency exam. Mickey says he'd been leading a life of crime sticking up telephone booths, but he's been in prison for six years for a murder he didn't commit. He used to be a tough guy, but now he's frightened of the streets and is just getting used to being with girls again. He's down on dope, "tragic magic" he calls it, but he thinks the college program saved him from addiction. Many of the students talk about the brutality and racism of prison, an entirely different world, where people don't think the same, don't act the same, but Chris remembers some funny things about the Women's House of Detention in Greenwich Village—like pinning candy and other food up on a clothesline at night so the mice couldn't get it, or sprinkling Rice Krispies on the corridor floor so she could hear the night officer coming around.

And they talk about adjusting to life on the streets and in college, often an almost impossible transition from prison—trying to find jobs when they are forbidden by law to practice occupations they may have been trained for in prison because they still bear the label of convicted felons, trying to stay away from drugs when many regular students are really into that scene. It costs up to $5000 a year to keep a person in prison, just about what it would cost to send him to Harvard. Long Island University isn't Harvard, but Marc says, "It's just about the best thing the state or federal government ever thought of. It's a shot at life." Not all of them make the shot, but they all have a real story to tell.

Joan Ariel

TO RACE THE WIND
By HAROLD KRENTS

Hal grew up in Scarsdale, New York, went to school, learned how to read and write, and became a hero in the first grade because of the demonstration he led against his teacher. He went to high school, was elected student-body president when he was a senior, learned to drive a car, graduated with honors, went to Harvard, played touch football in the Harvard quad, and was nicknamed "Cannonball Krents" because when he got the ball, he'd duck his head and charge for the goal line as fast as he could go, and if you got in his way, it was like being hit by a cannonball. He graduated with honors, went to Harvard Law School, was classified 1A for the draft, and almost had to drop out of school to join the Army! He graduated, was admitted to the New York Bar, and went to England for a year on a scholarship. When he returned he married a beautiful woman named Kit, joined a law firm in Washington, D.C., and began to practice law. He and Kit now have a son Jamie, who's about three and who loves to have his daddy read picture books to him. Hal and Kit have divided the labor in their marriage—Hal takes out the garbage and Kit drives the car and rides in the front seat of their tandem bike. The one detail I've left out that makes this very ordinary life something special, and also explains why Kit is always in the driver's seat, is the fact that since Hal was about eight years old, *he has been totally blind*.

He's done all of these things without being able to see. He decided to not let the fact that he eyes don't work keep him from enjoying life to its fullest—and he has succeeded. He has lots of funny stories about the scrapes he's gotten into because he can't see, but the funniest, I think, is the story about how he learned to drive a car.

Hal and some friends were spending a fall evening partying, and it was about midnight when they ran out of booze and decided to go get some more. They were all so drunk they could hardly walk, and most of them forgot all about the mud puddle at the end of the sidewalk. Five people fell in—Hal wasn't one of them, but by the time he'd pulled them all out and loaded them into the car, he was as muddy as they were. It was a little cramped in the car—it was a VW *Beetle!* Hal was in the back seat, with a 103-pound cheerleader on his lap. Any other time, Hal would have been delighted, but she was covered with mud, and when she threw her arms around him, squealed, "Oh Hal, I liiikke youuu!" and gave him a great big kiss, it was like being kissed by a 103-pound mudpie! Yick!

But suddenly Hal realized they had another problem—"We're not on the road!" he said. The driver stopped the car, opened the door, looked out, and said, "Whaddaya know? The blind guy's right!" "Huh! I bet even Hal could drive better than you." "Yeah, why don't we let Hal drive?" Hal said, "Oh no, that's okay." "Come on and drive, Hal—" "No, no, I'm fine right here." "Whatsa matter Hal—you chicken?" "*I'll drive.*" So, everyone got out so Hal could get in the driver's seat; they showed him the wheel, the pedals on the floor, the gearshift; then everyone piled back in and they started off. Have you ever been in a car with someone who's just learning to drive a standard transmission? First gear is awful—rather like a motorized earthquake! Everyone started shouting, "Shift! Shift! Put the clutch in!" After a few false tries, Hal managed to find the clutch and even got into second. Like magic, it all smoothed out, and they were going down the road just fine. Hal was thinking, "Huh, there's not so much to driving a car—." Just then one of the girls screamed, "There's a curve up ahead! We're all going to *die*!" Then everyone started screaming hysterically, and no one remembered they had to tell Hal two things—when to turn and which way! So he had to depend on his good old Krents intuition—which was also drunk that night. He made a *beautiful* turn. Unfortunately, it had nothing to do with the turn in the road. They went through some underbrush, cutting a new road as they went, through someone's front lawn and into a large bush next to their front porch. There was a short silence, then someone in the back seat said, "Thank God—we're alive!" "Right—but what're we going to do about that cop?" "What cop?" "The one that's been following us—and here he comes!" "I know! I know! We'll tell him we picked up a blind hitchhiker, and he kidnapped us and held us at gunpoint and forced us to let him drive our car!" "No, I don't think that'll work."

Just then the cop walked up and knocked on Hal's window. He rolled it down and the beer fumes drifted out. "Okay, lemme see your license!" "I haven't got a license." "Aha! I *knew* you weren't eighteen!" "Oh I'm eighteen all right—I just don't have a license." "Okay, let's hear your excuse!" "I'm blind." "Huh? *Sure* you are—*you* can't be blind!" It took Hal and his friends five or ten minutes to convince that policeman that it was true. Then he decided not to give Hal a ticket—if anyone at the station ever found out he'd given a drunk-driving ticket to a *real* blind drunk, he'd never hear the last of it! So if Hal would promise he'd never drive again, he'd let him go. Hal promised, and that's why Kit is the one in their marriage who does the driving today!

TRANSLATION

By STEPHEN MARLOWE

Sometimes you can say, "It all started when...," but with this book you can't. Was it when the exchange students from Martinsburg, Connecticut, went to Bourg St. Martin, France, because residents of the French town had long ago emigrated to New England to found Martinsburg? The students went to learn about their heritage, but perhaps found more than that. Or did it start when one of the students, Melody, made friends with the gypsy boy Rawl, or when his grandmother gave her an ancient diary, supposedly written by Jean-Baptiste Columbine, the artist who painted gypsies during the 1700s? Perhaps it all started with the collection of Columbine's paintings that was sent to Martinsburg for a special display, and the strange new painting that showed up when the shipping crates were unpacked. Or maybe it didn't really begin until Melody began to translate the old diary.

But people definitely knew something was wrong when Melody began to starve herself to death and a police officer began beating up on the local hoods. Other things, like murders and rapes, began to happen, and it looked as though respectable citizens of the town were responsible for them. And the new painting began to change and to grow older—it had looked freshly painted when they found it. That's one reason it was given to Melody, who hung it over the fireplace in her living room, where she could see it every day. It was obviously a fake—or *was* it?

Something was definitely, horribly wrong. But what was it? And could it be stopped?

TRIPLE BOY

By DALE CARLSON

He lost time—that was the only way he could explain it. There were whole chunks of time that he couldn't remember. He would black out while taking a test. He went out for baseball and he wasn't even very good but he made the team, and his girlfriend—*what was he doing with a girlfriend?*

Then there were his wood carvings—left, and when he came to—finished, but differently from how he would have done them.

Paul was sixteen and increasingly upset about his life. Oh, his mom was an alcoholic, he finally faced that, and his father an unsuccessful author—they were divorced. He tried not to think about the time when he was six and his little brother was three and ran in front of a train and got killed. If only he, Paul, had run faster! Maybe he could have saved Stevie . . . even his father said so.

Still, losing time was getting serious. One day when he was wandering down the beach wondering where the afternoon had gone, he met a new friend, John, who was studying to be a psychiatrist. John was friendly, not pushy, and seemed to understand Paul when he blurted out his problem of "losing time." For Paul was a multi-personality. There were two others who lived inside his body—Mike and George—all struggling for control. How the three personalities are integrated, with a lot of help from John and a lot of hindrance from Paul's parents, is the story of the Triple Boy.

by Carol Starr

THE WATER IS WIDE

By PAT CONROY

Yamacraw is an island off the South Carolina coast, not far from Savannah, Georgia. The twentieth century has basically passed by Yamacraw. The people who live there are black, dependent on the sea or on their small farms for a living. No bridges connect the island with the mainland; anyone who goes there or who leaves must travel by boat. The islanders have electricity, but no telephones or indoor plumbing. People live there much as they did a hundred years ago; indeed, many of them have never heard of the Emancipation Proclamation. Pat Conroy grew up in South Carolina, became a teacher, and taught at the high school he'd graduated from in Beaufort. However, he began to realize that South Carolina wasn't the world, and that not everything was right in the world. So he applied to the Peace Corps, and when he didn't hear from them, applied for a teacher's position on Yamacraw. When he began teaching there, he discovered that his students had great gaps in their knowledge—besides being nearly illiterate, they didn't even know who was President! [Read excerpts from the question-and-answer session—pp. 44, 47, paperback edition; pp. 34, 35, 37, hardback edition.]

Pat Conroy taught and learned and fought for his students against overwhelming odds. To find out why and how he fought, and what the outcome was, read *The Water Is Wide*, by Pat Conroy.

TWO FROM GALILEE

By MARJORIE HOLMES

Jesus' parents were just people, not much different from other people, and according to this book, they were rebellious, stubborn people who were determined to be married in spite of everything. Hannah, Mary's mother (Jesus' grandmother), had great plans for her beautiful daughter, and they didn't include Joseph the carpenter, poor as anyone could be and son of a drunken father besides. But Mary knew that Joseph was the only man for her, and he had been waiting for her for years. Together they defied both sets of parents and endured the scorn of the whole village when Mary became pregnant. They kept faith with each other and with God until their son was born.

In this book Mary and Joseph are real people—who wondered and prayed and dreamed and loved, and who were given the greatest blessing and heaviest burden two people could ever have—being the parents of Jesus, the Christ.

THE WANDERERS

By RICHARD PRICE

Richie Gennaro at seventeen is high warlord of the Wanderers. His is the cold, logical, mind behind the Wanderers' war machine, one of the most formidable in the Bronx. His girl friend, C, blasts the Shirelles on her record player, tries not to hear her parents fighting, dreams of marrying, and practices writing her name as Mrs. Richie Gennaro.

Then there's Joey Capra, star of the football team. Joey has really fast moves—he has to, his father tries to use him for a punching bag. There's Buddy Borsolino and Despie Carabella, who met at the pizza parlor and are in love. And Eugene Capito, the handsome super-stud. Everyone, including Eugene's father, is convinced that Eugene is an expert lover, and he's terrified to admit to anyone that he's still a virgin.

Early one evening as Richie is walking toward the clubhouse, he sees a big group of people. At first he thinks "Cops!" but no, it's the Wongs, a Chinese gang, all named Wong, who are supposed to be the best fighters around. They warn the Wanderers that although the black gangs don't want to rumble, they do want Richie's ass. In panic Richie asks what he's done. The Wongs tell him not to play dumb, everyone has seen the high-school sidewalk. The Wanderers rush off to the school and there in big letters is painted, NIGGERS STINK, signed Richie Gennaro. How Richie gets out of this mess and the just and hilarious revenge he wreaks on the sign painters are just a few of the many adventures described in this sad, tough, and funny book about a New York City teenage gang.

Nancy Kellum-Rose

WHAT DO YOU SAY AFTER YOU SAY HELLO?

By ERIC BERNE

Have you ever wondered why you do what you do? Why you handle your life one way when you really want something totally different? Did you ever think about the influence your parents have had on you? Do you represent their thwarted goals and ambitions, or do you represent yourself? Is it their intent to make you live out their dreams, so that they can have them vicariously, through you? Can you change your script— the role you're playing in your own life-play? How much can you change? Can you discard the role your parents have chosen for you and take control of your own life? Can you write your own script?

Eric Berne, author of *Games People Play* and the originator of the transactional analysis ideas in *I'm OK, You're OK*, has some unusual ideas about controlling your own life. You aren't at the mercy of your script, he says—you can write your own lines!

WHEN MICHAEL CALLS

By JOHN FARRIS

Helen Conally picked up the phone. "Hello?" "Auntie Helen, I missed the school bus. Will you come and get me?" "Wrong number," she thought. "Who is this?" "It's Michael, Auntie Helen. Are you coming?" "Just a minute.... Now who is this?" But the connection was broken before she could finish. Not an unusual conversation—nothing in it to inspire absolute terror. Nothing, that is, except the fact that Michael had died fifteen years ago in a blizzard, though no body was ever found. And the voice, which sounded like Michael's, was that of a ten-year-old boy. Helen wasn't unduly concerned at first, but the boy kept calling—and he knew things about her that only Michael could have known.

Then one day Michael said that something was going to happen to one of Helen's friends, something bad. And a man died, stung to death by bees, although he was an experienced beekeeper.

Who was Michael? Why did he keep calling? Why did he want so badly to terrify Helen? For the answer, read *When Michael Calls*, by John Farris.

WHEN THE LEGENDS DIE

By HAL BORLAND

"When the legends die, the dreams end. When the dreams end, there is no more greatness." This novel is about what happens when an American Indian rejects his heritage and the beliefs of his fathers. Although it's about an Indian, it could be true for anyone else—black, chicano, oriental—whatever the heritage.

Tom Black Bull grew up with his parents in the old Indian way. When his father died, he and his mother continued in the way, and when she died Tom continued alone, until Blue Elk, an old Indian, found him and took him to the Indian school. Tom hated living inside, acting as the white men forced him to act, but he was a boy and had no choice. He was kicked out of the school and was helping an old man herd sheep when he discovered he could ride broncos. He was a natural. A cowboy tricked him into riding a horse that was unrideable, and Red Dillon saw it, brought Tom from the reservation, and set him on his way to becoming a star. Tom won prizes, but he didn't make many friends, and he rode as if there were a demon on his shoulders. It was a long time before Tom realized it and could start to deal with it, so he could find out just who this person named Tom Black Bull really was—a bronc rider famed for his rough treatment of horses? or an Indian named Tom Black Bull, who lived in harmony with nature, in the old way?

WHERE ARE THE CHILDREN?

By MARY H. CLARK

TALK 1

On her birthday, seven years ago, Nancy Harmon's children disappeared. They were found when their bodies washed ashore, with plastic bags tied over their heads. They had been smothered and thrown into the ocean. Nancy was accused of murdering her children, and no one believed her when she said she was innocent. The DA was convinced she was guilty and Rod Legler, the key witness, testified that Nancy told him she was going to smother her children. Not even her husband believed her. The jury found her guilty, and she was sentenced to die in the gas chamber. But suddenly Legler disappeared, her husband committed suicide, and the court had to let her go on a technicality. The DA swore that if it took him the rest of his life, he'd get a conviction that would stick. Nancy cut her hair, dyed it, and fled across the country to Cape Cod. Here people didn't know her and wouldn't recognize her. She had heard that New Englanders were reserved and wanted nothing to do with strangers. This was a good place to hide, heal her wounds, and hope that Legler wouldn't show up again, because if he did, the DA could push for another trial.

Seven years later, she is Nancy Eldredge, married again and with two more children. She is relatively happy, although she still keeps very much to herself outside her family. On the morning of her thirty-second birthday, Nancy turns to the second section of the *Cape Cod Community News* and glaring back at her is a feature story, written anonymously, that reads: "Can this be a happy birthday for Nancy Harmon? Somewhere today Nancy Harmon is celebrating her thirty-second birthday and the seventh anniversary of the deaths of the children she was found guilty of murdering." There are also pictures of her then and now. She has been exposed and revealed to the Cape Cod community! To add to Nancy's terror, her children, the children she has now, have disappeared, and the police have located Legler. The nightmare is beginning all over again, and once more no one believes her—"Come on Nancy, tell the truth. You can't get away with it. Where are the children?" Someone on Cape Cod had known her, written the article, and someone, once again, had taken her children.

But *why*?

Talk 2

Almost seven years ago, Nancy Eldredge ran away from California, changed her name, cut and dyed her hair, and began a new life in an old house on Cape Cod. Now she is happily married to Ray Eldredge, a real estate man, and has two lovely children, Missy and Michael, but she's still haunted by the tragedy that had occurred seven years ago on her twenty-fifth birthday.

Then she had been Nancy Harmon, the wife of a university professor and the mother of three-year-old Lisa and five-year-old Peter. She had taken Lisa and Peter with her to get candles and chocolate for her birthday cake but had left them in the car while she went into the store. When she came back, Lisa and Peter were gone, and she was charged with murder when their mutilated bodies, their heads covered by plastic bags, were washed up on the shore of the ocean.

Nancy Harmon was sentenced to die in the gas chamber, but her conviction was overturned because two women jurors were overheard discussing the case in a bar midway through her trial and saying she was guilty as sin. By the time a new trial was ordered, the leading prosecution witness had disappeared. Nancy was released with the prosecuting attorney's promise that her nightmare wasn't over, that someday he would find a way to convict her.

Now, seven years later, the nightmare is beginning again. Today is Nancy's thirty-second birthday and Missy and Michael—her and Ray's two children—are outside playing on the swing at the edge of the woods behind the house. Fifteen minutes to do some housework, look at the paper, and then time to call the children in. Nancy picks up the paper and there is the story—"Somewhere today Nancy Harmon is celebrating her thirty-second birthday and the seventh anniversary of the deaths of the children she was found guilty of murdering."

In a panic Nancy runs outside to the children, but they are gone—only Missy's red mitten is left behind, caught on the swing. She runs to the lake and plunges into the icy water, but there is nothing. Where *are* the children and will they ever be seen again—alive?

Marianne Tait Pridemore

[Marianne takes only brief notes into the classroom with her. She copies the outline below onto three by five cards to make it easier to use.]

7 years ago Nancy Eldredge had run away from Calif.—changed her name—new life old house Cape Cod.

Happily married to Ray Eldredge, real estate—2—Missy and Michael

Haunted by tragedy 7 years ago on her birthday—25th Nancy Harmon—U. prof—Lisa 3, Peter 5—taken with her in car

Charged with their murder—mutilated bodies—heads covered by plastic bags—washed up on shore of lake

Sentenced to die—conviction overturned—two women jurors heard discussing the case in bar—guilty as sin.

By time new trial ordered, leading prosecution witness disappeared

Prosecuting attorney's promise that her nightmare not over—find a way to convict her

7 years later nightmare beginning again—32nd birthday—Missy & Michael—swing—15 min. housework—look at paper—"Somewhere today N. Harmon celebrating birthday & 7th anniversary of death of children."

Panic—runs outside to children—gone—Missy red mitten

Runs to lake—plunges into icy water—nothing
Where are the children?
Will they ever be seen again—alive?

WHERE ARE YOU GOING, WHERE HAVE YOU BEEN?
STORIES OF YOUNG AMERICA

By JOYCE CAROL OATES

This is a collection of stories about growing up in America, but they are not what you might expect. The realities are often harsh: Maryliz is in love with Ly Cooper, a rock star who plays on the same bill as the Jefferson Airplane. They're going to get married, but then she finds out Ly is sick, very sick.

Connie is home alone on Sunday afternoon when the guy who smiled at her at the drive-in movie the night before shows up with a friend to ask if she'd like to go for a ride. But after a while Connie realizes that despite his hip talk, he's probably over thirty and he wants more than a Sunday drive.

Not exactly fun stories—in fact, some of them may leave you with a sinking feeling in the pit of your stomach. I'm not saying you'll like this book, but it will probably haunt you.

Joan Ariel

WHY AM I SO MISERABLE IF THESE ARE
THE BEST YEARS OF MY LIFE?

By ANDREA B. EAGAN

The title of this book tells it all—and I wish I'd had it when I was a teenager! This is how the author starts out [p. 19, hardback edition: "Someone, at some time... and then you have to practice"]. That's more or less what becoming an adult is all about. Most people do it when they're teenagers—but then, some never do! The author survived being a teenager, and when she'd recovered, ten years later, she wrote this book about it, so you can survive too!

WIN ME AND YOU LOSE

By PHYLLIS ANDERSON WOOD

"Well, Matt, how do you feel about the custody situation?" said the judge. Matt Bristow is seventeen, and has to live with one of his parents for a year—but he knows neither of them is really interested in having him. Being "willing to take custody" is different from wanting someone. "Just like the old game, Button Button," Matt thought to himself. "Pass me around, and whoever has me when the bell rings is the unlucky loser. Mom . . . Dad . . . Mom . . . Dad. . . ." Just then a phone rang down the hall—"That's it," he said aloud. "Dad's the one, I guess"—and it was decided. Now two strangers have to learn to live together, and with all the bad memories they share, it isn't easy. Neither are cooking and housekeeping, when you've never had to do them before. There are lots of disasters before anything gets any better.

But Matt and his father discover they have something in common. They've made friends with Rebecca Javez and her mother, who live across the hall. And they've both seen the strange man who follows Rebecca to school and hangs around the hallway when she's home— and when he isn't around, sometimes the phone rings, and there's no one there. . . .

A WRINKLE IN TIME

A WIND IN THE DOOR

A SWIFTLY TILTING PLANET

By MADELEINE L'ENGLE

It was a dark and windy night; Meg Murray was in her attic bedroom being miserable about the fact that she always seemed to be an oddball and never fit in anywhere. Her little brother Charles Wallace was the only person who really understood her. Sometimes he even seemed to know what she was thinking—and on this particular night, when she went downstairs to get some cocoa, he was already in the kitchen with the milk on, enough for both Meg and her mother, who appeared shortly. A noise in the basement a few minutes later announced Mrs.

Whatsit, a very strange old lady who looked rather like a tramp in an assortment of rags, and who ate a liverwurst sandwich and left. But just as she walked out, she turned around and said to Mrs. Murray, "By the way, there *is* such a thing as a tesseract." Mrs. Murray nearly fainted, because the tesseract—the wrinkle in time—was the secret project she and her husband had been working on when he suddenly disappeared.

The next day, Meg and Charles Wallace went to the old house where Mrs. Whatsit and her friends were staying and met Calvin O'Keefe as well. He was to be the third human member of the rescue party. That's why Mrs. Whatsit, Mrs. Who, and Mrs. Which had come to earth—to take these three kids to the planet where the black thing and a force called "It" were holding Mr. Murray prisoner.

A Wind in the Door continues Meg and Charles Wallace's story—and describes their adventures with a cherub who looks more like a drove of dragons than an angel, a dark personage called a Teacher, and an old enemy of Meg's—Mr. Jenkins, the elementary school principal. Once again, Meg, Calvin, and Charles Wallace are all called to battle the dark shadow that surrounds the earth.

A Swiftly Tilting Planet is the last book of the trilogy. It takes place years after the first two. Charles Wallace is now a teenager, and this is his adventure. Meg helps, but she's pregnant with her and Calvin's first child and so can't do too much. This time, Charles Wallace is pretty much on his own.

Madeleine L'Engle's books are like the Narnia Chronicles. There's more to them than just surface action. Every time I read them, I find something new.

A ZOO IN MY LUGGAGE

By GERALD DURRELL

Gerald Durrell is an animal collector. He goes to strange places and captures exotic animals for various zoos. Then he writes hilarious books about his trips, which are guaranteed to have you rolling on the floor.

This book is about one of Durrell's expeditions to collect animals; he

went to the island of Bafut in the British Cameroons in West Africa.
However, he didn't do his collecting in a logical fashion—first he picked
out the animals, then he proceeded to look for a zoo to put them in,
resulting in the title of this book, *A Zoo in My Luggage*. There were
marvelously funny consequences, and in the end Durrell kept some of
the animals and opened his own zoo. Ralph Thompson illustrates most
of Durrell's books, and if Durrell's descriptions don't make the animals
come alive, these sketches surely do!

To give you an idea of what the animals were like—[read excerpts].

It takes someone with a particular sense of humor to appreciate these
books—they aren't the run-of-the-mill animal stories. But if you get
hooked, it may be a lifetime thing. I am, and one of my goals in life is to
visit Durrell's zoo in Jersey, begun with the animals that are described
in this book.

A Zoo in My Luggage, by Gerald Durrell

BIBLIOGRAPHIES

JUNIOR HIGH SCHOOL

General
(4th–8th grade reading levels)

Brown, Roy. *The Cage*. Seabury 1977.

Cleaver, Vera and Cleaver, Bill. *The Mimosa Tree*. Lippincott 1970, NAL 1977.

Conford, Ellen. *The Alfred G. Graebner Memorial High School Handbook of Rules and Regulations*. Archway (PB) 1977.

Danziger, Paula. *The Cat Ate My Gymsuit*. Delacorte 1974, Dell 1975.

———. *The Pistachio Prescription*. Delacorte 1978, Dell 1978.

Duncan, Lois. *I Know What You Did Last Summer*. Little 1973, Archway (PB) 1975.

———. *Summer of Fear*. Little Brown 1976, Dell 1977.

Elfman, Blossom. *The Girls of Huntington House*. Houghton 1972, Bantam 1973.

———. *A House for Jonnie O*. Houghton 1977, Bantam 1978.

Hinton, S. E. *Outsiders*. Viking 1967, Dell 1968.

———. *Rumble Fish*. Delacorte 1975, Dell 1976.

———. *That Was Then, This Is Now*. Viking 1971, Dell 1972.

Holman, Felice. *Slake's Limbo*. Scribner 1974, Dell 1977.

Lipsyte, Robert. *One Fat Summer*. Harper 1977, Bantam 1978.

Madison, Winifred. *Bird on the Wing*. Little 1973, Dell 1975

Mazer, Norma Fox. *Dear Bill, Remember Me?* Delacorte 1976, Dell 1978.

Peck, Richard. *Dreamland Lake*. Holt 1973, Avon 1974.

———. *Father Figure*. Viking 1978.

———. *The Ghost Belonged to Me*. Viking 1975, Avon 1976.

———. *Ghosts I Have Been*. Viking 1977, Dell 1979.

———. *Through a Brief Darkness*. Viking 1973, Avon 1974.

Peck, Robert Newton. *A Day No Pigs Would Die*. Knopf 1973, Dell 1974.

Pope, Elizabeth. *The Sherwood Ring*. Houghton 1958.

Roth, Arthur. *Iceberg Hermit*. Four Winds 1974.

Savitz, Harriet M. *The Lionhearted*. Day 1975, NAL 1977.

Sleator, William. *House of Stairs*. Dutton 1974, Avon 1975.

Wells, Rosemary. *None of the Above*. Dial 1974, Avon 1975.

White, Robb. *Deathwatch*. Doubleday 1972, Dell 1973.

Wood, Phyllis Anderson. *A Five-Color Buick and a Blue-Eyed Cat*. NAL 1977.

————. *I Think This Is Where We Came In*. Westminster 1976, NAL 1977.

————. *I've Missed a Sunset or Three*. Westminster 1973, NAL 1975.

————. *Song of the Shaggy Canary*. Westminster 1974, NAL 1976.

————. *Win Me and You Lose*. Westminster 1977, NAL 1978.

Science Fiction and Fantasy
(grades 7–8)

Alexander, Lloyd. *The Book of Three*. Holt 1964.

Asimov, Isaac. *I, Robot*. Doubleday 1963, Fawcett 1978.

Bonham, Frank. *The Missing Persons League*. Dutton 1976, Scholastic 1978.

Christopher, John. *Beyond the Burning Lands*. Macmillan 1971, 1976.

————. *City of Gold and Lead*. Macmillan 1967, 1970.

————. *Empty World*. Dutton 1978.

————. *Pool of Fire*. Macmillan 1968, 1970.

————. *The Prince in Waiting*. Macmillan 1970, 1974.

————. *The Sword of the Spirits*. Macmillan 1972, 1976.

————. *White Mountains*. Macmillan 1967, 1970.

Claire, Keith. *The Otherwise Girl*. Holt 1976.

Heinlein, Robert. *Between Planets*. Scribner 1957, Ballantine 1978.

————. *The Farmer in the Sky*. Ballantine 1975.

————. *Have Space Suit, Will Travel*. Scribner 1958, Ballantine 1977.

————. *Star Beast*. Scribner 1977, Ballantine 1977.

Juster, Norton. *The Phantom Tollbooth*. Random 1961.

Kurland, Michael. *Princes of Earth*. Nelson 1978.

Le Guin, Ursula K. The Earthsea Trilogy (3 vols). Bantam 1975. (*A Wizard of Earthsea, The Tombs of Atuan, The Farthest Shore*)

L'Engle, Madeleine. *A Swiftly Tilting Planet*. Farrar 1978.

————. *A Wind in the Door*. Farrar 1973, Dell 1976.

————. *A Wrinkle in Time*. Farrar 1962, Dell 1973.

Lewis, C. S. The Chronicles of Narnia (7 vols). Macmillan 1970. (*The Lion, the Witch, and the Wardrobe; Prince Caspian; The Voyage of the Dawn Treader; The Silver Chair; The Horse and His Boy;*

The Magician's Nephew; The Last Battle)

Norton, Andre. *Here Abide Monsters*. Atheneum 1973, DAW 1974.

————. *Plague Ship*. Ace 1976.

————. *Star Man's Son*. Fawcett 1978.

————. *Witch World*. Ace 1977.

O'Brien, Robert C. *Z for Zachariah*. Atheneum 1975, Dell 1977.

Peck, Richard. *The Ghost Belonged to Me*. Viking 1975, Avon 1976.

————. *Ghosts I Have Been*. Viking 1977, Dell 1979.

Rogers, Michael. *Mindfogger*. Knopf 1973, Dell 1976.

Saint Exupéry, Antoine de. *The Little Prince*. Harcourt © 1943, 1968.

Sleator, William. *House of Stairs*. Dutton 1974, Avon 1975.

Tolkien, J.R.R. *The Hobbit*. Houghton 1966, Ballantine 1976.

Townsend, John Rowe. *Noah's Castle*. Lippincott 1976, Dell 1978.

HIGH SCHOOL

General
(hi/lo readers to 8th grade reading level)

Barnes, Richard. *Listen to Me!* Lerner 1976.

Bethancourt, T. Ernesto. *The Dog Days of Arthur Cane*. Holiday 1976.

Blum, Ralph. *Old Glory and the Real-Time Freaks*. Delacorte 1972.

Blume, Judy. *Forever*. Bradbury 1975, PB 1976.

Claire, Keith. *The Otherwise Girl*. Holt 1976.

Cormier, Robert. *The Chocolate War*. Pantheon 1974, Dell 1975.

————. *I Am the Cheese*. Pantheon 1977, Dell 1978.

Higgins, Colin. *Harold and Maude*. Avon 1975.

Hinton, S. E. *Outsiders*. Viking 1967, Dell 1968.

————. *Rumble Fish*. Delacorte 1975, Dell 1976.

————. *That Was Then, This Is Now*. Viking 1971, Dell 1972.

Holland, Isabelle. *Of Love and Death and Other Journeys*. Lippincott 1975, Dell 1977.

Holman, Felice. *Slake's Limbo*. Scribner 1974, Dell 1977.

Juliusburger, Susanna. *Beginnings*. Coward 1974.

Kerr, M. E. *If I Love You, Am I Trapped Forever?* Harper 1973, Dell 1974.

————. *I'll Love You When You're More Like Me*. Harper 1977, Dell 1979.

Madison, Winifred. *Bird on the Wing*. Little 1973, Dell 1975.

Neufeld, John. *Lisa, Bright and Dark*. Phillips 1969, NAL 1970.

Patterson, Sarah. *The Distant Summer*. S&S 1976, PB 1977.

Peck, Richard. *Are You in the House Alone?* Viking 1976, Dell 1977.

————. *Father Figure*. Viking 1978.

————. *Ghosts I Have Been*. Viking 1977, Dell 1979.

————. *Representing Superdoll*. Viking 1974, Avon 1975.

————. *Through a Brief Darkness*. Viking 1973, Avon 1974.

Samuels, Gertrude. *Run, Shelley, Run!* T.Y. Crowell 1974, NAL 1975.

Savitz, Harriet M. *The Lionhearted*. Day 1975, NAL 1977.

Swarthout, Glendon. *The Shootist*. Doubleday 1975.

Wells, Rosemary. *None of the Above*. Dial 1974, Avon 1975.

White, Robb. *Deathwatch*. Doubleday 1972, Dell 1973.

Wood, Phyllis A. *A Five-Color Buick and a Blue-Eyed Cat*. Westminster 1975, NAL 1977.

————. *Song of the Shaggy Canary*. Westminster 1974, NAL 1976.

Zindel, Paul. *I Never Loved Your Mind*. Harper 1970, Bantam 1972.

————. *My Darling, My Hamburger*. Harper 1969, Bantam 1978.

Adventure, Suspense, and Mystery
(grades 10–12)

Asimov, Isaac. *Murder at the ABA*. Doubleday 1976, Fawcett 1978.

Barthel, Joan. *A Death in Canaan*. Dutton 1976, Dell 1977.

Bugliosi, Vincent and Gentry, Curt. *Helter Skelter*. Norton 1972, Bantam 1975.

Bugliosi, Vincent and Hurwitz, Ken. *Till Death Us Do Part*. Norton 1978.

Cussler, Clive. *Raise the Titanic!* Viking 1976, Bantam 1977.

Duncan, Lois. *I Know What You Did Last Summer*. Little 1973, Archway (PB) 1975.

————. *Killing Mr. Griffin*. Little 1978.

Elder, Lauren and Streshinsky, Shirley. *And I Alone Survived*. Dutton 1978, Fawcett 1979.

Farris, John. *When Michael Calls*. PB nd.

Forsyth, Frederick. *The Odessa File*. Bantam 1974.

Gallico, Paul. *The Poseidon Adventure*. Dell 1972.

Graham, Robin Lee. *Dove*. Harper 1972, Bantam 1978.

Higdon, Hal. *The Crime of the Century*. Putnam 1975.

————. *Finding the Groove*. Putnam 1973.

Higgins, Jack. *The Eagle Has Landed*. Holt 1975, Bantam 1976.

Hintze, Naomi. *You'll Like My Mother*. Fawcett © 1969.

King, Stephen. *Carrie*. Doubleday 1974, NAL 1976.

————. *Night Shift*. Doubleday 1978, NAL 1979.

———. *The Shining.* Doubleday 1977, NAL 1978.

Le Carré, John. *The Spy Who Came In From the Cold.* Coward 1964, Bantam 1975.

Levin, Ira. *The Boys From Brazil.* Random 1976, Dell 1978.

MacLean, Alistair. *Circus.* Doubleday 1975, Fawcett 1976.

———. *The Guns of Navarone.* Fawcett 1977.

———. *Ice Station Zebra.* Fawcett 1978.

Michaels, Barbara. *Ammie, Come Home.* Fawcett 1977.

Read, Piers Paul. *Alive!* Lippincott 1974, Avon 1975.

Robertson, Dougal. *Survive the Savage Sea.* Praeger 1973.

"Tey, Josephine" (Elizabeth Mackintosh). *The Daughter of Time.* Macmillan 1952, PB 1977.

Westlake, Donald. *Bank Shot.* S&S 1972, PB 1973.

White, Robb. *Deathwatch.* Doubleday 1972, Dell 1973.

Wood, Bari. *The Killing Gift.* Putnam 1975, NAL 1977.

American Government
(grades 11–12)

Archer, Jeffrey. *Shall We Tell the President?* Viking 1977, Fawcett 1978.

Barthel, Joan. *A Death in Canaan.* Dutton 1976, Dell 1977.

Bernstein, Carl and Woodward, Bob. *All the President's Men.* S&S 1974, Warner 1976.

Bova, Ben. *The Multiple Man.* Bobbs 1976, Ballantine 1977.

Bryan, C. D. B. *Friendly Fire.* Putnam 1976, Bantam 1977.

Drury, Allen. *Advise and Consent.* Doubleday 1959, Avon 1977.

Kovic, Ron. *Born on the Fourth of July.* McGraw 1976, PB nd.

Knebel, Fletcher and Bailey, Charles W. II. *Seven Days in May.* Harper 1962, Bantam 1969.

MacLaine, Shirley. *You Can Get There From Here.* Norton 1975, Bantam 1976.

Mills, James. *One Just Man.* S&S 1975, PB 1976.

Newcomb, Kerry and Schaefer, Frank. *Pandora Man.* Morrow 1979.

Safire, William. *Full Disclosure.* Doubleday 1977, Ballantine 1978.

Serling, Robert. *The President's Plane Is Missing.* Doubleday 1967, Dell 1977.

Stein, Sol. *The Magician.* Dell 1972.

Trudeau, Gary. *The Doonesbury Chronicles.* Holt 1975.

Wallace, Irving. *The Man.* Bantam 1974.

American History, American Studies
(grades 10–11)

Borland, Hal. *When the Legends Die*. Lippincott 1963, Bantam 1972.

Bristow, Gwen. *Calico Palace*. T.Y. Crowell 1970, PB 1973.

————. *Jubilee Trail*. T.Y. Crowell 1950, Pop Lib 1969.

Brown, Dee. *The Gentle Tamers*. University of Nebraska Press 1968, Bantam 1974.

Brown, Joe D. *Paper Moon* (originally entitled *Addie Pray*). NAL 1973 © 1971.

Coleman, Lonnie. *Orphan Jim*. Doubleday 1975, Dell 1977.

Conroy, Pat. *The Water Is Wide*. Dell 1972, 1974.

Fast, Howard. *The Hessian*. Morrow 1972.

Fields, Jeff. *A Cry of Angels*. Atheneum 1974, Ballantine 1975.

Finney, Jack. *Time and Again*. S&S 1970, 1978.

Fitzgerald, Tamsin. *Tamsin*. Dial 1973, Pop Lib 1976.

Fox, Paula. *The Slave Dancer*. Bradbury 1973, Dell 1975.

Gipe, George. *Coney Island Quickstep*. T. Y. Crowell 1977, Ballantine 1979.

Heyman, Abigail. *Growing Up Female*. Holt 1974.

Horan, James. *New Vigilantes*. Crown 1975, Avon 1976.

Houston, Jeanne Wakatsuki. *Farewell to Manzanar*. Houghton 1973, Bantam 1974.

Kavanagh, Paul. *Not Comin' Home to You*. Putnam 1974.

Magnuson, James and Petrie, Dorothea. *Orphan Train*. Dial 1978.

Majerus, Janet. *Grandpa and Frank*. Lippincott 1976, PB 1977.

Matheson, Richard. *Bid Time Return*. Ballantine 1976.

Maynard, Joyce. *Looking Back*. Avon 1974.

Medved, Michael and Wallechinsky, David. *What Really Happened to the Class of '65*. Random 1976, Ballantine 1977.

Pope, Elizabeth. *The Sherwood Ring*. Houghton 1958.

Powers, J. R. *Do Black Patent Leather Shoes Really Reflect Up?* Contemporary 1975, Pop Lib 1976.

Rushing, Jane. *Mary Dove*. Doubleday 1974, Avon 1975.

Saroyan, William. *The Human Comedy*. Harcourt 1944, Dell nd.

Shaw, Arnold. *The Rockin' '50s*. Hawthorn 1974.

Starkey, Marion. *The Visionary Girls*. Little 1973.

Tidyman, Ernest. *Dummy*. Little 1974.

"Twain, Mark" (Samuel Clemens). *The Adventures of Huckleberry Finn*. many editions.

——. *The Adventures of Tom Sawyer*. many editions.

——. *Roughing It*. many editions.

Vidal, Gore. *1876*. Random 1976. Ballantine 1977.

Vliet, R. G. *Rockspring*. Viking 1974.

Wagoner, David. *The Road to Many a Wonder*. Farrar 1974, Avon 1975.

Ward, Robert. *Cattle Annie and Little Britches*. Morrow 1977, Ace 1979.

Wilder, Laura Ingalls. *West From Home*. Harper 1974.

Biographies
(grades 10–11)

Angelou, Maya. *Gather Together in My Name*. Random 1974, Bantam 1975.

——. *I Know Why the Caged Bird Sings*. Random 1970, Bantam 1971.

——. *Singin' and Swingin' and Gettin' Merry Like Christmas*. Random 1976, Bantam 1977.

Armes, Jay J. *Jay J. Armes, Investigator*. Macmillan 1976, Avon 1977

Barthel, Joan. *A Death in Canaan*. Dutton 1976, Dell 1977.

Conn, Canary. *Canary*. Bantam 1977.

Durrell, Gerald. *The Whispering Land*. Penguin 1975.

——. *A Zoo in My Luggage*. Penguin 1976.

Fitzgerald, Tamsin. *Tamsin*. Dial 1973, Pop Lib 1976.

Frank, Anne. *The Diary of a Young Girl*. Doubleday 1952, PB nd.

Gaines, Stephen S. *Marjoe*. Harper 1973, Dell 1974.

Jacobs, Frank. *The Mad World of William M. Gaines*. Lyle 1973.

Heyman, Abigail. *Growing Up Female*. Holt 1974.

Herriot, James. *All Creatures Great and Small*. St. Martins 1972, Bantam 1973.

——. *All Things Bright and Beautiful*. St. Martins 1974, Bantam 1975.

——. *All Things Wise and Wonderful*. St. Martins 1977, Bantam 1978.

Ipswitch, Elaine. *Scott Was Here*. Delacorte 1979.

Juliusburger, Susanna. *Beginnings*. Coward 1974.

Kopay, David, and Young, Perry D. *The David Kopay Story*. Arbor 1977.

Krents, Hal. *To Race the Wind*. Putnam 1972, Bantam 1972.

Levit, Rose. *Ellen: A Short Life Long Remembered*. Chronicle 1974.

Lund, Doris. *Eric*. Lippincott 1974, Dell 1975.

Nasaw, Jonathan. *Easy Walking*. Lippincott 1975.

Petty, Richard. *King of the Road*. Macmillan 1977.

Sal Sayers, Gale and Silverman, Al. *I Am Third*. Viking 1970, Bantam nd.

Smith, Dennis. *Report From Engine Company 82*. Dutton 1972, PB 1973.

Specht, Robert. *Tisha*. St. Martins 1976, Bantam 1977.

Sullivan, Tom and Gill, Derek. *If You Could See What I Hear*. Harper 1975, NAL 1976.

Thompson, Thomas. *Richie*. Bantam, 1974.

Gothic Novels
(grades 10–12)

Aldiss, Brian. *Frankenstein Unbound*. Random 1974.

Brautigan, Richard. *The Hawkline Monster*. S&S 1974, PB 1976.

Brontë, Charlotte. *Jane Eyre*. many editions.

Brontë, Emily. *Wuthering Heights*. many editions.

Daniels, Dorothy. *The Unlamented*. PB 1975.

Hintze, Naomi. *You'll Like My Mother*. Fawcett 1969.

Holland, Isabelle. *Tower Abbey*. Rawson 1978, Fawcett 1979.

Holt, Victoria. *King of the Castle*. Doubleday 1967, Fawcett 1978.

———. *Kirkland Revels*. Doubleday 1962, Fawcett 1977.

———. *Shadow of the Lynx*. Doubleday 1971, Fawcett 1977.

King, Stephen. *'Salem's Lot*. Doubleday 1975, NAL 1976.

Marasco, Robert. *Burnt Offerings*. Delacorte 1973, Dell 1976.

Michaels, Barbara. *Ammie, Come Home*. Fawcett 1977.

———. *Witch*. Dodd 1973, Fawcett 1978.

Peck, Richard. *Through a Brief Darkness*. Viking 1973, Avon 1974.

Shelley, Mary. *Frankenstein*. many editions.

Stewart, Mary. *My Brother Michael*. Morrow 1960, Fawcett 1978.

Minorities
(grades 9–12)

Black

Angelou, Maya. *Gather Together in My Name*. Random 1974, Bantam 1975.

———. *I Know Why the Caged Bird Sings*. Random 1970, Bantam 1971.

———. *Just Give Me a Cool Drink of Water 'Fore I Diiie*. Random 1971, Bantam 1973.

———. *Oh Pray My Wings Are Gonna Fit Me Well*. Random 1975, Bantam 1977.

———. *Swingin' and Singin' and Gettin' Merry Like Christmas*. Random 1976, Bantam 1977.

Baldwin, James. *If Beale Street Could Talk*. Dial 1974, NAL 1975.

Childress, Alice. *A Hero Ain't Nothin' But a Sandwich*. Coward 1973, Avon 1977.

Conroy, Pat. *The Water Is Wide*. Houghton 1972, Dell 1974.

Frazier, Walt and Berkow, Ira. *Rockin' Steady*. Prentice 1974.

Gaines, Ernest J. *The Autobiography of Miss Jane Pittman*. Dial 1971, Bantam 1972.

Griffin, John Howard. *Black Like Me*. Houghton 1961, NAL nd.

Guy, Rosa. *The Friends*. Holt 1973.

———. *Ruby*. Viking 1976.

Hunter, Kristin. *The Soul Brothers and Sister Lou*. Scribner 1968, Avon 1976.

Mathis, Sharon Bell. *A Teacup Full of Roses*. Viking 1972, Avon 1973.

Meriwether, Louise. *Daddy Was a Numbers Runner*. Prentice 1970, Pyramid 1976.

Myers, Walter D. *Fast Sam, Cool Clyde, and Stuff*. Viking 1975.

Rushing, Jane. *Mary Dove*. Doubleday 1974, Dell 1975.

Tidyman, Ernest. *Dummy*. Little 1974.

Walker, Margaret. *Jubilee*. Houghton 1966, Bantam 1975.

Hispanic

Harth, Dorothy and Baldwin, Lewis M., eds. *Voices of Aztlan*. NAL 1974.

Mohr, Nicholasa. *El Bronx Remembered.* Harper 1975.
O'Dell, Scott. *Child of Fire.* Houghton 1974.
Villarreal, Jose A. *Pocho.* Doubleday 1970.

Jewish

Frank, Anne. *The Diary of a Young Girl.* Doubleday 1952, WSP 1972, PB
    nd.
Howe, Irving. *World of Our Fathers.* Harcourt 1976, S&S 1977.
Jacot, Michael. *Last Butterfly.* McClelland 1973, NAL 1975.
Joffo, Joseph. *A Bag of Marbles.* Houghton 1975, Bantam nd.

Native American

Borland, Hal. *When the Legends Die.* Lippincott 1963, Bantam 1972.
Harris, Marilyn. *Hatter Fox.* Random 1973, Bantam 1974.
Momaday, N. Scott. *House Made of Dawn.* Harper 1968, 1977.

Oriental

Houston, Jeanne Wakatsuki. *Farewell to Manzanar.* Houghton 1973,
    Bantam 1974.
Kingston, Maxine Hong. *The Woman Warrior.* Knopf 1976, Random
    1977.

Occult and Psychic Sciences
(grades 10–12)

Anson, Jay. *The Amityville Horror.* Prentice 1977, Bantam 1978.
Bartell, Jan. *Spindrift.* NAL 1975.
Blum, Ralph and Blum, Judy. *Beyond Earth.* Phillips 1974, Bantam
    1976.
Claire, Keith. *The Otherwise Girl.* Holt 1976.
Cline, Terry C., Jr. *Death Knell.* Putnam 1977, Fawcett 1978.
Cooper, Arnold and Leon, Coralee. *Psychic Summer.* Dial 1976, Dell
    1977.
De Felitta, Frank. *Audrey Rose.* Putnam 1975, Warner 1977.
Duncan, Lois. *Summer of Fear.* Little 1976, Dell 1977.
Erlich, Max. *The Reincarnation of Peter Proud.* Bantam 1975.
Fuller, John G. *The Airmen Who Would Not Die.* Putnam 1979.
———. *The Ghost of Flight 401.* Berkley 1976, 1978.
Goodavage, Joseph. *Write Your Own Horoscope* (rev. ed.). NAL 1978.

Goodman, Linda. *Linda Goodman's Love Signs*. Harper 1978.

————. *Linda Goodman's Sun Signs*. Taplinger nd, Bantam 1975, 1979.

Harris, Marilyn. *The Conjurers*. Dell 1976.

Jackson, Shirley. *The Haunting of Hill House*. Viking 1959, Pop Lib 1977.

Janifer, Laurence. *Survivor*. Ace 1977.

King, Stephen. *Carrie*. Doubleday 1974, NAL 1976.

————. *Night Shift*. Doubleday 1978, NAL 1979.

————. *'Salem's Lot*. Doubleday 1975, NAL 1977.

————. *The Shining*. Doubleday 1977, NAL 1978.

Konvitz, Jeffery. *Sentinel*. S&S 1974, Ballantine 1977.

Levin, Ira. *Rosemary's Baby*. Random 1967, Fawcett 1976.

Marasco, Robert. *Burnt Offerings*. Delacorte 1973, Dell 1976.

Marlowe, Stephen. *Translation*. Prentice 1976, Ballantine 1977.

Michaels, Barbara. *Ammie, Come Home*. Fawcett 1977.

Miedaner, Terrel. *The Soul of Anna Klane*. Coward 1977, Ballantine 1978.

Montandon, Pat. *The Intruders*. Coward 1975, Fawcett 1977.

Moody, Raymond, Jr. *Life After Life*. Stackpole 1976, Bantam 1976.

Nathan, Robert. *Portrait of Jennie*. Knopf 1940, Dell 1977.

Peck, Richard. *The Ghost Belonged to Me*. Viking 1975, Avon 1976.

————. *Ghosts I Have Been*. Viking 1977, Dell 1979.

Pope, Elizabeth. *The Sherwood Ring*. Houghton 1958.

Rudorff, Raymond. *Dracula Archives*. Arbor 1972.

St. Clair, David. *Watseka*. Playboy 1977.

Sutphen, Dick. *You Were Born Again To Be Together*. PB 1976.

————. *Past Lives, Future Loves*. PB 1978.

Wood, Bari. *The Killing Gift*. Putnam 1975, NAL 1977.

Poetry
(grades 9–12)

Angelou, Maya. *Just Give Me a Cool Drink of Water 'Fore I Diiie*. Random 1971, Bantam 1973.

————. *Oh Pray My Wings Are Gonna Fit Me Well*. Random 1975, Bantam 1977.

Giovanni, Nikki. *My House*. Morrow 1972.

————. *Ego Tripping*. Laurence Hill 1973.

Lee, Mary. *Tender Bough*. Crown 1969.

Lueders, Edward and St. John, Primus, eds. *Zero Makes Me Hungry.* Lothrop 1976.

Morse, David. *Grandfather Rock.* Delacorte 1972, Dell 1973.

Nimoy, Leonard. *You and I.* Celestial Arts 1973, Avon 1973.

———. *Will I Think of You?* Celestrial Arts 1974, Dell 1975.

Peck, Richard, ed. *Pictures That Storm Inside My Head.* Avon 1976.

———. *Sounds and Silences.* Dell 1970.

Rinder, Walter. *Love Is an Attitude.* Celestial Arts 1970.

Singer, Frieda, ed. *Daughters in High School.* Daughters 1974.

Psychology and Sociology
(grades 10–12)

Axline, Virginia M. *Dibs: In Search of Self.* Houghton 1965, Ballantine 1976.

Barthel, Joan. *A Death in Canaan.* Dutton 1976, Dell 1977.

Brown, Rita Mae. *Rubyfruit Jungle.* Daughters 1973, Bantam 1977.

Bugliosi, Vincent and Hurwitz, Ken. *Till Death Us Do Part.* Norton 1978.

Conn, Canary. *Canary.* Bantam 1977.

Cormier, Robert. *The Chocolate War.* Pantheon 1974, Dell 1975.

———. *I Am the Cheese.* Pantheon 1977, Dell 1978.

D'Ambrosio, Richard. *No Language But a Cry.* Doubleday 1970.

Eagan, Andrea Boroff. *Why Am I So Miserable If These Are the Best Years of My Life?* Lippincott 1976, Pyramid 1977.

Elder, Lauren and Streshinsky, Shirley. *And I Alone Survived.* Dutton 1978, Fawcett 1979.

Elliot, David. *Listen to the Silence.* Holt 1969.

Fishel, Elizabeth. *Sisters.* Morrow 1979.

Gordon, Sol and Conant, Roger. *You! A Teenager Survival Book.* Time 1975.

Green, Hannah. *I Never Promised You a Rose Garden.* Holt 1964, NAL 1977.

Guest, Judith. *Ordinary People.* Viking 1976, Ballantine 1977.

Hanes, Mary. *Lovechild.* NAL 1973.

Harris, Thomas. *I'm OK, You're OK.* Harper 1969, Avon 1976.

Heyman, Abigail. *Growing Up Female.* Holt 1974.

Higdon, Hal. *The Crime of the Century.* Putnam 1975.

Hobson, Laura. *Consenting Adult.* Doubleday 1975, Warner 1976.

Holmes, Beth. *Whipping Boy.* Marek 1978.

Jury, Mark and Jury, Dan. *Gramp.* Penguin 1978.

Kellogg, Marjorie. *Like the Lion's Tooth.* Farrar 1972, NAL 1973.

———. *Tell Me That You Love Me, Junie Moon.* Farrar 1968, Pop Lib 1975.

Kesey, Ken. *One Flew Over the Cuckoo's Nest.* Viking 1962, NAL 1975, Penguin 1976.

Lichtenberg, Jacqueline. *House of Zeor.* PB 1977.

McCracken, Mary. *A Circle of Children.* Lippincott 1973.

———. *Lovey.* Lippincott 1976, NAL 1977.

Peck, Richard. *Are You in the House Alone?* Viking 1976, Dell 1977.

———. *Representing Superdoll.* Viking 1974, Avon 1975.

Read, Piers Paul. *Alive!* Lippincott 1974, Avon 1975.

Rubin, Theodore. *Jordi, Lisa, and David.* Ballantine 1973.

Stirling, Nora. *You Would If You Loved Me.* Evans 1969, Avon 1974.

Tidyman, Ernest. *Dummy.* Little 1974.

Walton, Todd. *Inside Moves.* Doubleday 1978, NAL 1979.

Warren, Patricia Nell. *The Beauty Queen.* Morrow 1978.

———. *The Fancy Dancer.* Morrow 1976, Bantam 1977.

———. *The Front Runner.* Bantam 1975.

Wood, Phyllis Anderson. *Win Me and You Lose.* Westminster 1977, NAL 1978.

Religion and Philosophy
(grades 10–12)

Andrew, Brother and others. *God's Smuggler.* NAL 1968, Revell nd.

Caldwell, Taylor. *Dialogues With the Devil.* Fawcett 1978.

———. *Grandmother and the Priests.* Fawcett 1978.

Castaneda, Carlos. *Journey to Ixtlan.* S&S 1972, PB 1976.

———. *A Separate Reality.* S&S 1971.

———. *Tales of Power.* S&S 1974, PB 1976.

———. *The Teachings of Don Juan.* University of California Press 1968, PB 1976.

Cruz, Nicky. *Run Baby Run.* Logos 1968, Pyramid 1969.

Forsyth, Frederick. *The Shepherd.* Viking 1976, Bantam 1977.

Gibran, Kahlil. *The Prophet.* Knopf 1923.

Hesse, Hermann. *Siddartha.* New Directions 1951, Bantam nd.

Holmes, Marjorie. *Two From Galilee.* Revell 1972, Bantam 1976.

L'Engle, Madeleine. *A Swiftly Tilting Planet*. Farrar 1978.

————. *A Wind in the Door*. Farrar 1973, Dell 1976.

————. *A Wrinkle in Time*. Farrar 1962, Dell 1973.

Lewis, C.S. The Chronicles of Narnia (7 vols.). Macmillan 1970.

————. *The Screwtape Letters and Screwtape Proposes a Toast*. Macmillan 1964.

Patrick, Ted and Dulack, Tom. *Let Our Children Go!* Dutton 1976, Ballantine 1977.

Pirsig, Robert. *Zen and the Art of Motorcycle Maintenance*. Morrow 1974, Bantam 1976.

Potok, Chaim. *The Chosen*. S&S 1967, Fawcett 1978.

————. *The Promise*. Knopf 1969, Fawcett 1978.

St. Johns, Adela Rogers. *Tell No Man*. Doubleday 1966.

Ten Boom, Corrie and Sherrill, John. *Hiding Place*. Bantam 1974.

West, Morris. *The Shoes of the Fisherman*. Morrow 1963, PB 1974, 1978.

Wilkerson, David. *Beyond the Cross and the Switchblade*. Chosen 1974.

————. *The Cross and the Switchblade*. BJ 1970, Revell nd, Pillar 1976.

Science Fiction and Fantasy
(grades 9–12)

Adams, Richard. *Watership Down*. Macmillan 1974, Avon 1976.

Asimov, Isaac. *I, Robot*. Doubleday 1963, Fawcett 1978.

————. *Foundation Trilogy*. Avon 1974.

————. *The Rest of the Robots*. Doubleday 1964.

Beagle, Peter. *The Last Unicorn*. Ballantine 1976.

Blish, James. *Cities in Flight*. Avon nd.

Clarke, Arthur C. *Childhood's End*. Harcourt 1963, Ballantine 1976.

————. *Imperial Earth*. Harcourt 1976, Ballantine 1976.

————. *Rendezvous With Rama*. Harcourt 1973, Ballantine 1976.

————. *2001: A Space Odyssey*. NAL 1968.

Dickson, Gordon. *The Dragon and the George*. Ballantine 1978.

Eckert, Allan. *Hab Theory*. Little 1976, Pop Lib 1977.

Ellison, Harlan. *Approaching Oblivion*. Walker 1974, NAL 1976.

————. *Deathbird Stories*. Harper 1975, Dell 1976.

————. *Strange Wine*. Harper 1978.

Finney, Jack. *Time and Again*. S&S 1970, 1978.

Heinlein, Robert. *The Past Through Tomorrow*. Putnam 1967, Berkley 1975.

Herbert, Frank. *Children of Dune*. Berkley 1976.

————. *Dune*. Chilton 1965, Berkley 1975.

————. *Dune Messiah*. Putnam 1969, Berkley 1975.

Hogan, James. *The Genesis Machine*. Ballantine 1978.

————. *The Left Hand of Darkness*. Ace 1976.

Le Guin, Ursula K. *Earthsea Trilogy* (3 vols.). Bantam 1975.

————. *The Wind's Twelve Quarters*. Harper 1975, Bantam 1976.

Lichtenberg, Jacqueline. *House of Zeor*. PB 1977.

Lockley, Ronald. *Seal-Woman*. Bradbury 1975, Avon 1977.

McCaffrey, Ann. *Dinosaur Planet*. Ballantine 1978.

————. *Dragonflight*. Ballantine 1975.

————. *Dragonsong*. Atheneum 1976, Bantam 1977.

————. *The Ship Who Sang*. Ballantine 1976.

Matheson, Richard. *Bid Time Return*. Ballantine 1976.

Miedaner, Terrel. *The Soul of Anna Klane*. Coward 1977, Ballantine 1978.

Nathan, Robert. *Heaven and Hell and the Megas Factor*. Delacorte 1975.

————. *Portrait of Jennie*. Knopf 1940, Dell 1977.

Niven, Larry and Pournelle, Jerry. *Lucifer's Hammer*. Playboy 1977, Fawcett 1978.

————. *The Mote in God's Eye*. S&S 1974, PB 1975.

Sargent, Pamela. *More Women of Wonder*. Random 1976.

————. *New Women of Wonder*. Random 1978.

————. *Women of Wonder*. Random 1975.

Schmitz, James H. *The Witches of Karres*. Ace 1966, 1977.

Scortia, Thomas N. And Robinson, Frank M. *The Prometheus Crisis*. Doubleday 1975.

Stewart, Mary. *The Crystal Cave*. Morrow 1970, Fawcett 1978.

————. *The Hollow Hills*. Morrow 1973, Fawcett 1978.

Stickgold, Bob and Noble, Mark. *Gloryhits*. Ballantine 1978.

Thane, Elswyth. *Tryst*. Aeonian 1974 (reprint of 1939 ed.)

Tiptree, James. *Star Songs of an Old Primate*. Ballantine 1978.

Tolkien, J. R. R. *The Lord of the Rings* (3 vols.). Houghton 1967, Ballantine 1976.

Wheeler, Thomas. *Loose Chippings*. Phillips 1969, Avon 1971.

White, T. H. *The Once and Future King*. Putnam 1958, Berkley nd.

Short Stories
(grades 10–11)

Allingham, Marjorie. *The Allingham Minibus*. Manor 1977.

Asimov, Isaac. *I, Robot*. Doubleday 1963, Fawcett 1978.

──── . *100 Great Science Fiction Short Short Stories*. Doubleday 1978.

──── . *The Rest of the Robots*. Doubleday 1964.

Brown, Dee. *The Gentle Tamers*. Putnam 1958, Bantam 1974.

Doyle, Arthur Conan. *The Complete Sherlock Holmes*. Doubleday 1953.

Ellison, Harlan. *Approaching Oblivion*. Walker 1974, NAL 1976.

──── . *Dangerous Visions*. NAL 1975.

──── . *Deathbird Stories*. Harper 1975, Dell 1976.

──── . *Strange Wine*. Harper 1978.

"Henry, O." (William S. Porter). *The Gift of the Magi*. Bobbs 1978.

King, Stephen. *Night Shift*. Doubleday 1978, NAL 1979.

Le Guin, Ursula. *The Wind's Twelve Quarters*. Harper 1975, Bantam 1976.

Maupassant, Guy de. *Guy de Maupassant's Short Stories*, translated by Marjorie Laurie. Dutton 1934.

Mazer, Norma Fox. *Dear Bill, Remember Me?* Delacorte 1976, Dell 1978.

"Saki" (H. H. Munro). *The Best of Saki*, edited by Graham Greene. Penguin 1977.

Sargent, Pamela. *More Women of Wonder*. Random 1976.

──── . *New Women of Wonder*. Random 1978.

──── . *Women of Wonder*. Random 1975.

Singer, Frieda. *Daughters in High School*. Daughters 1970.

Vonnegut, Kurt, Jr. *Welcome to the Monkey House*. Delacorte 1968, Dell 1974.

Women's Studies
(grades 10–12)

Angelou, Maya. *I Know Why the Caged Bird Sings*. Random 1970, Bantam 1971.

──── . *Gather Together in My Name*. Random 1974, Bantam 1975.

──── . *Singin' and Swingin' and Gettin' Merry Like Christmas*. Random 1976, Bantam 1977.

Blume, Judy. *Forever*. Bradbury 1975, PB 1976.

Boston Women's Health Book Collective. *Our Bodies, Ourselves*, rev. ed. S&S 1976.

Brown, Dee. *The Gentle Tamers*. Putnam 1958, Bantam 1974.

Brown, Rita Mae. *Rubyfruit Jungle*. Daughters 1973, Bantam 1977.

──── . *Six of One*. Harper 1978.

Carlson, Dale. *Girls Are Equal Too.* Atheneum 1973, 1977.

Clark, Mary H. *Where Are the Children?* S&S 1975, Dell 1976.

Conn, Canary. *Canary.* Bantam 1977.

Eagan, Andrea B. *What Am I So Miserable If These Are the Best Years of My Life?* Lippincott 1976, Pyramid 1977.

Elfman, Blossom. *The Girls of Huntington House.* Houghton 1972, Bantam 1973.

———. *A House for Jonnie O.* Houghton 1977, Bantam 1978.

Engdahl, Sylvia. *Enchantress From the Stars.* Atheneum 1970.

Fishel, Elizabeth. *Sisters.* Morrow 1979.

Fitzgerald, Tamsin. *Tamsin.* Pop Lib 1976.

Freedman, Benedict and Freedman, Nancy. *Mrs. Mike.* Coward 1947, Berkeley 1968.

Friday, Nancy. *My Mother/Myself.* Delacorte 1977, Dell 1978.

Gordon, Sol and Conant, Roger. *You! The Teenage Survival Book.* Time 1975.

Green, Hannah. *I Never Promised You a Rose Garden.* Holt 1964, NAL 1977.

Guy, Rosa. *The Friends.* Holt 1973.

———. *Ruby.* Viking 1976.

Hahn, Harriet. *The Plaintain Season.* Norton 1976.

Hanes, Mary. *Lovechild.* NAL 1973.

Heyman, Abigail. *Growing Up Female.* Holt 1974.

Holt, Victoria. *My Enemy the Queen.* Doubleday 1978, Fawcett 1979.

Juliusburger, Susanna. *Beginnings.* Coward 1974.

Kerr, M. E. *Love Is a Missing Person.* Harper 1975, Dell 1977.

Klein, Norma. *It's OK If You Don't Love Me.* Dial 1977, Fawcett 1978.

———. *Give Me One Good Reason.* Avon 1977.

Konigsberg, E. L. *A Proud Taste for Scarlet and Miniver.* Atheneum 1973, 1977.

Le Guin, Ursula. *The Left Hand of Darkness.* Walker 1969, Ace 1976.

Lofts, Norah. *The Maude Reed Tale.* Nelson 1972, Dell 1974.

McCullough, Colleen. *Tim.* Harper 1974, Pop Lib 1977.

MacLaine, Shirley. *You Can Get There From Here.* Norton 1975, Bantam 1976.

Margolies, Marjorie and Gruber, Ruth. *They Came to Stay.* Coward 1976.

Miller, Isabel. *Patience and Sarah.* Fawcett 1976.

Patterson, Sarah. *The Distant Summer.* S&S 1976, PB 1977.

Peck, Richard. *Are You in the House Alone?* Viking 1976, Dell 1977.

———. *Representing Superdoll.* Viking 1974, Avon 1975.

Sargent, Pamela, ed. *More Women of Wonder.* Random 1976.

———. *New Women of Wonder.* Random 1978.

———. *Women of Wonder.* Vintage 1975.

Sheehy, Gail. *Passages.* Dutton 1976, Bantam 1977.

Singer, Frieda, ed. *Daughters in High School.* Daughters 1974.

Specht, Robert. *Tisha.* St. Martin 1976, Bantam 1977.

Stirling, Nora. *You Would If You Loved Me.* Evans 1969, Avon 1974.

Vliet, R. G. *Rockspring.* Viking 1974.

World History and Geography
(grades 10–11)

Andrew, Brother and others. *God's Smuggler.* NAL 1968.

Burnford, Sheila. *Bel Ria.* Little 1978, Bantam 1979.

Crichton, Michael. *Eaters of the Dead.* Knopf 1976.

———. *The Great Train Robbery.* Knopf 1975, Bantam 1976.

Durrell, Gerald. *Two in the Bush.* Viking 1966, Penguin 1977.

———. *The Whispering Land.* Penguin 1975.

———. *A Zoo in My Luggage.* Penguin 1976.

Frank, Anne. *The Diary of a Young Girl.* Doubleday 1952, PB nd.

Graham, Robin Lee. *Dove.* Harper 1972, Bantam 1978.

Grohskopf, Bernice. *Blood and Roses.* Atheneum 1979.

Hawkins, Gerald S. *Beyond Stonehenge.* Harper 1973.

———. *Stonehenge Decoded.* Doubleday 1965, Dell 1966.

Herriot, James. *All Creatures Great and Small.* St. Martins 1972, Bantam 1973.

———. *All Things Bright and Beautiful.* St. Martins 1974, Bantam 1978.

Heyerdahl, Thor. *Aku-Aku.* Rand McNally 1958, Ballantine 1974.

———. *Kon-Tiki.* Rand McNally 1950, PB 1977.

Higgins, Jack. *The Eagle Has Landed.* Holt 1975, Bantam 1976

Holmes, Marjorie. *Two From Galilee.* Revell 1972, Bantam 1976.

Holt, Victoria. *My Enemy the Queen.* Doubleday 1978, Fawcett 1979.

Jacot, Michael. *The Last Butterfly.* McClelland 1973, Ballantine 1975.

Johnston, Jennifer. *How Many Miles to Babylon?* Avon 1975.

Konigsberg, E. L. *A Proud Taste for Scarlet and Miniver.* Atheneum 1973, 1977.

Lofts, Norah. *The Maude Reed Tale.* Nelson 1972, Dell 1974.

Patterson, Sarah. *The Distant Summer.* S&S 1976, PB 1977.

Peters, Elizabeth. *The Murders of Richard III.* Dodd 1974.

Read, Piers Paul. *Alive!* Lippincott 1974, Avon 1975.

Rhodes, Evan. *An Army of Children.* Dial 1978.

Robertson, Dougal. *Survive the Savage Sea*. Praeger 1973.

Speare, Elizabeth. *The Bronze Bow*. Houghton 1961, 1973.

Sutcliff, Rosemary. *Tristan and Iseult*. Dutton 1971, Penguin 1976.

"Tey, Josephine" (Elizabeth Mackintosh). *The Daughter of Time*. Macmillan 1952, PB 1977.

White, T. H. *The Once and Future King*. Putnam 1958, Berkley nd.

Zassenhous, Hiltgunt. *Walls: Resisting the Third Reich*. Beacon 1974, 1977.

"BOOKS SOMEONE THOUGHT WERE EASY TO BOOKTALK"

(compiled by the Alameda County YA staff)

Admission to the East - Beckmann
Are You in the House Alone? - Peck
Bird on the Wing - Madison
Burnt Offerings - Marasco
Carrie - King
Cassandra Crossing - Katz
Daughters in High School - Singer
Dr. Hip's Natural and Unnatural Acts - Schoenfield
Forever - Blume
Gift - Dickinson
Growing Up Female - Heyman
Harold and Maude - Higgins
House of Stairs - Sleator
I Know What You Did Last Summer - Duncan
I Never Promised You a Rose Garden - Green
In Search of Dracula - McNally
Intruders - Montandon
Logan's Run - Nolan
My Darling, My Hamburger - Zindel
No Language But a Cry - D'Ambrosio
Portrait of Jennie - Nathan
Richie - Thompson
Reincarnation of Peter Proud - Ehrlich
'Salem's Lot - King
Shootist - Swarthout
Tamsin - Fitzgerald
Through a Brief Darkness - Peck
To Race the Wind - Krents
Where Are the Children? - Clark

LIST OF PUBLISHERS

Ace. Ace Books, 360 Park Ave. S., New York, NY 10010

Aeonian. Aeonian Press, Inc., Box 1200, Mattituck, NY 11952

Arbor. Arbor House, 641 Lexington Ave., New York, NY 10022

Archway (PB). Archway Paperbacks, c/o Pocket Books, 1230 Avenue of the Americas, New York, NY 10020

Atheneum. Atheneum Publishers, 122 East 42nd St., New York, NY 10017

Avon. Avon Books, 959 Eighth Ave., New York, NY 10019

Ballantine. Ballantine Books, Inc., 201 East 50th St., New York, NY 10022

Bantam. Bantam Books, Inc., 666 Fifth Ave., New York, NY 10019

BJ. BJ Publishing Group, 200 Madison Ave., New York, NY 10016

Beacon. Beacon Press, Inc., 25 Beacon St., Boston, MA 02108

Berkley. Berkley Publishing Corporation, 200 Madison Ave., New York, NY 10016

Bobbs. Bobbs-Merrill Co., Inc., 4300 West 62nd St., Indianapolis, IN 46206

Bradbury. Bradbury Press, 2 Overhill Rd., Scarsdale, NY 10583

Celestial Arts. Celestial Arts Publishing Co., 231 Adrian Rd., Millbrae, CA 94030

Chosen. Chosen Books Publishing Co., Ltd., Lincoln, VA 22078

Chronicle. Chronicle Books, 870 Market St., San Francisco, CA 94102

Contemporary. Contemporary Books, Inc., 180 N. Michigan Ave., Chicago, IL 60601

Coward. Coward, McCann & Geoghegan, Inc., 200 Madison Ave., New York, NY 10016

T. Y. Crowell. Thomas Y. Crowell Co., Publishers, 521 Fifth Ave., New York, NY 10017

Crown. Crown Publishers, Inc., 1 Park Ave., New York, NY 10016

Daughters. Daughters Publishing Co., Inc., MS 590, P.O. Box 4299, Houston, TX 77042

DAW. DAW Books, New American Library, 1301 Avenue of the Americas, New York, NY 10019

Day. John Day Co., Inc., c/o Harper & Row, Publishers, 10 East 53rd St., New York, NY 10022

Delacorte. Delacorte Press, c/o Dell Publishing Co., 1 Dag Hammarskjold Plaza, 245 East 47th St., New York, NY 10017

Dell. Dell Publishing Co., Inc., 1 Dag Hammarskjold Plaza, 245 East 47th St., New York, NY 10017

Dial. Dial Press, 1 Dag Hammarskjold Plaza, 245 East 47th St., New York, NY 10017

Dodd. Dodd, Mead & Co., 79 Madison Ave., New York, NY 10016

Doubleday. Doubleday & Co., Inc., 501 Franklin Ave., Garden City, NY 11530

Dutton. E. P. Dutton, 2 Park Ave., New York, NY 10016

Evans. M. Evans & Co., Inc., 216 East 49th St., New York, NY 10017; orders to Lippincott, 521 Fifth Ave., New York, NY 10017

Farrar. Farrar, Straus, & Giroux, Inc., 19 Union Square West, New York, NY 10003

Fawcett. Fawcett Book Group, 1515 Broadway, New York, NY 10036

Four Winds. Four Winds, Scholastic Book Services, 50 West 44th St., New York, NY 10036

Harcourt. Harcourt Brace Jovanovich, Inc., 757 Third Ave., New York, NY 10017

Harper. Harper & Row Publishers, Inc., 10 East 53rd St., New York, NY 10022

Hawthorn. Hawthorn Books, Inc., 260 Madison Ave., New York, NY 10016

Holiday. Holiday House, Inc., 18 East 53rd St., New York, NY 10022

Holt. Holt, Rinehart, and Winston, Inc., 383 Madison Ave., New York, NY 10017

Houghton. Houghton Mifflin Co., 2 Park St., Boston, MA 02107

Knopf. Alfred A. Knopf, Inc., 201 East 50th St., New York, NY 10022

Laurence Hill. Laurence Hill & Co., Inc., 24 Burr Farm Rd., Westport, CT 06880; orders to Independent Publishers Group, 60 East 55th St., New York, NY 10022

Lippincott. J. B. Lippincott Co., 521 Fifth Ave., New York, NY 10017

Little. Little, Brown & Co., 34 Beacon St., Boston, MA 02114

Logos. Logos International, 201 Church St., Plainfield, NJ 07060

Lothrop. Lothrop, Lee & Shepard Co.,105 Madison Ave., New York, NY 10016; orders to William Morrow & Co., Inc., Wilmor Warehouse, 6 Henderson Dr., West Caldwell, NJ 07006

Lyle. Lyle Stuart, Inc., 120 Enterprise Ave., Secaucus, NJ 07094

McClelland. McClelland & Stewart, Ltd., 25 Hollinger Rd., Toronto, Ontario M4B 3G2 Canada

McGraw. McGraw-Hill Book Co., 1221 Avenue of the Americas, New York, NY 10020

Macmillan. Macmillan Publishing Co., Inc., 866 Third Ave., New York, NY 10022

Manor. Manor Books, Inc., 432 Park Ave. S., New York, NY 10016

Marek. Richard Marek, Publisher, 200 Madison Ave., New York, NY 10016

Morrow. William Morrow & Co., Inc., 105 Madison Ave., New York, NY 10016

NAL. New American Library, 1301 Avenue of the Americas, New York, NY 10019

Nelson. Thomas Nelson, Inc., P.O. Box 946, 407b Seventh Ave. S., Nashville, TN 37203

New Directions. New Directions Publishing Corp., 80 Eighth Ave., New York, NY 10011

Norton. W. W. Norton & Co., Inc., 500 Fifth Ave., New York, NY 10036

Pantheon. Pantheon Books, 201 East 50th St., New York, NY 10022

PB. Pocket Books, Inc., 1230 Avenue of the Americas, New York, NY 10020

Penguin. Penguin Books, Inc., 625 Madison Ave., New York, NY 10022

Phillips. Phillips Publishing Co., 1562 Main St., Suite 713, Springfield, MA 01103

Pillar. Pillar Books, c/o Harcourt Brace Jovanovich, Inc., 757 Third Ave., New York, NY 10017

Playboy. Playboy Press, 747 Third Ave., New York, NY 10017; distributed by Harper & Row Pubs., Inc., Keystone Industrial Park, Scranton, PA 18512

Pop Lib. Popular Library, Inc., 1515 Broadway, New York, NY 10036

Praeger. Praeger Publishers, c/o Holt, Rinehart & Winston, 383 Madison Ave., New York, NY 10017

Prentice. Prentice-Hall, Inc., Englewood Cliffs, NJ 07632

Putnam. G. P. Putnam's Sons, 200 Madison Ave., New York, NY 10016; orders to 390 Murray Hill Pkwy., East Rutherford, NJ 07073

Pyramid. Pyramid Press Publishing Co., 1686 Marshall St., Benwood, WV 26031

Rand McNally. Rand McNally & Co., P. O. Box 7600, Chicago, IL 60680

Random. Random House, Inc., 201 East 50th St., New York, NY 10022; orders to 400 Hahn Rd., Westminster, MD 21157

Rawson. Rawson Wade Publishers, Inc., 630 Third Ave., New York, NY 10017; distributed by Atheneum Publishers, 122 East 42nd St., New York, NY 10017

Revell. Fleming H. Revell Co., 184 Central Ave., Old Tappan, NJ 07675

S&S. Simon & Schuster, Inc., 1230 Avenue of the Americas, New York, NY 10020

St. Martins. St. Martin's Press, Inc., 175 Fifth Ave., New York, NY 10010

Scholastic. Scholastic Book Services, 50 West 44th St., New York, NY 10036

Scribner. Charles Scribner's Sons, 597 Fifth Ave., New York, NY 10017

Seabury. Seabury Press, Inc., 815 Second Ave., New York, NY 10017; orders to Seabury Service Center, Somers, CT 06071

Stackpole. Stackpole Books, Cameron and Keller Sts., Harrisburg, PA 17105

Taplinger. Taplinger Publishing Co., Inc., 200 Park Ave. S., New York, NY 10003

Time. Time-Life Books, Alexandria, VA 22314; distributed by Little, Brown & Co., 34 Beacon St., Boston, MA 02106 and Morgan & Morgan, 400 Warburton Ave., Hastings on Hudson, NY 10706

University of California Press. University of California Press, 2223 Fulton St., Berkeley, CA 94720

University of Nebraska Press. University of Nebraska Press, 901 N. 17th St., Lincoln, NE 68588

Viking. Viking Press, Inc., 625 Madison Ave., New York, NY 10022

Walker. Walker & Co., 720 Fifth Ave., New York, NY 10019

Warner. Warner Books, Inc., 75 Rockfeller Plaza, New York, NY 10019

Westminster. Westminster Press, 925 Chestnut St., Philadelphia, PA 19107

WSP. Washington Square Press, Inc., 1230 Avenue of the Americas, New York, NY 10020

INDEX

Numbers in **boldface** type refer to pages where booktalks appear.

Action, in narrative, 9, 12, 13
Ad-libbing, 16, 61, 62
"Adult picture books," 39, 66
Advance notice for class visit, 34-5
Age levels, 23, 37, 54
Aku-Aku (Heyerdahl), 85
Alfred G. Graebner Memorial High School Handbook of Rules and Regulations (Conford), 10, **85-6**
Alive! (Read), 10
All Creatures Great and Small (Herriot), 7, **87**
All Things Bright and Beautiful (Herriot), 7
American Library Association. *Doors to More Mature Reading*, xi
Amityville Horror (Anson), 13, 41, 57, **87-8**
Ammie, Come Home (Michaels), 9, 42, **88-9**
And I Alone Survived (Elder), **89-90**
Annotation of booklists, 48, 71
Anson, Jay. *The Amityville Horror*, 13, 41, 57, **87-8**
Appointment calendar, 27, 48, 50
Are You in the House Alone? (Peck), 7, 9, **20**, 42
Ariel, Joan, talks by, **197, 201-2, 213**
Armes, J. J. *Jay J. Armes, Investigator*, 42, 63
Art Department, 27
Artwork by students, 27, 70
Asimov, Isaac. *I, Robot*, **136-7**
Attention span, 21, 37, 74
Audience participation, 65, 83; in workshops, 75-8
Audience reaction, 3, 7, 9, 11, 17, 19, 28, 31-2, 41-3, 44, 48-53, 54-5, 60, 62-5, 83
Audio-visual materials, 22, 42-4
Author's style, 4, 10
Authors, information about, 11

Bad Bad Leroy Brown (film), 43
A Bag of Marbles (Joffo), **90-91**
Bailey, Maralyn and Maurice. *Staying Alive!* 193
BAYA Hip Pocket Reading Survey, 42
Baldwin, James. *If Beale Street Could Talk*, **138**
Barthel, Joan. *A Death in Canaan*, **104-5**
Beginnings (Juliusberger), 42
Berne, Eric. *What Do You Say After You Say Hello?* **208-9**
Best sellers, 82
Bethancourt, T. E. *The Dog Days of Arthur Cane*, **107-9**
Bibliographies, 217-35. *See also* Booklists
Bid Time Return (Matheson), 9, **93-4**
Bird on the Wing (Madison), 13, 80, **91-3**
Black Like Me (Griffin), **94**
Blaze Glory (film), 43
Blum, Ralph. *Old Glory and the Real-Time Freaks*, **158-9**
Blume, Judy. *Forever*, **118**
Blurb, 13
Body language, 52-3, 63
Book Bait (Walker), xi
Book reports, 3, 24, 37, 53, 57
Books: to borrow in class, 44, 48-50; to borrow in library, 23-4, 45, 69; to use in school visits, 39, 45-6, 47, 53-4. *See also* Selecting books for booktalks
Booklists, 45, 46, 48, 53, 54, 70-71, 73, 78-9, 83
Booktalking: purpose of, 1-3, 37, 73, 83-4; in schools, 22-68; teaching of, 74-81; uses for, xiii, 82. *See also* Booktalks; Mistakes in booktalking
"Booktalking: You Can Do It" (Chelton), 84

Booktalks: long, 3, 5-20; memorized, 3-4; short, 3, 13, 20-21. *See also* Booktalking; Exchange of booktalks; Preparation of booktalks; Selecting books for booktalks

Boredom, 10, 14, 23, 25, 62, 83

Borland, Hal. *When the Legends Die*, **209-10**

Borrowing: of booklists, 73; of booktalks, xi, 5, 19-20

The Boys From Brazil (Levin), 7, 9, 41, **94-5**

Bradford, Richard. *Red Sky at Morning*, 13, **170-2**

Bradley, M. Z. *Hunters of the Red Moon*, **132-3**

Brautigan, Richard. *The Hawkline Monster*, **127**

Breathing, 18

Brontë sisters, 42

Brooks, Jerome. *The Testing of Charlie Hammelman*, **198-9**

Brooks, Terry. *The Sword of Shannara*, **195-6**

Brown, Claude. *The Children of Ham*, **99-100**

Bryan, C.D.B. *Friendly Fire*, **119-20**

Burn-out, 31, 34

Callahan's Crosstime Saloon (Robinson), **95-6**

Cancellation of a school visit, 44

Carlson, Dale. *Triple Boy*, **205-6**

Carpio, Virginia, 75, 76n

Carr, Terry. *Science Fiction for People Who Hate Science Fiction*, 179

The Cat Ate My Gymsuit (Danziger), **97-8**

Carrie (King), 7, 11, **96-7**

Cattle Annie and Little Britches (Ward), 14, **98-9**

Catton, Bruce. *Glory Road*, **123**

Chelton, Mary Kay, 4; "Booktalking: You Can Do It," 84

Children of Ham (Brown), **99-100**

Children's librarians, 31, 44, 70-71, 74, 82

The Chocolate War (Cormier), 9

Christie, Agatha, 42

Circulation, 22, 69

Claire, Keith. *The Otherwise Girl*, **161**

Clapp, Patricia. *I'm Deborah Sampson*, **138-9**

Clark, M. H. *Where Are the Children?* **210-13**

Class Visit Information Card, 39-40, 48, 71

Class Visit Summary Sheet, 71

Classics, 42

Clothing, 37, 50-52, 79. *See also* Grooming

Coleman, Lonnie. *Orphan Jim*, **159-60**

Collections of booktalks, xi, 23. *See also* Exchange of booktalks

Combined classes, 36

Composition of class, 37-8, 39, 41-2

Conford, Ellen. *The Alfred G. Graebner Memorial High School Handbook of Rules and Regulations*, **85-6**

Conroy, Pat. *The Water Is Wide*, **206-7**

Cooperation with school librarians, 24-5, 35-6, 44, 73

Copper Arnold. *Psychic Summer*, **165-9**

Cormier, Robert. *The Chocolate War*, 9

The Crime of the Century (Higdon), **100-101**

The Crystal Cave (Stewart), **101-2**

Cussler, Clive. *Raise the Titanic!* 7, **169-70**

Czubiak, Edith, talk by, **114-15**

D'Ambrosio, Richard. *No Language But a Cry*, 7, **156**

Danziger, Paula. *The Cat Ate My Gymsuit*, **97-8**

Daughter of Time (Tey), **102**

A Day No Pigs Would Die (Peck), 13

Dear Bill, Remember Me? (Mazer), **102-4**

A Death in Canaan (Barthel), 41, **104-5**

Deathwatch (White), 14, 41, 62, **105-6**

Demonstration booktalk, 25, 26, 79
Department heads, 26-8
Dialect, 4
Diamond, G. R. *The Haven*, 2
Dickens, Charles, 42
Dickinson, Peter. *The Gift*, **121-2**
Display of books during talk, 18, 45-6, 53-4
Displays, library, 27, 45, 70
Dickson, Gordon. *The Dragon and the George*, 2, 9, **110-11**
Discipline, 27, 28, 36, 62-5, 67-8, *See also* Troublesome students
A Distant Summer (Patterson), 42, **106-7**
The Dog Days of Arthur Cane (Bethancourt), **107-9**
Doors to More Mature Reading (ALA), xi
Dracula Archives (Rudorff), **109-10**
The Dragon and the George (Dickson), 2, 9, **110-11**
Dragonsong (McCaffrey), **111-12**
Dreamsnake (McIntyre), **112-13**
Dress. *See* Clothing; Grooming
Duckwall, Larry, talks by, **127, 175-6, 180-81, 195-6**
Duncan, Lois. *Five Were Missing*, **117-18**; *I Know What You Did Last Summer*, 7, **133-5**; *Killing Mr. Griffin*, 7, **144-5**
Dune (Herbert), **113-14**
Durrell, Gerald. *A Zoo in My Luggage*, **215-16**
Dust jacket, 13

Eagan, A. B. *Why Am I So Miserable If These Are the Best Years of My Life?* 24, **213**
"Easy YA Booktalking," 76n, 84
Edwards, Margaret. *The Fair Garden and the Swarm of Beasts*, 84
Elder, Lauren. *And I Alone Survived*, **89-90**
Elfman, Blossom. *The Girls of Huntington House*, **122-3**; *A House for Jonnie O.*, **129-30**
Ending of booktalk, 14
English classes, 27, 42, 74
English department, 27

Enunciation, 18
Episodic plots, 7
Equipment for lecture, 79-80; for school visit, 34, 42-50
Evaluation forms, 48, 52
Evaluation of presentation, xiii, 48, 54-5, 69, 80-81
Excerpts: memorized, 3-4; read, 10-11
Exchange: of advice, 55, 80-81; of booktalks, xi, 5, 19-20; of ideas for booklists, 70-71
Eye contact, 17

Faculty. *See* Teachers
Faculty meetings, 25-7
The Fair Garden and the Swarm of Beasts (Edwards), 84
Farris, John. *When Michael Calls*, **209**
Feedback, 48, 55, 80-1
Feral (Roueché), **114-15**
Filing: of booktalks, 20, 71; of information cards, 40
Films, 42-3
First sentence of booktalk, 12
Fitzgerald, Tamsin. *Tamsin*. **196-7**
A Five-Color Buick and a Blue-Eyed Cat (Wood), 7, **115-17**
Five Were Missing (Duncan), **117-18**
Forever (Blume), **118**
Forgetting. *See* Memory, failure of
The Forgotten Beasts of Eld (McKillip), **118-19**
Formality, 25, 26, 51, 52
Format of written talk, 14-15
Foster, A. D. Splinter of the Mind's Eye, 2
Fox, Paula. *Slave Dancer*, **188**
Frank Film, 43
Friendly Fire (Bryan), **119-20**
Frosty (Weaver), 11

Gallico, Paul. *The Poseidon Adventure*, 10
Gestures, 18, 52-3
Ghosts I Have Been (Peck), 7, 8, **120-21**
The Gift (Dickinson), **121-2**
The Gift of the Magi (O. Henry), **122**
Gillett, Charlie. *Rock Almanac*, 54

The Girls of Huntington House
(Elfman), 122-3
Glory Road (Catton), **123**
Green, Hannah. *I Never Promised
You a Rose Garden*, **136**
Greene, A. C. *The Santa Claus
Robbery*, **178-9**
Griffin, J. H. *Black Like Me*, **94**
Grooming, 34
Gruber, Ruth. *They Came to Stay*,
199
Guest, Judith. *Ordinary People*, 9
Guy de Maupassant's Short Stories
(Maupassant), **124**

Habenstreit, Barbara. *To My Brother
Who Did a Crime*, **201-2**
Hall, Lynn. *Sticks and Stones*, **193-4**
Hallahan, William. *The Search for
Joseph Tully*, **180**
Hangin' Out With Cici (Pascal),
124-5
Hanson, Gloria, talk by, **176-8**
Hargrove, Marion, 15, 33
Harold and Maude (Higgins), **125-6**
Harris, Marilyn. *Hatter Fox*, **126**
Hatter Fox (Harris), **126**
The Haven (Diamond), 2
The Hawkline Monster (Brautigan),
127
Head, Ann. *Mr. and Mrs. BoJo Jones*,
152-3
*Heaven and Hell and the Megas
Factor* (Nathan), **127-8**
Heinlein, Robert. *The Past Through
Tomorrow*, **162-3**
Henry, O. *The Gift of the Magi*, **122**
Herbert, Frank. *Dune*, **113-14**
Herriot, James, 11; *All Creatures
Great and Small*, 7, **87**; *All Things
Bright and Beautiful*, 7
Heyerdahl, Thor. *Aku-Aku*, **85**
Higdon, Hal. *The Crime of the
Century*, **100-101**
Higgins, Colin. *Harold and Maude*,
125-6
Hi/lo readers, 39, 44; books for,
217-18, 219-20
Hinton, S. E. *The Outsiders*, **161-2**
Hip Pocket Reading Survey, 42

The Hobbit (Tolkien), 2, **128-9**
Holland, Isabelle. *Of Love and Death
and Other Journeys*, **158**
The Hollow Hills (Stewart), **101-2**
Holman, Felice. *Slake's Limbo*, **20**
Holmes, Marjorie. *Two From Galilee*,
207
Honesty, 5, 7, 61
A House for Jonnie O. (Elfman),
129-30
House of Stairs (Sleator), 42, 58-9,
130-32
Humor, 26, 61, 70
Hunters of the Red Moon (Bradley),
132-3

I, Robot (Asimov), **136-7**
I Know What You Did Last Summer
(Duncan), 7, 14, 41, **133-5**
I Never Loved Your Mind (Zindel),
135
I Never Promised You a Rose Garden
(Green), **136**
Ice Station Zebra (MacLean), 42, **137**
If Beale Street Could Talk (Baldwin),
138
Illustrations, 53-4. *See also* Adult
picture books
I'm Deborah Sampson (Clapp), **138-9**
Improvement in booktalking, 80-81
Improvisation, 61, 82-4. *See also*
Ad-libbing
Individual style, xi, xii, 4, 50, 82-4
Informality, 25, 26, 51, 52
Information about libraries, 29, 38-9,
43, 56-7
Injelmo, Ilene, talk by, **165-6**
Inside Moves (Walton), **140-41**
Interlibrary loans, 57
Interruptions in presentation, 66-7
Interview With the Vampire (Rice),
10, 11, **141**
Introduction of booktalker, 51-2
Introduction to presentation, 38-9
Intruders (Montandon), 7, **142-3**
Involvement of audience. *See*
Audience participation; Audience
reaction
Involvement of library staff, 23, 31,
45-6, 55-7, 69-71, 73

Jacot, Michael. *Last Butterfly*, 146
James, Mary, talks by, **87**, **94**, 121-2, 135, 138-9, 180, 181-2
Jay J. Armes, Investigator (Armes) 42, 63
Joffo, Joseph. *A Bag of Marbles*, **90-91**
Johnson, G. C. *Logan's Run*, **148**
Journalism department, 27
Junior high classes, 32, 54; books for, 217-19

Kavanagh, Paul. *Not Comin' Home to You*, **157-8**
Kellum-Rose, Nancy, talk by, **207-8**
Killing Gift (Wood), **143-4**
Killing Mr. Griffin (Duncan), 7, 57, **144-5**
King, Stephen, 7; *Carrie*, 7, **96-7**; *Night Shift*, **154-5**; *'Salem's Lot*, 7, **175-8**; *The Shining*, 7, **186-7**
Krents, Harold. *To Race the Wind*, 8, 11, **20**, **202-4**
Kurland, Michael. *Princes of Earth*, **164-5**
Kuykendall, Judy, 4

Landlady (Raucher), **145-6**
Lapides, Linda, 83
Last Butterfly (Jacot), 146
Last sentence of booktalk, 14
Le Guin, U. K. *The Left Hand of Darkness*, **147**
Learning booktalking, 57, 74-81
Lectures on booktalking, 78-80
Lee, Joanna. *Mary Jane Harper Cried Last Night*, **150**
The Left Hand of Darkness (Le Guin), **147**
L'Engle, Madeleine. *A Swiftly Tilting Planet*, **214-5**; *A Wind in the Door*, **214-5**; *A Wrinkle in Time*, **214-5**
Length of talks, 15, 21, 39; of presentation, 33-4
Leon, Coralee. *Psychic Summer*, **165-9**
Levin, Ira. *The Boys From Brazil*, 7, 9, 41, **94-5**
Librarian image, 22, 50

Librarians. *See* Children's librarians; Reference librarians; School librarians; YA librarians
Libraries: information about, 29, 38-9, 43, 56-7; public relations for, 20, 22, 24, 38-9, 44-5
Library associations, 74
Library staff, involvement of, 23, 31, 45-6, 55-7, 69-71, 73
Lisa, Bright and Dark (Neufeld), **147-8**
Lists, in booktalks, 10
Literary qualities, 3, 6, 12
Lockley, Ronald. *Seal-Woman* **180-82**
Lofts, Norah. *The Maude Reed Tale*, **150-51**
Logan's Run (Nolan and Johnson), **148**
Loose Chippings (Wheeler), **148-9**
Lucifer's Hammer (Niven and Pournelle), **149**

Maas, Peter. *Serpico*, **182-5**
McCaffrey, Anne. *Dragonsong*, **111-12**
McIntyre, V. K. *Dreamsnake*, **112-13**
McKillip, Patricia. *The Forgotten Beasts of Eld*, **118-19**
MacLean, Alistair. *Ice Station Zebra*, **137**
Madison, Winifred. *Bird on the Wing*, 13, 80, **91-3**
Magazines, 38-9, 66
Magnuson, James. *Orphan Train*, **160**
Margolies, Marjorie. *They Came to Stay*, **199**
Marlowe, Stephen. *Translation*, **205**
Mary Jane Harper Cried Last Night (Lee), **150**
Materials for school visit, 42-50
Matheson, Richard. *Bid Time Return*, **93-4**
Mathis, S. B. *A Teacup Full of Roses*, **197-8** .
The Maude Reed Tale (Lofts), **150-51**
Maupassant, Guy de. *Guy de Maupassant's Short Stories*, **124**
Mazer, N. F. *Dear Bill, Remember Me?* **102-4**

Memorization, 3-4, 60
Memory, failure of, 16, 17, 47, 59-62
Meyer, R. G., 18; talks by, **102-4, 145-6, 154-5, 166-7**
Michaels, Barbara. *Ammie, Come Home*, 9, 42, **88-9**; *Patriot's Dream*, **163**
Mindfogger (Rogers), **151-2**
Mirrors, 17, 18
Mistakes in booktalking, xii, 3, 5, 9-10, 43, 53, 57, 58-62, 65-6, 76
Mr. and Mrs. BoJo Jones (Head), **152-3**
Montandon, Pat. *The Intruders*, 7, **142-3**
Moore, Mary, 15, 30, 35, 48, 55, 62; talks by, **130-31, 133-5**
Multi-session workshops, 75-7
Murray, Peggy, talks by, **90-91, 118-19, 132-3, 173-4**
Music, in presentation, 43-4
My Darling, My Hamburger (Zindel), 42, **153-4**

Nathan, Robert. *Heaven and Hell and the Megas Factor*, **127-8**; *Portrait of Jennie*, **164**
Neufeld, John. *Lisa, Bright and Dark*, **147-8**
NICEM indexes, 43
Nicholas, Charles, illus. *Star Wars*, 2
Night Shift (King), **154-5**
Niven, Larry. *Lucifer's Hammer*, **149**
No Language But a Cry (D'Ambrosio), 7, **156**
Noise, 36, 43, 62-5, 67
Nolan, W. F. *Logan's Run*, **148**
None of the Above (Wells), **156-7**
Not Comin' Home to You (Kavanagh), **157-8**
Notes: taking of, 6 82-3; use of, in presentation, 14-15, 19, 52, 60, 82-3
Nugent, Stephen. *Rock Almanac*, 54
Number of presentations per day and week, 32-4
Number of talks per class, 39

Oates, J. C. *Where Are You Going, Where Have You Been?* **213**
Observers, 55-7

Of Love and Death and Other Journeys, (Holland), **158**
Old age homes, 82
Old Glory and the Real-Time Freaks (Blum), **158-9**
The Olympia Diving Sequence (film) 43
"Openers," 41
Ordinary People (Guest), 9
Orphan Jim (Coleman), **159-60**
Orphan Train (Magnuson and Petrie), **160**
The Otherwise Girl (Claire), **161**
Outlines of talks, 15, **108-9, 124, 130-31, 184-5, 192, 212-13**
Outsiders (Hinton), **161-2**

Page, Thomas. *The Spirit*, **191-2**
Pair visiting, 55, 80-81
Panshin, Alexei. *Rite of Passage*, **173-4**
Paperbacks, 23-4, 44, 46
Participation by audience: in class, 65, 83; in workshop, 75-8
Partners, 55, 80-81
Pascal, Francine. *Hangin' Out With Cici*, **124-5**
The Past Through Tomorrow (Heinlein), **162-3**
Patriot's Dream (Michaels), **163**
Patterson, Sarah. *The Distant Summer* **106-7**
Peck, Richard. *Are You in the House Alone?* **20**, 42; *Ghosts I Have Been*, 7, 8, **120-21**; *Representing Superdoll*, 11, **172**; *Through a Brief Darkness*, 42, 59, **199-201**
Peck, Robert. *A Day No Pigs Would Die*, 13
Persistence, xiii, 61, 63, 83
Personal material in talks, 11-12
Personal preferences, xii, 7
Personal style. *See* Individual style
Petrie, Dorothea. *Orphan Train*, **160**
Picture books, adult, 39, 66
Pictures in books, 54
Plot, treatment of in booktalk, 8-9, 21
Poetry, 11
Pope, Elizabeth. *The Sherwood Ring*, **185**

Portrait of Jennie (Nathan), **164**
The Poseidon Adventure (Gallico), 10
Posture, 18, 52-3
Pournelle, Jerry. *Lucifer's Hammer*, **149**
Practice, 16-19, 47, 76, 78
Preparation: of a booktalk, 5-21; of a class presentation, 38-42
Price, Richard. *The Wanderers*, **207-8**
Pridemore, Marianne, 15; talks by, **107-8, 182-4, 191-2, 211-13**
Princes of Earth (Kurland), **164-5**
Principals, 24, 25
Priorities in YA work, 29-31, 73
Problems in booktalking, 43, 58-68. *See also* Mistakes in booktalking
Psychic Summer (Copper and Leon), 8, **165-9**
Public relations for libraries, 20, 22, 24, 38-9, 44-5
Public service desks, 70-71

Raise the Titanic! (Cussler), 7, **169-70**
Raucher, Constance. *Landlady*, **145-6**
Read, P. P. *Alive!* 10
Reader's advisory work, xiii, 3, 20, 71, 74
Reading, for booktalks, 6
Reading aloud, 10-11
Reading classes, 74
Reading skills, 1-2, 38, 65-6
Recordings, 22, 43-4, 83. *See also* Audio visual materials; Tape recorders; Videotapes
Records of class visits, 39-40, 71
Red Sky at Morning (Bradford), 8, 13, **170-2**
Reference librarians, 31, 44, 56-7, 70-71, 74, 82
Representing Superdoll (Peck) 11, **172**
Request cards, 24, 48-50, 54
Requests, 23-4, 48, 54, 57, 69-70
Research procedures, teaching of, 56
Responses of students. *See* Audience reaction
Reta, Karmann, talks by, **138, 196-7**

Revision of talks, 15
Rice, Anne. *Interview With the Vampire*, 10, 11, **141**
Richie (Thompson), **173**
Rite of Passage (Panshin), **173-4**
Rivera, Geraldo. *A Special Kind of Courage*, **190-1**
Road to Many a Wonder (Wagoner), 10, **174**
Roberts, Kay, talk by, **188-9**
Robertson, Dougal. *Survive the Savage Sea*, 10, **194-5**
Robinson, Spider. *Callahan's Crosstime Saloon*, **95-6**
Rock Almanac (Nugent and Gillett), 54
Rock music, 22, 44
Rogers, Michael. *Mindfogger*, **151-2**
Roueché, Berton. *Feral*, **114-15**
Rudorff, Raymond. *Dracula Archives*, **109-10**
Run Shelley Run (Samuels), **175**
Russo, Richard, talks by, **151-2, 193-4**

'Salem's Lot (King), 7, **175-8**
Samuels, Gertrude. *Run Shelley Run*, **175**
The Santa Claus Bank Robbery (Greene), **178-9**
Scheduling class visits, 27-35, 50, 64, 68
Scenes, for booktalks, 7-8
School librarians, 24-5, 28, 29, 35-6, 44, 51, 71
School library, xiii, 36
School Library Journal, 4, 43
School visiting, xiii, 3, 22-68; in pairs, 55, 80-81; priority of, 29-31; purpose of, 24, 37. *See also* Scheduling class visits
Schools: contacting, 24-29; relations with, 5-6, 51; visits to, 22-68
Science Fiction for People Who Hate Science Fiction (Carr), **179**
Seal-Woman (Lockley), **180-82**
The Search for Joseph Tully (Hallahan), **180**
Selecting books for booktalks, 6-7, 37-9, 41-2, 65-6

Senior citizens, 82
Senior high classes, 32, 54; books for, 219-35
Sequence of booktalks, 41-2, 63
Serpico (Maas), **182-5**
Sex of students, 37-8, 41-2, 65
Sexism in students, 42
The Sherwood Ring (Pope), 14, **185**
The Shining (King), 7, 41, **186-7**
The Shootist (Swarthout), **187**
Short booktalks, 13, 20-21
Single-session workshops, 77-8
Size: of classes, 36; of workshops, 75
Skills: booktalking, 80-81; reading, 1-2, 38, 65-6
Slake's Limbo (Holman), **20**
Slave Dancer (Fox), **188**
Sleator, William. *House of Stairs*, 42, 58-9, **130-32**
Slides, 43-4
A Slipping-Down Life (Tyler), **188-9**
Social studies department, 27
Song of the Shaggy Canary (Wood), **189**
Specht, Robert. *Tisha*, 8
A Special Kind of Courage (Rivera), **190-1**
Speech, 18
The Spirit (Page), **191-2**
Splinter of the Mind's Eye (Foster), 2
Spontaneity, 19, 23
Staff, library, involvement of, 23, 31, 44-6, 55-7, 69-71, 73
Stage fright, 41, 53, 77, 80
Stage-setting, in a booktalk, 10
Stamina, 31-4
Star Wars (Nicholas), 2
Starr, Carol, 30, 51-2, 70, 75, 76, 80; talks by, **99-100, 111-12, 129-30, 147-8, 153-4, 198-9, 205-6**
Staying Alive! (Bailey and Bailey), **193**
Steinbeck, John, 42
Stewart, Mary. *The Crystal Cave*, **101-2**; *The Hollow Hills*, **101-2**
Sticks and Stones (Hall), **193-4**
Storytelling, 4, 74
Student art, 27
Students. *See* Age levels; Audience participation; Audience reaction;

Junior high classes; Senior high classes; Sex of students; Sexism in students; Troublesome students
Style, author's, 4, 10
Style, personal. *See* Individual style
Subjects, class, 24, 35, 37, 56, 73
Subject files, 71
Survive the Savage Sea (Robertson), 10, **194-5**
Swarthout, Glendon. *The Shootist*, **187**
A Swiftly Tilting Planet (L'Engle), **214-5**
The Sword of Shannara (Brooks), **195-6**

Tait, Sue, 34, 83
Talbot, Elizabeth, 11, 26, 71, 82-3; talk by, **167-8**
Tamsin (Fitzgerald), **196-7**
Tape recorders, 17, 18-19
Teachers, 24-9, 43, 51, 69, 74, 75, 82; problem, 62-4, 67-8
Teachers' Class Visit Evaluation Forms, 48, 52
Teaching booktalking, 74-81
A Teacup Full of Roses (Mathis), **197-8**
Teenagers. *See* Age levels; Audience participation; Audience reaction; Junior high classes; Senior high classes; Sex of students; Sexism in students; Troublesome students
Term papers, 56
The Testing of Charlie Hammelman (Brooks), **198-9**
Tey, Josephine. *Daughter of Time*, 102
Team booktalking, 55, 80-81
That Rotten Teabag (film), 43
They Came to Stay (Margolies and Gruber), **199**
Thompson, Thomas. *Richie*, **173**
Through a Brief Darkness (Peck), 13, 42, 59, **199-201**
Timing booktalks, 15, 39
Timing of visits. *See* Scheduling of class visits
Tisha (Specht), 8

To My Brother Who Did a Crime
(Habenstreit), **201-2**
To Race the Wind (Krents), 8, 11, 20,
80, **202-4**
Tolkien, J.R.R., 2; *The Hobbit*, 2,
128-9
Translation (Marlowe), **205**
Triple Boy (Carlson), **205-6**
Troublesome students, 36, 62-5, 67
Turned On (film), 43
Two From Galilee (Holmes), **207**
Tyler, Anne. *A Slipping-Down Life*,
188-9

Videotape, 17, 75, 77
Visualization, 19, 83
Voice, tone of, 18

Wagoner, David. *Road to Many a
Wonder*, 10, **174**
Walker, Elinor. *Book Bait*, xi
Walton, Todd. *Inside Moves*, **140-1**
The Wanderers (Price), **207-8**
Ward, Robert. *Cattle Annie and Little
Britches*, 14, **98-9**
The Water Is Wide (Conroy), **206-7**
Weaver, Harriet E. *Frosty*, 11
Wells, Rosemary. *None of the Above*,
156-7
*What Do You Say After You Say
Hello?* (Berne), **208-9**
Wheeler, Thomas. *Loose Chippings*,
148-9

When Michael Calls (Farris), **209**
When the Legends Die (Borland),
209-10
Where Are the Children? (Clark),
210-13
*Where Are You Going, Where Have
You Been?* (Oates), **213**
White, Robb. *Deathwatch*, 14, 41, 62,
105-6
*Why Am I So Miserable If These Are
the Best Years of My Life?* (Eagan),
24, **213**
A Wind in the Door (L'Engle), **214-15**
Win Me and You Lose (Wood), **214**
Wood, Bari. *The Killing Gift*, **143-4**
Wood, P. A. *A Five-Color Buick and a
Blue-Eyed Cat* 7, **115-17**; *Song of
the Shaggy Canary*, **189**; *Win Me
and You Lose*, **214**
Workshops in booktalking, 75-8
A Wrinkle in Time (L'Engle), **214-15**
Writing booktalks, 12-16

YA librarians, xi, 22-3, 29-31, 43-4,
57, 70, 71, 75
YA services, 20, 29, 43-4

Zindel, Paul. *I Never Loved Your
Mind*, **135**; *My Darling, My
Hamburger*, 42, **153-4**
A Zoo in My Luggage (Durrell),
215-16